Trad Online Books

www.tradonline-books.com

The World in Words
50 professional translators provide a unique insight into their country's culture

with Notes and Appendixes by Aurelia Popescu

First edition, France 2013

Copyright © **Trad Online**

All rights reserved.

www.tradonline.fr

Coordinator – Aurelia Popescu

Cover – Anne-Catherine Dufros

ISBN-13: 978-2-9543940-0-8

ISBN-10: 2954394005

A FEW WORDS FROM THE EDITOR

This work is dedicated to all the translators worldwide whose help and support made this book possible. We are all trying to do our bit in helping the environment and promoting cultural awareness. All benefits will go to Planète Urgence, a French NGO committed to fighting climate change and empowering people to act in their local communities.

Contents

Foreword 10

North America & Canada.15

Canada 16

U.S.A. 22

Mexico 29

Dominican Republic 36

Central America 42

Costa Rica 43

Honduras 49

Nicaragua 55

South America.63

Argentina 64

Bolivia 71

Brazil 79

Chile 91

Colombia 100

Ecuador 106

Peru 112

Uruguay 120

Venezuela 126

Northern & Eastern Africa.133

Algeria 134

Ethiopia 141

Kenya 148

Uganda 157

Central, Southern & Western Africa.163

Cameroon 164

South Africa 172

Mali 183

Senegal 190

Europe.198

Armenia 199

Belgium 209

Bulgaria 217

Estonia 231

France 238

Italy 247

Ukraine 286

Asia/Pacific 302

China 303

Indonesia 312

Japan 319

Lebanon 331

Malaysia 340

Pakistan 346

Thailand 354

South Korea 361

Vietnam 368

Yemen 377

Russia 384

Turkey 390

New Zealand 397

The Response.405

The Authors 406

FOREWORD

THE IDEA...

Three months ago, Trad Online's team started this exciting writing project about the world with the help of a community of linguists worldwide. One of our team members had a great idea and we decided to turn this idea into reality – what if we created a crowd-written book like no other and showed the world cultural facts that cannot be found on Wikipedia or in any standard book? We could share unique insights, features and new perspectives on countries, provided directly from the people living there. We sometimes only get a very shallow image of other countries, so we wanted to make sure that the project went beyond conventional cultural boundaries.

For translators, even though this is a volunteer project, it is a unique opportunity to participate in creating a book with many others linguists from all over the world. Linguists, in their daily work on localisation (translation with transformation into a local culture), are at the very heart of this issue. They understand, collect and list cultural differences to be good at their jobs and find the best translation solution. And now they can do their part in helping the planet, as all profits from sales of this "crowd-sourced" book will be donated to Planète Urgence, an NGO committed to fighting climate change through reforestation projects in developing countries.

The project...

It all started after an exciting brainstorming session with the French team. We came up with a list of cultural topics, all those little (or not so little) "tidbits" that make each country unique - society, values, traditions, language, music, cuisine, people, history, etiquette, etc. We focused on those topics that could eventually allow translators to share the wide range of experiences they have had growing up in their country:

- A typical conversation – what are the common/universal topics people go for (weather, politics, etc.)? And topics that you should avoid discussing with the locals?
- Events of great significance for the community, deeply stored in everyone's mind
- Nouns and figures from the past/present that you use in colloquial expressions
- Words used to designate a type of person, animal or thing
- Common phrases and fun expressions in your native language, and their translation in English
- Songs and games you remember from your childhood, that are generally passed on to the next generation

- Legends/stories or famous characters of the imaginary; folk tales
- Products or goods that represent a "national treasure"

The last item has been kept as open as possible, to let translators write about something that is little known outside the "inner circle" of their culture.

Each country chapter in this book has the same template, a basic requirement to maintain consistency. Having a single template gave the writers the freedom to compose in their own style, following the list of cultural topics we created. It was also an interesting way to analyze the similarities between cultures, a way of expressing the fact that no matter where we come from or no matter what the angle we see reality from, human experience is universal and beauty lies in difference. This unity-in-diversity approach helped the translators share some interesting experiences and allowed us to see cultural differences in how reality is perceived. In this way, we can better understand human nature and dignity, as seen from 50 different perspectives. You might notice some topics are missing for certain countries. Even if our contributors couldn't think of anything special for them, if you're a native why not mail your ideas to us? You might just find them on the blog, where we add all extra material.

THE BOOK...

When we set out on our journey to research and prepare this book, we had no idea it would take three months to complete it. The list of translators participating was always changing as many of them were already involved in huge localisation projects. The ones who agreed to contribute to this collaborative book needed time and documentation, and sometimes topics were difficult to understand. What you see in this book is essentially what we collected from the start - names, stories, experiences, final versions of the templates and many other interesting things. It is an honour to share the stories of these remarkable people, and the untold part of their country's history. You will see different registers and varieties of English throughout; this we left intact, to better reflect the diversity out there in the world! A specific example is that of the words "soccer" and "football," which our contributors have used according to their preference; both refer to European football- or as American English would have it, soccer.

Because of the number of responses we received, some contributions may instead be used in an alternative collaborative project (a potential sequel to this book).

The book will be promoted on all the major social networks, such as LinkedIn, Viadeo, Facebook, Orkut, Twitter and Pinterest so that everyone can enjoy it. A special blog has been created, www.tradonline-books.com/, where we will be posting extras such as texts, pictures and even videos.

The general layout was created on CreateSpace, an Amazon service, whose team we would especially like to thank for their prompt response and support.
To find out more about Trad Online, about this project and Planète Urgence, the nonprofit organisation receiving the profits from the sales of the book, please use the links below:

The blog related to this project: www.tradonline-books.com

Trad Online's general blog: www.tradonline.fr/blog/

Trad Online's Facebook page: http://www.facebook.com/tradonline.translations

Trad Online's company page on LinkedIn: www.linkedin.com/company/trad-online

Planète Urgence's website: www.planete-urgence.org/

NORTH AMERICA & CANADA

- Canada
- United States of America
- Mexico
- Dominican Republic

Canada

FIRST NAME: JOHANNE
FAMILY NAME: TREMBLAY
JTREMBLAY@PLEINEPAGE.CA

Capital	Ottawa	Population	34,300,000
Government	Parliamentary democracy, federation, and constitutional monarchy	Currency	Canadian Dollar (CAD)
Religion(s)	Roman Catholic, Protestant		
Language(s)	English (official), French (official) and others		

I was born in Granby, in Québec, Canada, and my family lived in numerous places in Québec, from Baie Comeau to Saint-Jean-sur-Richelieu, and Pincourt (near Montréal) to Loretteville (near Québec city). I have been telling stories since my childhood, first with pictures and photos cut from magazines and glued on paper, then as a freelance journalist for mainstream and corporate magazines and as a writer of all sorts of texts, including short stories. Nowadays I work mostly as a self-employed translator (from English to French) of textbooks, website content and software, and on personal writing projects.

I live and thrive in Québec, one of Canada's ten provinces and three territories. As with any big country, Canada has many facets. My story is rooted in Québec and is probably very different from those of people living in Ontario, Western Canada, the Maritimes or Nunavut.

1 - A typical conversation – what are the common/universal topics people go for? (weather, politics, etc.) - And some topics that you should avoid discussing with the locals?

Here in Québec (and probably in the rest of Canada, aka the ROC), weather and hockey are fundamental conversation starters. We marvel at the nice weather all through summer, the Indian summer (3-4 days at the end of October), the warm spells in February and early spring in April, and the beautiful snow of December. But we complain about the heat waves in June and July, the rain in May and November, and, most of all, the never-ending snow in March. As hockey is Canada's national sport, people spend a lot of time discussing every aspect of the game. The Montreal's Canadien (with an e please!) team is a staple of our culture and we have a long love story with it, even for those of us who are not crazy about hockey. The Québec city hockey fans used to cheer for their beloved Nordiques until their team was sold and moved to the States, but they might get a brand new one sometime soon, and then, the old Montréal-Québec rivalry will start up again and keep us warm throughout the year.

Of course, everyone here knows better than to bring up the topic of Canada's two divisions – English and French Canadian communities – in a formal conversation. Politics is a very sensitive subject and best kept for later, between people with a solid friendship!

2 - Events of great significance for the community, deeply stored in everyone's mind

The first major event that defined Quebec's community was the British Conquest (la Conquête) of New France in 1759, during the Seven Year's War, at the end of which France ceded New France to Great Britain. This event put an end to the French regime, replaced it with the British regime and eventually led to the Canadian Confederation in 1867. Today, French communities are found in every province and territory, but the vast majority live in Québec.

The Quiet Revolution, which occurred during the 1960s, was the defining moment for modern Québec. Best known as la Révolution tranquille, it refers to the major political, economic, social and cultural changes that occurred when the new Lesage government launched various programmes in addition to taking charge of education and health, which had been in the hands of the Roman Catholic Church since the early days of the colony. The Quiet Revolution allowed Québec to blossom by promoting its institutions, economy, common language (French), culture and values.

Of course, not all Canadians have the same defining moment, as First Nation people, Acadians, Newfies and Westerners will tell you.

3 - Nouns and Figures from the past / present that you use in colloquial expressions

La tête à Papineau: Louis-Joseph Papineau was a politician and the leader of the Patriotes, a protest movement behind what is known as the Patriotes Rebellion of 1837-1838 against the British colonial administration. He was an educated man and a brilliant speaker. Today it is common to say that one doesn't need to have Papineau's brain (or to be very smart) to understand something quite simple (*Pas besoin de la tête à Papineau pour comprendre ça*).

4 - Words used to designate a type of person, animal, things

A *Séraphin* refers to a greedy person. It is also the name of the main character of a famous novel from Claude-Henri Grignon, Un homme et son péché (1933). The novel inspired a serial drama that lasted 24 years on radio before being adapted for television in the 50s and 60s as Les belles histoires des pays d'en haut. Reruns of the show are still very popular today.

A *Jo connaissant* (Joe knows all) is someone who acts as if he knows everything, but doesn't.

Avoir l'air de la chienne à Jacques (to look like Jacques'dog) describes someone who is not well dressed or groomed.

A *Roger bon temps* (literally Roger good time) describes someone who is always in a good mood, a happy-go-lucky type of guy.

A *Germaine* refers to a bossy woman who takes the lead in every situation, whether people want it or not. The pun-name is made from two verbs, as a Germaine is someone who manages (gère) and leads (mène). Note that Germaine is really a girl's name, although it is not so common these days.

5 - Common phrases and fun expressions in your native language and their translation in English

Coller au plafond (stick to the ceiling) probably comes from "go through the roof" and means to be very irritated very quickly by something or someone.

Avoir la broue dans le toupet (to have foam in one's tuft) means to be very busy for a short time: a waiter at lunch time for example, or a mother of three toddlers at 7am.

Sirop de poteau (post syrup) refers to the syrup made from sugar and sold in grocery stores as opposed to maple syrup, one of Québec's emblematic products (see below). Years ago, manufacturers called their product "maple syrup" even if no maple sap was used to produce it, and real maple syrup fans would make a point of calling it contemptuously "post syrup," in reference to the telephone posts seen everywhere along streets and roads.

6 - Songs and games you remember from your childhood, that are generally passed on to the next generation

Songs and games that children play here are probably the same as in other countries. Today video games take up a large part of the day (and heart) of many kids, but here are a few more traditional ones.

Skipping rope and rubber band are popular among girls in school yards in spring; boys play street hockey (with a ball in summer or a puck in winter) year round.

At the end of summer, some kids collect stones from horse chestnut fruit. Using a big nail, they thread a string through the stone, make a knot and play a game whose winner is the one who can hit and break the opponent's stone without breaking his or hers.

Halloween is a very popular celebration here and everywhere in

Canada.

During winter, snow provides a great playground. Kids build forts, launch snowball battles and slide on any snowdrift available. A splendid movie from André Melançon, Roger Cantin and Daniele Patenaude captures the spirit of it: *La guerre des tuques* (The Dog Who Stopped the War).

8 - Products or goods that come to mind as 'the national treasure'

Water is definitely Québec and Canada's national treasure. Québec holds 3% of the world's freshwater storage in 4,500 rivers, plus half a million lakes and the Saint-Laurent River.

Maple syrup, made from the sweet water that turns into sap in early spring, is a staple food in many pantries.

Actually, natural resources have featured heavily in Québec's economy and still do. These include minerals, forests, water (supplying major hydroplants) and numerous performers and creators. Some say our geographic location and being surrounded by English culture are key factors in our tremendous creative output.

U.S.A.

First name: Katherine
Family name: Parks
INFO@ENANGLAIS.COM
WWW.ENANGLAIS.COM

Capital	Washington, DC	Population	313,847,400
Government	Constitution-based federal republic	Currency	US dollar (USD)
Religion(s)	Protestant, Roman Catholic and other		
Language(s)	English and others		

I grew up in Oklahoma (U.S.A.) and from an early age I always had my nose in a book, dreaming of faraway places. After studying abroad in several different countries during high school and college (or "university" in the rest of the world), I chose to attend graduate school at the Institute of Political Studies of Paris (Sciences Po). My master's program (Human Resource Management) allowed me to combine work and school. My apprenticeship in an international executive search firm gave me close access to the nuclear energy sector and taught me how to juggle different cultures and languages while meeting clients' needs. After obtaining my M.A., I began working at the OECD, a bilingual international organization based in Paris. During my work I was required to do a lot of "ad hoc" translation, which I adored. After much consideration and research, I decided to make the scary but exciting leap into a new career as a French-to-English translator. Three years later, I am completing a Certificate in Translation from NYU while working as a full-time translator (with a particular fondness for legal and technical documents). My lifelong love of reading and learning has served me extremely well in this field, where every new document presents its own set of challenges (client needs, terminology, and research) and rewards (learning about everything from real estate contracts to how an airplane flies).

1 - A typical conversation - what are the common/universal topics people go for? (weather, politics, etc.) - And some topics that you should avoid discussing with the locals?

The first thing I should point out – and this applies to all my answers – is that the U.S.A. is still an extremely young, diverse country. There are not as many unspoken boundaries, hierarchical layers, and implicit rituals in the U.S. as in some countries. We believe strongly in the freedom of speech and of religion, so as long as you are polite and friendly, you can discuss a wide variety of topics with Americans, including politics and religion.

I have often heard people from other countries say that Americans are kind but a bit superficial. They say that they never know where they stand with Americans, and the constant smiling comes across as insincere. I try to explain that – in only a few generations – immigrants from every region of the world had to learn to work together, understand each other, and find new ways of cooperating, to build this huge country from scratch[1]. Being friendly, direct, and trusting was not an option – it was requirement for survival. In my opinion, this might be part of why Americans tend to say what they mean and try to look others directly in the eye. Unlike what I have heard some people claim, Americans are perfectly capable of forming deep friendships and can be extremely loyal to the ones they love. However, due to a tradition of immigration, in-country migration, and a love of independence, these bonds can sometimes shift, change, or end. Above all, Americans are a pragmatic people who adapt quickly, without a lot of reverence for ancient traditions or social codes. No topics of conversation are off-limits if you remain polite and curious.

2 - Events of great significance for the community, deeply stored in everyone's mind

Americans tend to be proud of their Revolutionary War (1775-1883). The date of July 4 became an important national holiday celebrating independence from Great Britain. (Of course, the true details of why and how this war was won are extremely complex, but every country needs its own traditions and symbols of pride.)

Another event, the Civil War (1861-1865), left much more painful scars on the country. This war killed more people than all other American wars combined and left lasting divisions between the North and the South. Its one positive outcome was the thirteenth Constitutional amendment, which outlawed slavery.

---

[1] Of course there was already a large population of Native Americans that was almost eliminated in the process, but that history deserves its own, separate attention.

There are so many events from the twentieth century that could be included in this list, but I will mention an event that is unforgettable for the people of my generation: September 11, 2001. I was in high school when it happened and I remember it very clearly. I walked into my first class of the day and was confused to see that the television was on, showing images of a burning building. My teacher had turned it on because (according to the reports at the time) one of the World Trade Center towers had been hit by a plane, probably a confused pilot. This meant that we were all watching live when, unexpectedly, a second plane hit the second tower. My teacher, a Vietnam War veteran, stood up told us, "I don't know what just happened, but I do know that this just became the defining moment for your entire generation. Your lives will never be the same after today, and I'm sorry for that." He was right – that event has defined our generation to a large extent, and its repercussions will continue for a long time to come.

3 - Nouns and Figures from the past / present that you use in colloquial expressions

One of the greatest American cities is New York City, known as the "Big Apple." Few people know the meaning behind this nickname. Although there are several theories, the most likely answer is that in the early 20th century, people had come to recognize this booming city's position of influence and importance. On a "tree" (the United States) of many "apples" (or cities), this one was the biggest (and was the recipient of the most "sap," or money and attention). Another alternative suggests that "apple" was a term that referred to the prizes given out for races at New York racetracks. These were some of the largest prizes in the country, so many jockeys aspired to race in New York – the biggest "apple" of them all!

4 - Words used to designate a type of person, animal, things

"Average Joe" and "Plain Jane" – a person who is average and unexceptional

"Keeping up with the Joneses" – the act of constantly comparing oneself to one's neighbors and striving to match or exceed their levels of spending

"No kidding, Sherlock" – an ironic expression used to mock a person who has made an idiotic remark

5 - Common phrases and fun expressions in your native language and their translation in English

Benjamin Franklin, one of the Founding Fathers of the U.S., was known for his witty phrases that imparted knowledge and commonsense advice. Many of these uniquely American quotations have become such a part of American culture that most people do not realize that they were invented by Mr. Franklin. Some of the most common phrases attributed to Benjamin Franklin include:

"Early to bed and early to rise makes a man healthy, wealthy, and wise."

"They that can give up essential liberty to obtain a little temporary safety deserve neither safety nor liberty."

"In this world nothing can be said to be certain, except death and taxes."

6 - Songs and games you remember from your

childhood, that are generally passed on to the next generation

Games (which are not uniquely American) include: ring around the rosy, hide-and-seek, capture the flag, hopscotch, dodgeball, musical chairs, Simon says.

Children's songs in America are generally the same as in the UK. Yankee Doodle, however, is a uniquely American song. Legend has it that this song was originally sung by British soldiers to mock their American counterparts in the late 18th century. Americans soon made it their own and it became a patriotic children's song.

7 - Legends/ stories or famous characters of the Imaginary / Folk tales

Famous American legends include two by Washington Irving: **"The Legend of Sleepy Hollow"** and **"Rip Van Winkle."** In the first story, a man named Ichabod Crane fights with another man for the love of a local girl. After she rejects him, he rides home alone. He meets a headless man on horseback, supposedly the ghost of a man killed in the Revolutionary War. He is seized with terror and before he can run away, the ghostly man rears his horse, and throws his head in Ichabod's face. The next morning, no-one in town can find Ichabod, and he is never seen again. The main character of the second story is, of course, Rip Van Winkle, a very lazy man who hates hard work and never does anything around the farm. One day he wanders away from his village and, after meeting some unusual characters and drinking their liquor, falls asleep. He wakes up twenty years later to find that he has missed the Revolutionary War and the entire world has changed.

8 - *Products or goods that represent 'the national treasure'*

This is a difficult question. When people think of the U.S.A., they generally think of things like automobiles, hamburgers, Hollywood movies, and more. To find relatively unknown goods or products that represent America, it is best to start at the local level. Over the last few decades, locally made "artisan" food products have become more popular. Specially made cheeses in Wisconsin, fine wines from California, various styles of barbecued meats in every state from Texas to Tennessee, and even bison burgers have gained in popularity as Americans have become more accepting of and interested in locally made products.

Of course, nothing is more American than the many Native American cultures themselves. While most Native Americans no longer live in the regions their ancestors inhabited, many tribes have fought to maintain their native traditions and languages. Native American baskets, paintings, jewelry, sculptures, dolls, and more have always been popular in the American southwest, while ingredients such as corn, squash, and beans have become staples of many regional diets.

***

The United States of America is a breathtakingly vast and diverse country. This was a fun but challenging assignment, since it is so hard to summarize in a few short paragraphs this country that is based on the premise of bringing together people from almost every culture in the world. Although it is a country that elicits strong reactions – positive and negative – in the rest of the world, I know that the U.S. has a lot of good qualities, ideas, and products to share with others.

Mexico

FIRST NAME: OSVALDO
FAMILY NAME: ROCHA
OSVALDR@GMAIL.COM
TIEMPOSNORDICOS.COM

Capital	Mexico City	Population	114,975,400
Government	Federal republic	Currency	Mexican pesos (MXN)
Religion(s)	Roman Catholic and others		
Language(s)	Spanish and indigenous languages		

I am a writer, translator and lecturer. I hold a master's degree in Old Norse language and literature from the University of Iceland and studied history and German at the University of Guadalajara (Mexico). I am currently a lecturer at the University of the Atemajac Valley (Mexico) and a freelance translator working from English, German and the Scandinavian languages. I have also published essays, poems and translations in magazines and journals from Mexico, Columbia, Venezuela, Chile, Argentina, Spain, the Netherlands, and Singapore. I also manage the news-blog tiemposnordicos.com.

1 - A typical conversation – what are the common/universal topics people go for? (weather, politics, etc.) - And some topics that you should avoid discussing with the locals?

Unlike other regions of the world, the weather is quite stable in most parts of Mexico (warm throughout the year) and thus it is not the most typical subject to start a conversation. People usually discuss sports –mostly football, politics, the economy and public insecurity due to crime. Religion is not a big issue in Mexico since the majority of the population is Catholic, at least from a sociocultural point of view. Nevertheless, religious fervour is stronger in some regions of the country and so is crime, which makes them delicate topics in certain contexts.

2 - Events of great significance for the community, deeply stored in everyone's mind

Events such as independence from Spain (started on 16 September 1810), the revolution (started on 20 November 1910) and victory against the French at the Battle of Puebla (on 5 May 1862), the Tlatelolco Massacre (2 October 1960) and the 1985 earthquake have left a very significant imprint on Mexico's collective memory. More recently, the economic crisis in 1994 was a traumatic event for many families in the country. This crisis eventually affected other economies through the so-called 'Tequila Effect.' Also in 1994 the EZLN (Zapatista Army of National Liberation) started a revolutionary leftist movement against the Mexican government, and later in that year the presidential candidate Luis Donaldo Colosio was assassinated at a campaign rally, one of the most shocking events in recent history.

3 - Nouns and Figures from the past / present that you use in colloquial expressions

Malinchista, Malinchismo

Named by the Spanish conquerors as 'La Malinche' or 'doña Marina,' Malintzin was a Nahua woman who became Hernán Cortés' interpreter (she knew Nahuatl, Mayan and Spanish) ...and mistress. She helped him eventually achieve the conquest of Mexico and gave birth to one of the first mestizos babies – half Spanish, half native – in Mexico: Martín Cortés. Despite her short life – about 30 years – her actions turned her name into a Spanish adjective, *malinchista* (noun: *malinchismo*), which denotes someone who betrays his or her country or sells out to foreigners. This term can also apply to anyone who prefers something coming from abroad rather than anything coming from Mexico. For logical reasons, Malintzin was portrayed as a respectable historical character by the Spanish conquerors and chroniclers, whereas the indigenous peoples and even modern Mexicans have viewed her as a despicable woman responsible for the European colonisation.

Cantinflear, Cantinfleada

Mario Moreno (1911-1993), better known as 'Cantinflas,' was a Mexican humourist and actor who became an icon in the Mexican culture. Praised even by Chaplin as the best comedian alive, Cantinflas created his persona – just like Chaplin's Charlot – to represent different social roles. One of his main features was a very creative use of wordplay, often viewed as incongruous and nonsensical speech. This kind of speech would eventually be called *cantinfleada* (verb: *cantinflear*). The Royal Spanish Academy officially included the verb *cantinflear* in its dictionary in 1992.

4 - Words used to designate a type of person, animal, things

- Don Juan or donjuán: After a legendary character famous for seducing women. It means 'womaniser,' similar to Casanova, and is used all over the Spanish-speaking world.

- Dondiego or dompedro: From 'Don Diego' and 'Don Pedro' respectively, it is the name for the flowering plant known in English as 'morning glory.'

- Magdalena: Used especially in the expression Llorar como una Magdalena, literally to cry like Mary Magdalene, as depicted in the Bible.

- María or galleta maría: literally 'Mary cookie,' a particular kind of cookie.

- Martín pescador: literally Martin the fisher, a bird known in English as 'kingfisher' or 'river kingfisher.'

- Moisés: Spanish variant of the name Moses. It means 'bassinet,' a lightweight basket with handles used as a portable crib.

- Séneca: After the Roman philosopher Lucius Annaeus Seneca. Used to denote a very wise man.

- Nerón: After the Roman emperor Nero. Used to denote a very cruel man.

5 - Common phrases and fun expressions in your native language and their translation in English

Enchilado (lit. spiced with chilli) can also mean 'angry' or 'irritated.'

Cotorrear (lit. to act like a cotorra –Spanish for parrot–) means to chat or to hang out with someone for a little while.

Padre (lit. father) also means 'cool,' 'nice,' 'awesome.'

- Mexico -

Echar un taco de ojo (lit. to have an eye taco – taco made of eye) means to enjoy oneself by looking at something or someone, usually good-looking people.

Mordida (lit. a bite) also means bribe.

6 - Songs and games you remember from your childhood, that are generally passed on to the next generation

Although many traditional games have passed away since the arrival of video games, there are some that refuse to leave. One of these is the Mexican Lottery Card Game, known as Lotería in Spanish, which works pretty much like Bingo. Nevertheless, the players in this game must wait for the name of each card to be read aloud by a sort of referee until they match all their pictures on their illustrated 4x4 matrices. Smashing piñatas is also very popular among young and old. Other older traditional games include variants of very well-known games such as jump rope (brincar la cuerda), freeze tag (encantados), hide and seek (escondidas), rock, paper, scissors (piedra, papel, tijera), marbles (canicas), London Bridges (la víbora de la mar) and the yoyo. Finally, there are also singing games in which children repeat previous lines and songs get longer, for instance Hay un hoyo en el fondo de la mar (lit. There's a hole in the bottom of the sea) and Mientras el lobo no está (lit. While the wolf is away). Among traditional children songs are those composed by Francisco Gabilondo, better known as Cri Cri, el Grillo Cantor (Cri Cri, the Singing Cricket), in the mid-twentieth century.

7 - *Legends/ stories or famous characters of the Imaginary / Folk tales*

The most popular Mexican folktale might be that of **La Llorona** (The weeping woman). The story is also known in other Latin American countries and tells about a woman who killed her children by drowning them or stabbing them and then killed herself. The most common version told in Mexico starts from this woman's unrequited love toward a man, which eventually makes her kill her three children, allegedly also his children, and then take her own life because of her guilty conscience. She then became a ghost that wanders through the streets during the night mourning the death of her children, searching for other children to make up for her loss. This story has been used to scare and warn children for many years.

8 - *Products or goods that represent 'the national treasure'*

Tequila, mariachi, food and aboriginal handcrafts are regarded as distinctive national products by many Mexicans. Widely recognized abroad, they are also reasonably popular inside the country, although handcrafts are usually not as admired as they are abroad. Beaches and indigenous ruins are also highly regarded among Mexicans.

***

As occurred in other Latin American countries, Mexican culture – including religion, music, food and folktales – was strongly influenced by the European (Spanish) colonization, which led to massive miscegenation. After an intense campaign devoted to revitalize the indigenous people's values in the early twentieth century, Mexico is still in search of its own identity as a mixed people. While Mexico has the largest Spanish-speaking population in the world, there are also 68 indigenous languages recognized by the Mexican State. Even though these native languages – particularly Nahuatl– have influenced Mexican Spanish, they are spoken by only 6% of the population and are rarely learned by Spanish speakers. For obvious geographical reasons, the United States has become a major influence on Mexican society, particularly after the second half of the twentieth century.

Dominican Republic

First name: Marie
Family name: Benzo
MBENZO@GMAIL.COM

Capital	Santo Domingo	Population	10,088,500
Government	Democratic republic	Currency	Dominican pesos (DOP)
Religion(s)	Roman Catholic		
Language(s)	Spanish (official)		

Marie Benzo: Dominican linguist; born in the Dominican Republic in 1981; specialised in the Conference Services Communication Field, in the areas of Translation and Interpretation with 10+ years of experience, combined with a natural talent for languages, and a knack for working with people. Specialised in working English<> Spanish Interpretation (CI & SI) and written translation.

Founder of Voice, Ink- Editorial, Translation & Interpretation Solutions in Santo Domingo; a young translation and localization company featuring a customer portfolio comprising Multinationals, NGOs, and private entities in the US, Canada, Europe and the UAE.

Within my field, I have had the opportunity to contribute to many interesting projects with people from all over the world. I can only describe these experiences as priceless.

I would describe my work as "the best of both worlds put together." Why? Because translation is an art not just a discipline, and as an art, it introduces you to a world of knowledge in a vast array of fields, makes an interesting study tool, because in the field, there must be a willingness to learn new things constantly, and communicate them, so, not only is it a tool for education but also for communication; it is an art because a translator is an "artist in relaying a clear message from one language to another," whereas the interpreter reenacts that message from one language to another; and this requires not only willingness and mastery of the field, but also openness to culture, and more essentially, love for what you do.

1 - A typical conversation – what are the common/universal topics people go for? (weather, politics, etc.) - And some topics that you should avoid discussing with the locals?

When starting a conversation in a Latin American country, it is always a sign of good education to ask the other participant in the dialogue how they are, how their life is treating them, how their family is, and what they are currently doing professionally.

Followed by a short summary of what you are doing, and working on, always remembering to respond after the other person has asked you.

Topics to avoid:

- Conversations about religion

- Conversations about the Vatican controversy
- General issues on politics
- Current government issues (especially the differences between the past government and the new government).

2 - Events of great significance for the community, deeply stored in everyone's mind

February 27, 1844: The Independence of the Dominican Republic

1863-1865: War of Restoration of the Dominican Republic, 17 years after its independence, led by General Gregorio Luperón; in response to the Republic's annexation to Spain by its first Constitutional President, Pedro Santana.

May 30, 1961: The assassination of Generalissimo Trujillo, the dictator who governed the Dominican Republic for 31 years.

1962: Celebration of the 1st Open Presidential Election

The Civil War of 1963 and the deposition of President Juan Bosch, first democratic president elected after the assassination of dictator Trujillo.

The revolution of 1965

The 12 years of President Balaguer 1966-1978: The President who took office after the assassination of Trujillo.

The elections of 2012: the third consecutive term in government of the Dominican Liberation Party (PLD) as President Leonel Fernández passes command to President elect Danilo Medina, confirming 12 years of mandate; the longest a political party has governed since Balaguer's 12 years from 1966 to 1978.

3 - Nouns and Figures from the past / present that you use in colloquial expressions

Regarding "name legacies," it is a folk custom for many members of the local population, more specifically, inhabitants who have a poor level of education, to name their children by combining names of former governors, dictators, characters from TV and movies, and even popular figures.

Example:

1) Usnavy: name very much used in Washington Heights, known as Little Dominican Republic in N.Y.; when deconstructed, the name is just the initials of the U.S. Navy put together.

2) Hitler, Stalin, and Mussolini: This combination of names has been used by many families to name their sons. In some cases they are unaware that their sons have been named in homage to three of history's best-known dictators.

4 - Words used to designate a type of person, animal, things

- Doña: used to refer respectfully to the lady of the house, a married woman, or an older woman (past the age of 60)
- Don: the same as previous but for a man. Ref: to a superior at work, an important official, an executive within a company, an older man, an old friend or acquaintance of the family.
- Cochita: an affectionate way of saying "Cosita"; usually when we first meet a newborn baby we say "Que cochita más linda" (what a cute little thing)
- Mishu Mishu: a way of referring to a cat, regardless of whether you know its name or not.
- Mi amor: (My love) is not just a way of addressing your

loved one, it is also used by men trying to flirt with an attractive woman, or denoting confidence with someone you just met.

5 - Common phrases and fun expressions in your native language and their translation in English

Las enfermedades entran a caballo y salen a pie (meaning: illness races its way in, but crawls its way out)

Ay! Mi madre (literally: oh my mother! meaning: oh man!)

Pa'hambre vieja no hay pan duro (meaning: when there's hunger, no old bread is hard to eat)

Cuando cuca bailaba (referring to the good old days)

Ese huevo quiere sal (literally: that egg wants some salt; meaning: something's up)

Ahí hay gato entre macuto (the cat's in the bag; meaning: "there's something there we don't know about")

Curarse en salud (literally: to heal when still healthy; this means: "better safe than sorry")

La cosa ta' mala compadre (literally: it's bad my man; meaning: "things are not going well my friend")

Tiró la toalla (literally: dropped the towel; "giving up")

6 - Songs and games you remember from your childhood, that are generally passed on to the next generation

- La rueda rueda (Ring around the rosie)
- El topao'paralizao (Tag)
- El Escondío' (Hide and Seek)

7 - *Legends/ stories or famous characters of the Imaginary / Folk tales*

The legend of the **Ciguapa** (mythical character depicted as a beautiful woman with very long hair, whose feet are backwards)

El Cuco (the boogeyman)

8 - *Products or goods that represent 'the national treasure'*

Rum: Ron Brugal known as "Dominican white gold" in Europe, for its taste is unlike any other rum ever tasted.

Sancocho: our traditional Dominican dish, which consists of a stew involving seven types of meat, plantains and different types of produce (nams, manioc; also known as yucca).

***

When you talk about the Dominican Republic, you talk about a country that is a world of its own. Born out of the mixture of different colonies and thus cultures, when you visit the Dominican Republic, you meet people who are warm, hospitable, and embracing of foreign cultures.

The colorfulness of our ways enchants visitors, and many of them end up settling here. Be it our landscapes, our music, our rum, the flavors in our food or the passion we apply to everything, who knows really what the "true secret" may be, but it is definitely worth finding out.

CENTRAL AMERICA

- Costa Rica
- Honduras
- Nicaragua

Costa Rica

First name: Gabriela
Family name: Castro
mail@gabrielacastro.com
www.GabrielaCastro.com

Capital	San Jose	Population	4,636,300
Government	Democratic republic	Currency	Costa Rican colones (CRC)
Religion(s)	Roman Catholic, Evangelical		
Language(s)	Spanish (official), English		

I was born and raised in Costa Rica. My first contact with the English language was when I was in elementary school and my mom thought learning English was important for my future. Little did she know English was going to be the basis of my major and my life! After studying English Teaching as a major and getting a Bachelor's Degree in Translation at a local university, I became a teacher, studied to obtain a Master's Degree in English teaching and taught the language from pre-k to adults for ten years.

After that, I decided to switch my professional path and explore the language services market. That is how I ended up working as an in-house financial translator and two years later I started working on my own. Learning the ups and downs of the business has been quite an experience! I have had the opportunity to be the head of our national association of language service providers, I have experienced working directly with clients and there is still more to come!

Today, I am specialised in pharmaceuticals, finance and legal documents and my journey as a simultaneous interpreter is full of new topics. In a few months I will graduate with a Master's degree in English to Spanish Translation and I am starting to think about the next adventure!

1 - A typical conversation – what are the common/universal topics people go for? (weather, politics, etc.) - And some topics that you should avoid discussing with the locals?

Costa Ricans are very friendly and talkative. Although the country is not fully bilingual, tourists and visitors will always find a helping hand to assist them regardless of the language barrier. Costa Ricans tend to be openly sociable from the start and do not need a lot of time to be honest about their thoughts. As in many cultures, religion and money are conservative topics but it does not mean Costa Ricans will avoid these topics at all cost. Under our democratic regime, everyone in the country has their own opinion on politics and most are not afraid to express what they feel about politicians and the future of the country. Soccer and family are commons topics to discuss with friends and relatives.

2 - Events of great significance for the community, deeply stored in everyone's mind

Costa Rica has been an independent country since 1821 and

although our history holds a Civil War that lasted only 44 days and stories of national heroes, modern marches and social groups are also as well-rooted in the minds of ticos and ticas (Costa Rican men and women).

Since this was the only Civil War the country has ever experienced, Costa Ricans keep in their minds other types of events like the dates of destructive earthquakes, 1910 in Cartago, 1990 in Alajuela or 1991 in Limón. Something else in the mind of our population was the only time Costa Rica's national soccer team had the chance to participate in a World Cup in 1990.

A demonstration in favour of the privatization of the main Costa Rican energy provider, ICE, was held in the year 2000 causing thousands of Costa Ricans to join the march. People take pride in the fact that Óscar Arias Sánchez, former Costa Rican president from 1986 to 1990, received the Peace Nobel Prize in 1987 for his efforts to end civil wars in other Central American countries during that time.

3 - *Figures from the past / present*

Our national hero, **Juan Santamaría**, was a simple drummer boy. In 1855, William Walker, a Southerner who planned to enslave Central America, took over the Nicaraguan government. Juan Rafael Mora, Costa Rica's president back then, decided to fight the filibusters with an army of peasants. The enemy sought protection in a wooden fort and Juan Santamaría bravely volunteered to burn it forcing Walker and his group outside. Juan Santamaría carried a torch and he threw it at the fort and burned it down, although he was shot repeatedly.

A more contemporary hero is astronaut **Franklin Chang** who was also a poor boy who had the opportunity and eagerness to get far and became an astronaut at NASA. He currently runs a major company that develops and has commercialized the Variable Specific Impulse Magnetoplasma Rocket (VASMIR®).

Prominent writer **Carmen Lyra** (María Isabel Carvajal) was an active communist. In 1920, her famous collection of folk tales *Cuentos De Mi Tia Panchita* (Tales of My Aunt Panchita) was published and still exists as a reference in print nowadays.

These are just three examples of influential people from our past. Costa Ricans are certainly influenced by different public figures in many areas.

5 - *Common phrases and fun expressions in your native language and their translation in English*

"Tuanis" (cool or nice): an informal word. It is very commonly used in isolation to say hi. Some people say it possibly derived from the English phrase "too nice" used by Jamaican descended population in the Limón province.

"Pura vida" (nice or state of well-being): a phrase that is as much used in semiformal and informal contexts to express that something is good or nice, or someone is doing well.

The phrases below are used in very informal contexts or in everyday language. Costa Rica's official language is Spanish. Part of the population is bilingual (uses English at work or school) and we also have small indigenous groups that still speak their native languages.

- aguevado: bored or boring
- brete: work or job

- chunche: thing
- güila: a girl
- jumas: drunk
- choza: home
- vara: thing
- macha: a blond female, usually a foreigner
- por dicha: thank goodness
- que m'iche? what's up?

6 - Songs and games you remember from your childhood, that are generally passed on to the next generation

Hopscotch and sack races are still in fashion in schools. Games such as hide and seek and TV tag have also been around for ages and school teachers promote them to elementary school students. "Elástico" or jump ropes are used at children's parties. Back in the days, it was a lot more common to see boys playing with "bolinchas" or marbles than now but still some of them know what they are. Passing an egg on a spoon from one side of a room or area to another is still common even at adult office parties involving motivational and group work techniques. Soccer games have also stood the test of time.

Traditional songs are still taught at schools and to preschoolers. These songs include "Arroz con leche," "Los esqueletos," "Los pollitos dicen" and "Era una paloma."

7 - Legends/ stories or famous characters of the Imaginary / Folk tales

There are at least two famous Costa Rican legends from colonial times that everyone in the country knows about. They are "El Cadejos" and "La llorona."

El Cadejos is the story of a boy who disobeyed his parents and was turned into an old, black, lonely dog. This dog was seen very often following drunken men and those who arrived home late at night.

La llorona is the story of a pretty woman who fell in love with a married Spanish officer who broke her heart. The unbearable pain turned her into a horrible looking monster that hunted lonely travelers. They would come across a beautiful woman on the road with porcelain-like skin, black eyes and long hair. She would suddenly appear and ask lonely men for a ride. Once by their side, she would turn into monster with the skull of a horse, red eyes and sharp teeth.

8 - Products or goods that represent 'the national treasure'

If we were to prepare a basket with food products from Costa Rica for someone who is at home sick, that basket would definitely include Costa Rican coffee, which nowadays is famous and sold worldwide as one of the best coffees in the world. Other products include "Lizano" sauce made of fresh vegetables, "Pozuelo" cookies and crackers, "Gallito" chocolate and different flavors of jelly from "Ujarrás."

Our national treasure can also be measured in terms of natural resources. Costa Rica is one of the 20 countries in the world with the highest biodiversity including 500,000 animal species. We have plenty of pristine beaches, pre-Colombian art from indigenous regions and abundant national parks and volcanos.

Honduras

First name: Gabriela
Family name: Leveron
GLEVERON@HOTMAIL.COM

Capital	Tegucigalpa	Population	8,296,500
Government	Democratic constitutional republic	Currency	Lempiras (HNL)
Religion(s)	Roman Catholic		
Language(s)	Spanish (official), Amerindian dialects		

Hi, I'm Gabriela Leverón. I was born and raised in San Pedro Sula and am currently living there. Ever since I was a young girl, I could think of nothing more than to become a veterinarian, but through life's twists and turns found the joy of teaching and currently work as a full time teacher at a private bilingual school near my home. This prompted me to obtain a second undergraduate degree in teaching, which I'm currently working on. Teaching introduced me to a life of patience, volunteering, and big ideas, and has shaped the person I am today. I'm not really limited to teaching; I do translations when I can, and read, read, read.

I'm a lover of pasta, and the wife of a computer engineer whom I dated for almost nine years before agreeing to marry him. I can always be found with a good book in my hand.

1 - A typical conversation – what are the common/universal topics people go for? (weather, politics, etc.) - And some topics that you should avoid discussing with the locals?

In Honduras, nearly everyone's favourite topic is football, and having our national team get through to the final round of qualifying for the 2014 World Cup is a welcome conversation topic for anyone. Other than that, conversing about good food and places to eat with your family and friends is also popular.

The only topic that will gain you lifelong enemies is the events of June 2009 when the president was ousted from power and exiled.

2 - Events of great significance for the community, deeply stored in everyone's mind

As mentioned before, our most precious memories involve our national football team, which qualified for the 2010 World Cup in South Africa – it was even declared a national holiday when they did! Unfortunately, we got eliminated in the first round, but that was enough to keep us happy for many years to come. Qualifying for the Sydney Olympics was also a big event.

On a negative note, Hurricane Mitch in 1998 set us back 20 years in an already struggling economy: this event wiped out our second largest export, bananas, and we are still trying to get back to pre-Mitch. Then, in 2009, the coup which ousted President "Mel" Zelaya created great controversy worldwide and caused the falling out of many families and long-time friendships.

Of course, with the whole Mayan prediction of the end of the world, our small city of Copan draws a lot of attention from locals and foreigners.

3 - Figures from the past / present that you use in colloquial expressions

History has it that the name Honduras comes from an exclamation made by Christopher Columbus after having found shelter while caught in a storm at sea. He said, "Gracias a Dios que hemos salido de estas honduras!" (Thank god we've escaped these depths!) Henceforth, the territory where he docked was known as Gracias a Dios and the rest of it as Honduras.

Another person from our past who is used as the greatest role model for everyone is **Francisco Morazán**, who fought for the union of Central American countries, created the Constitution, established taxes, made military service obligatory and created schools. Even further back in history, Lempira, a Lenca chief and warrior, managed to unify Indian tribes to resist the Spanish conquerors. He remained invincible and was tricked into having a peace conference. With this, he was drawn out from his hiding place and shot with an arrow by a hidden archer. With his death, other Indians fled or surrendered.

4 - Words used to designate a type of person, animal, things

Hondurans are also known as "catrachos," which derives from General Florencio Xatruch who, around the 1800s, was an avid defender of Central American sovereignty. General Xatruch was proclaimed generalissimo for his bravery in a war against North American filibusters, and the men who served with him in battle were able to help him in reclaiming a large part of invaded Nicaraguan land. When they returned from battle, they were celebrated as heroes and people used the phrase: "Here come the catrachos," mispronouncing the general's difficult last name.

5 - Common phrases and fun expressions in your native language and their translation in English

Being a small, traditional country, we have a very colourful set of phrases that range from innocent to outright cheeky, and using them is considered to show a lack of education. Among them are the following:

- When referring to someone saying a lie, "¡paja!" (hay)
- Agreeing with someone about something or doing something, "cheque pues" (okay then)
- Someone who has expensive taste and is stuck-up, "fresa" (strawberry)
- Someone who acts or behaves as if they come from a small town, are overly shy and do not want to do something, "montuno" (coming from the grass)
- When someone does something dumb, "pataston" (big pataste) or "papo"

6 - Songs and games you remember from your childhood, that are generally passed on to the next generation

Unfortunately traditional games are being lost to the call of technology, but many small towns celebrate festivals where these games are honoured and kept in the minds of children. These include playing "cantarito" (hide and seek using a ball), "maules," mispronounced form for marbles in Spanish, jump rope, hopscotch, and the "trompo," a wooden conic object with a metal tip, that you "make dance" using a string.

7 - Legends/ stories or famous characters of the Imaginary / Folk tales

- Honduras -

Everybody in Honduras, including a few of my very close friends, swear they've seen him: a short, long eared man who always wears a big hat. He is called **"El duende"** (the dwarf) and stalks the homes of pretty girls by hiding among the shadows only to lure them away. They are taken to his dwelling in a cave and are never to be seen or heard from again. This story is a warning to young women that they should never go out alone, much less after dark. Another story for young women is about "el Sisimite," who resembles a shorthaired Bigfoot and whose aim is to steal away young women, take them to his cave and force them to procreate.

The majority of Honduran stories are meant to keep men from drinking or picking up women. Among these are:

- "El cadejo" is a large dog that is either black or white. If you encounter the white 'cadejo' then you should count your blessings, since it's considered a good spirit that protects the person it walks next to. The black 'cadejo,' on the other hand, tries to kill the people it appears to.

- "La sucia" is the dirty woman. She appears to men who are out late and is usually washing clothes and crying. Her hair always covers her face and when she lets a man kiss her, screams as she reveals her monstrous face and bad breath, causing men to go insane. There are many variations on this story, but it's always in the middle of the night and only happens to men.

- "La Sihuanaba" is a woman who stalks single men who are out alone after hours, seducing them from behind, then revealing long, sharp fingernails and a skeleton horse's head. After meeting her, men get fevers and become very sick. It's recommended to always travel with a red piece of cloth in your left pocket or wear a cross made of pins on your hat.

8 - *Products or goods that represent 'the national treasure'*

Honduras is famous around the world for the precious wood from our extensive forests, such as fine mahogany, cedar and coffee. In addition, we export many tropical fruits like pineapple, melons, mango, and bananas. On the Caribbean coast, "sopa de caracol" (conch soup) is the most sought after dish, followed by fried fish with fried plantain slices, "tajadas." After a day of hard work, when the sun has done its duty, a relaxing nap on a handmade hammock is a must.

Most of our food comes from corn: tortillas, tamales, atol. A representative dish of the city of San Pedro Sula is the "baleada," in its most basic form it is a wheat tortilla with pureed frijoles, a dollop of "mantequilla" and a sprinkle of hard cheese. You can add anything to it because it goes with everything: eggs, meat, onion, sausage, chorizo… the sky is the limit, but you must not forget to enjoy it with a hot, strong cup of black coffee.

Nicaragua

FIRST NAME: ANGELES
FAMILY NAME: BERMUDEZ
ANGELESMASAYA@GMAIL.COM
&
FIRST NAME: ROLANDO
FAMILY NAME: TELLEZ
EBACCA7@GMAIL.COM

Capital	Managua	Population	5,727,700
Government	Republic	Currency	Cordobas (NIO)
Religion(s)	Roman Catholic, Protestant		
Language(s)	Spanish (official), English and indigenous languages		

Angeles: I was born in Masaya, Nicaragua. I studied in the US during my early twenties, then became a staff member at the World Bank. I met my future husband who was a Conference Interpreter for the UN, we married and I moved to England, then France and Spain. I enriched my experience by living in the Basque Country, on both the French and Spanish sides, where I had close contact with the Basque people, their customs, language and traditions. I went back to the UK in the middle of the nineties and decided to study for a Degree in Bilingual Translation at the

University of Westminster. Europe gave me a great opportunity to plunge into four different cultures and in all I have lived 28 years away from my home country. Life brought me back to Nicaragua where I have a very close-knit family and where I work full-time as a freelance translator.

Rolando: I was born in Managua city, located in the heart of the Americas in 1961. I began to teach technical English at the National University (UNAN) in 1981, and then I had opportunities to work as an interpreter and translator. Since 1994, I worked only part time at other universities because of translation work. My first official translation course diploma was issued in 1988. This postgraduate course was taught by Belgium translators-trainers. In 1990, I studied at Indiana State University, and in 1992, I graduated in Speech Communication from Southern Illinois University in the United States of America.

When I came back to Nicaragua, I set up my translation office. Since then, I have provided translation and interpretation services to hundreds of companies, NGOs, and individuals.

1 - A typical conversation – what are the common/universal topics people go for? (weather, politics, etc.) - And some topics that you should avoid discussing with the locals?

- Weather: This is a topic that is not usually a conversation issue for me. You might get into a taxi cab, and then you can make a comment about traffic or about the weather. My country is prone to weather disturbances such as hurricanes, floods, landslides, etc. When Hurricane Mitch hit Nicaragua in 1998, I was almost swept away inside my car by a strong current and decided to take an active role in helping the most affected areas of Nicaragua. I had never experienced such a tragic moment in my life and curiously I was interviewed by different radio stations including Radio France. I never thought my conversation was being recorded and all of a sudden I started to receive calls from France and the UK, and my friends sent donations for the victims. At that time, weather was discussed daily.

- Family: Usually you can discuss with others about your family members and your place of origin.

- Sports: You can talk about soccer activities taking place in Europe; baseball is more popular in Nicaragua.

- Volcanology: It is a fascinating topic to me. I live near active volcanoes and lagoons of volcanic origin. The Pacific Coast of Nicaragua is dotted with a chain of volcanoes: some active, some inactive, some dormant. It is a fact of life for us to live and coexist with those volcanoes.

- Coffee: My family has been in the coffee business since the end of the nineteenth century. The farm has gone from generation to generation and now my sisters, my brother and I are dedicated to the coffee plantation. We work all year round to maintain a healthy farm. We avoid chemical products and try to create the best product we can. Our production is small but we are proud when the farmhands pick the coffee from the trees. It is magical to see the red grains grow from the beautiful white flowers that bloom in May, when the rains start here.

Topics to avoid:

- Politics

- Religion: Every time religion is a topic in a conversation, I notice people become uneasy.

- Sex: A difficult one to be included in a usual conversation.

- Financial issues: Local currency is always going down.

- Social status: You can make negative comments about the

rich.

2 - Events of great significance for the community, deeply stored in everyone's mind

At the end of the 1970s, the dictatorship in Nicaragua was ousted by a group of revolutionaries called the Sandinistas, who formed the Sandinista Front for National Liberation (FSLN). They overthrew the president and during the 1980s my country suffered a cruel civil war where brothers and sisters became enemies. The war is burned in the minds of the Nicaraguan people. The Sandinistas got the support of the people because Nicaragua was drained by a dictatorship for almost four decades. In 1979, when the Revolution triumphed, the revolutionaries were supported by the population. Had they called for free elections in 1980, they would have won unanimously. They didn't and began to govern in the direction of the left.

In 1985, when they called for an election, there was only one party and the elections were won by the FSLN. That provoked the embargo imposed on Nicaragua by the United States and the war became very crude with the Contras who were attacking Nicaragua from Honduras. There was rationing because there were not enough goods and even less food to feed the people. There was a Sandinista army recruiting men and women from the age of 16, which caused youngsters to flee to other countries. Families became broken and the brain drain was enormous with thousands of professionals leaving the country.

During the Revolution there was a literacy campaign conducted by a priest and it reached every nook and cranny of Nicaragua.

In 1990, elections were called and a strong "UNO" group led by

Mrs. Violeta Barrios de Chamorro, widow of our martyr and journalist, Pedro Joaquin Chamorro, won the elections, marking the end of the war on Nicaragua.

3 - Figures from the past / present

Rubén Darío Sarmiento, a Nicaraguan poet, began a Hispanic-American literary movement known as "modernismo." Rubén Darío influenced the Spanish language so much that he was called the "Prince of Castilian Letters."

Agusto Cesar Sandino, a Nicaraguan hero who drove U.S. troops out of Nicaragua. Sandino's tactics included a guerrilla warfare against Americans who occupied Nicaragua for several years. Sandino wanted Latin American countries to unite against U.S. intervention in Latin America, and to set the poor free from the oppression imposed by the capitalist system in Latin America. He was successful in defeating U.S. troops in Nicaragua. However local pro-American politicians finally assassinated him.

4 - Words used to designate a type of person, animal, things

- Chunche: can be any object for which somebody doesn't remember the real name.
- Mamita: term of endearment for mothers, friends and girlfriends.
- Cuchi-cuchi: a man who can be homosexual
- Melcocha: a person who is sweet
- Negro: a dog
- Se hace el sueco: Swedish people do not know much about local culture. The word "sueco" refers to any person who

does not want to understand what people tell him or her.

5 - Common phrases and fun expressions in your native language and their translation in English

- *Mi media naranja:* my better half (a boyfriend or girlfriend)
- *Tiene nave y billete:* It refers to a person who has a car and money; used in a positive way.
- *Ponéte chiva:* This means you have to be careful because you are in a place where other people may attack you. Young people use this expression a lot.
- *¡Estoy arrecho!* When somebody is very angry at someone or something. A person will say ¡Estoy aLas It can be translated to "I feel so pissed off!" or "It is driving me crazy!"
- *¡Ve que pinche!* An informal way of saying you don't like to spend your money.
- *¡Ponéte las pilas!* A way of saying, "Get a move on there!" or "Move fast." Don't miss this chance.
- *Te ves tuani.* "You look great! It's cool!"
- *Hablar a calzón quitado.* To talk honestly without euphemism.

6 - Songs and games you remember from your childhood, that are generally passed on to the next generation

Songs

Los pollitos dicen pio pio pio cuando tienen hambre cuando tienen frio, la gallina busca el maíz y el trigo les da su alimento y después su abrigo. This is almost the first song a child learns in Nicaragua and is about farm animals.

Dormito niñito que tengo que hacer, lavar tus pañales e irme a coser... - Mothers sing this song to put babies to sleep.

Caballito Chontaleño:

Caballito chontaleño de mi tierra tropical
corre corre que a la guelta ves aquel cañaveral
Ahora vengo satisfecho porque a mi negra he besado
traigo el corazón desecho y me siento desmayado.

Games

"OA – Sin moverme, sin reírme, en un pie, en una mano, adelante, atrás, media vuelta y vuelta entera." This game is played with a ball while saying this sentence and if you drop the ball, you lose.

"Tin marin de dos pinguin cucara macara títere fue." - This is a rhyming sentence used to choose the one who wins.

7 - Legends/ stories or famous characters of the Imaginary / Folk tales

The wailing woman. In the days of the colony, there was an Indian woman who fell pregnant to a white man. After giving birth she went and killed her child out of desperation in front of her people and her family for having committed the sin of having a baby with a white man. Feeling incredibly guilty for having killed the baby, she threw herself down Lake Masaya and killed herself. Those living next to the lake swear they can hear a woman screaming and wailing and that the screams are from the woman who drowned in the lake.

8 - Products or goods that represent 'the national treasure'

Ron Flor de Caña (rum): an internationally known liquor.

Marimba (simple piano-like instrument): It is used to sing folk music.

The *Gueguense*: Cultural Heritage of Humanity - The Gueguense is a yearly Nicaraguan popular play and dance in the streets of Diriamba town in January. This comedy-dance is about an old man who pretends not to hear what the Spanish authorities are saying, quid pro quo or play on words, obscene words, and pre-Colombian music and dance. Power relationships and Spanish influence are perceived in the dialogues that can make an interesting movie.

***

Los Ahuizotes: This has become the Nicaraguan Halloween, especially in the city of Masaya. In the old days, the procession of the Ahuizotes took place only in Monimbo, the indigenous enclave south of Masaya. It celebrated All Saints Day and the main characters were, and continue to be, la Mocuana (who cries inconsolably with her long hair and hidden face), el Padre sin Cabeza (who haunts everybody in the procession), la Carreta Nagua (a cart pulled by oxen making lots of noise and driven by a dead woman who usually predicts the death of someone who is in good health and all of a sudden becomes ill and dies), black devils, red devils. Everyone is disguised, frightening people and causing havoc in town. This takes place on the last Friday of October.

SOUTH AMERICA

- Argentina
- Bolivia
- Brazil
- Chile
- Columbia
- Ecuador
- Peru
- Uruguay
- Venezuela

Argentina

FIRST NAME: MARIELA
FAMILY NAME: CACURRI
AMCACURRI@YAHOO.COM.AR

Capital	Buenos Aires	Population	42,192,400
Government	Republic	Currency	Argentine pesos (ARS)
Religion(s)	Nominally Roman Catholic		
Language(s)	Spanish (official) and other European languages, indigenous (Mapudungun, Quechua)		

My full name is Adriana Mariela Cacurri, but everybody calls me by my second name (Mariela). I was born in Buenos Aires, Argentina, on the 30th of December 1977. I currently live in Rosario with my family. I'm married and the mother of two kids (Gerónimo and Victoria). Since I was a child, I knew that I wanted to be an English teacher when I grew up. My first job was in a Clinical Research Organisation where I started to translate medical and pharmaceutical material. I found it really interesting to research terms and interview professionals to discuss different technical words. Then, I realised that my true vocation was to be a translator. Consequently, I gave up my studies in English Teaching and started my studies in the fascinating world of literary, technical and scientific translation. I obtained my Degree in

- Argentina -

Translating and since then I've been working as a professional freelancer. I specialised in medical translation but I have also discovered a completely new area of translation: subtitling. I've subtitled more than 10,000 hours of video since 2007. Fortunately, I work for three well-known subtitling companies on a regular basis. I have translated documentaries, medical videos and even horror films.

My personal interests are: music, sport (jogging), movies and reading (literature and history).

1 - A typical conversation – what are the common/universal topics people go for? (weather, politics, etc.) - And some topics that you should avoid discussing with the locals?

When introducing a common conversation, it's a sign of politeness to ask how the other person is doing and about his or her family. After talking about how they're doing, people may then talk about football. I think this is the most common conversation topic, especially after a weekend in which all the teams play a football match in the annual championship league. Even women talk about football. It's a passion shared by people of all ages.

We are well informed people and we like talking about politics with family; however we tend to avoid this topic with people we don't know very well.

We are very vehement speakers, and we frequently interrupt one another. So interrupting is a sign of participation and interest.

2 - *Events of great significance for the community, deeply stored in everyone's mind*

1816 Independence from Spain

1982 The Falklands War: a war between Argentina and the United Kingdom due to a dispute over the sovereignty of the Falkland Islands (for us "Islas Malvinas"). The conflict ended with the Argentine surrender. Many young soldiers from Argentina died due to lack of experience and training. In addition, they were badly equipped.

1976-1983 A military dictatorship took power in 1976. The Dirty War is the name given to the extra-judicial kidnappings and murders of political dissidents by the Argentine military during 1976-1983. The Mothers of the Plaza de Mayo (las Madres de Plaza de Mayo) began a protest in the square to demand information about their missing children. Democracy was restored in 1983.

2001 Economical, social and political crisis occurred. President De la Rua resigned. There was a general crisis with unemployment, rioting, looting and emigration (especially to Spain and Italy). In the following two weeks, there were five different presidents.

3 - *Nouns and Figures from the past / present that you use in colloquial expressions*

- Maradona and Messi (both Argentinians): are synonyms of extraordinary football players
- Huevón (Big Egg): a silly person
- Grasa (Grease): someone with bad taste, or a rude or uneducated person.

- *Argentina* -

- Gato (Cat): a woman that dresses or behaves like a prostitute
- Careta (Mask): snobbish person

5 - *Common phrases and fun expressions in your native language and their translation in English*

"Ojo!" (Eye): Be careful!

"Onda" (Waves, vibes): It can be used with "buena" or "mala" to mean equivalent of "good vibes" (*buena onda*) or "bad vibes" (*mala onda*) in English. Onda can also be used preceded by "Qué" (what) as an equivalent for "How is it going?"

"Che" (Hey): Short for "escuchame," meaning "listen to me" or "hey." Used as an exclamation to call your attention to the rest of the sentence. Ernesto "Che" Guevara (Argentine revolutionary who had a major role in the Cuban Revolution) got the nickname "Che" from other Spanish speakers because he used to say it all the time.

"Quilombo" (Chaos): Meaning mess, disaster.

"Boludo" It can mean "idiot" or can also be used affectionately. This word is widely used, especially in the country's capital.

"Estar en el horno" (to be in the oven): To be stressed out or in a bad situation

"Le faltan algunos jugadores" (Some players are missing): He or she is out of his or her mind, he or she is dumb

"Mala leche" (Bad milk): Bad luck

"Tomalo con soda" (Drink it with soda water): Calm down, take it easy

"Calavera no chilla" (Skull doesn't yell): You get what you deserve

6 - Songs and games you remember from your childhood, that are generally passed on to the next generation

Most of María Elena Walsh's songs are very popular in Argentina, like *Canción de tomar el té* (Tea Time Song), *El reino del revés* (The Reverse Kingdom), *La Tortuga Manuelita* (Manuelita The Turtle), etc.

Other popular songs are *Arroz con leche* (Rice pudding), *Qué linda manito* (What a pretty hand), *Saco una manito* (I take out a little hand).

Games: Rayuela (hopscotch), gallito ciego (blindman's buff), huevo podrido (rotten egg), la popa o la mancha (tag game), las escondidas (hide and seek).

7 - Legends/ stories or famous characters of the Imaginary / Folk tales

Gauchito Gil is a legendary character of Argentina's popular culture. He is regarded as the most prominent "gaucho" saint in Argentina ("Gaucho" is a term commonly used to describe native residents of South American pampas, usually mixed Spanish and Indian ancestry).

La Difunta Correa is a semi-pagan mythical figure in folk-religion for which a number of people in Argentina feel a great devotion.

La Luz Mala is a ghostly light seen by travellers at night and is mostly seen in rural areas.

Pacha Mama is a fertility goddess who presides over planting and harvesting. She causes earthquakes.

Pombero is a mythical humanoid of small stature from Guaraní mythology. He is said to be a primarily nocturnal creature, generally viewed as a harmless troublemaker.

8 - Products or goods that represent 'the national treasure'

Asado (Barbecue): Argentina is not a place for vegetarians, but for those who love beef. The "asado" is the traditional meal to be eaten on Sundays with family and friends.

Dulce de Leche is a traditional dairy product and its literal translation is "Sweet Milk."

Empanadas are usually served as a starter or main course. The National Empanada Festival is celebrated in Tucumán Province every year.

Mate is our national drink and is best shared with friends.

Famous cartoon characters

Patoruzú is a character created in 1928 and is considered to be the most popular hero of Argentine comics.

Clemente is another comic strip character created by Caloi in 1973.

Hijitus (a comic strip character) is a normal child who can transform himself into a superhero called Super-Hijitus using his magic hat and the magic phrase "Sombrero, sombreritus, conviérteme en Super-Hijitus."

Mafalda: The comic features a 6-year-old girl named Mafalda, who is deeply concerned about humanity and world peace and rebels about the current state of the world. The character was created by Quino.

***

Argentina is a dynamic and charming nation that oscillates perpetually between crisis and boom. It has a vast territory and it is rich in natural resources. It has a great variety of topography and climates. In Argentina you can find one of the seven wonders of nature: Cataratas del Iguazú (Iguazu Falls).

This nation produced Che Guevara (Cuban revolutionary leader), Gardel (Tango singer), Maradona and Messi (football players), Favaloro (cardiac surgeon, creator of the coronary artery bypass surgery) and María Eva Duarte de Perón (the political leader known as "Evita").

Bolivia

FIRST NAME: GONZALO
FAMILY NAME: PALACIOS
GTRANSLATES@GMAIL.COM

Capital	La Paz (administrative) Sucre (constitutional)	Population	10,290,000
Government	Republic - the constitution defines Bolivia as a "Social Unitarian State"	Currency	Bolivianos (BOB)
Religion(s)	Roman Catholic		
Language(s)	Spanish (official), Quechua (official), Aymara (official)		

I was born in La Paz-Bolivia, located in the heart of South America, in 1977. After finishing my English studies at CBA (Centro Boliviano Americano, the highest accredited institution in my country) in 1998, I decided to work as an English teacher. Initially, I only worked in a small school, however in time, due to my extensive experience (over 10 years), I also worked in various and important local organisations.

In 2006, a student's husband, who was the president of an important company, contacted me to translate some documents and, since he knew that I also had a degree in Biotechnology

(Universidad Mayor de San Andres-Faculty of Medicine), he thought I was the right person to translate his documents. In fact, his company was one of the largest pharmaceutical companies in Bolivia. Initially, he only gave me a few documents to translate, but then he started giving me lots of documents so that as a result I gained more experience in translation (pharmaceutical and medical documents). I was really very fascinated with the world of translation because this was an amazing way to be involved in different fields (legal, financial, computing, sciences, biology, technology, etc.) as well as to meet a great variety of people of various ages, races and social statuses from different countries.

As a freelance translator I have now devoted 7 years to translation. Also, I am a registered member at ProZ.com: http://www.proz.com/translator/1377350, where you can find more details about me.

1 - A typical conversation – what are the common/universal topics people go for? (weather, politics, etc.) - And some topics that you should avoid discussing with the locals?

Common topics:

***Weather:** When you get into a taxi, and you want to discuss any topic with the taxi driver, you can start a conversation about how the weather is today or was yesterday.

***Family:** Usually you can discuss your family members with others, even including some specific details about their personality.

***Sports:** Every region has its favourite soccer team such as "The strongest," "Bolivar," "Oriente Petrolero" and "San José" and you might have a funny conversation glorifying your team and putting down the others.

***Politics:** It can lead to many hours of discussion and every person will take the time to defend his or her political party.

Topics to avoid:

***Religion**

***Sex:** Most families are still conservative so this topic would be a difficult one to include in a normal conversation.

***Financial issues and social status**

2 - Events of great significance for the community, deeply stored in everyone's mind

1825 Independence of Bolivia with Simon Bolivar as its first president, who also gave his name to the country (member of Congress Manuel Martín Cruz proposed: "If from Romulus comes Rome, then from Bolívar comes Bolivia").

1879–1883 War of the Pacific, Bolivia loses its sea access to Chile together with the port of Antofagasta

1932-35 Chaco War, Bolivia loses territory to Paraguay.

1952 The Revolutionary Nationalist Movement (MNR) leads a successful revolution and Víctor Paz Estenssoro, introduces far-reaching social and economic reforms.

2003 (September-October) Bolivian gas conflict. President Sanchez de Lozada resigns.

2005 Evo Morales wins the presidential elections, becoming the first indigenous Bolivian to take office.

2011 (August-September) Plans to build a major road through a rainforest reserve known as Isiboro Secure Indigenous Territory and National Park (TIPNIS) spark mass protests and later, in **2012,** President Morales rescinds the contract awarded to Brazil's OAS to build this controversial road.

3 - *Nouns and Figures from the past / present that you use in colloquial expressions*

Carlos Palenque (1944–1997) was a Bolivian musician, singer and politician popularly known as "the Compadre." In fact, he was the owner of RTP (Sistema de Radio Television Popular) which was one of the most important local broadcasters. It is very significant that in his program "La Tribuna Libre del Pueblo," he called his co-host (Remedios Loza) "**Comadre** Remedios" and she called him "**Compadre** Palenque." When people visited the programme, usually poor and humble people, Carlos Palenque and Remedios Loza received them warmly calling them "compadre" or "comadre" and as a result they felt more comfortable and confident talking about their particular issues. On one hand, locally both words "compadre/comadre" are used by parents for godparents of a new-born child. However, you can now also use these words for your best friends, in which case both words (compadre/comadre) might be translated as "my good friend" or "my brother/sister" for people with a stronger friendship.

Zambo Salvito (1838-1870) (Salvador Sea) was a notorious, wily thief who committed a variety of crimes including muggings, homicides and rape, terrorizing people travelling from La Paz to the Yungas (tropical valleys from Bolivia). As a result he was executed, but before dying the thief asked to say a few words to his stepmother. When he saw his stepmother, he bit her ear angrily and quickly removed it. He claimed that he acted in that way because when he was a child, she had allowed him to steal small things such as needles, threads and buttons and later he became a feared thief. That's why some grandparents usually advise their grandchildren not to take things from others because they will end up in trouble like Zambo Salvito.

4 - Words used to designate a type of person, animal, things

- Bobby: A general way to name a dog. You can usually hear "¿Puedo pasar? No hay un Bobby en la casa, ¿no?" (Could I get in? You don't have dogs, do you?)

- Don: A respectful way to call a man who is married or assuming formal responsibilities. But you should be careful when using the word "Doncito," a diminutive for the word "Don," as this may be interpreted as a scornful term for a man.

- Doña: A respectful way to call a woman who is married. And similar to the word "Doncito," the word "Doñita" is a diminutive for the word "Doña" and may be interpreted as a scornful term for a lady.

- Compadre/Comadre: If you have your child baptised then you have a "comadre" (godmother) and you have a "compadre" (godfather). And usually you can use both terms in a more affectionate way with your friends.

- Pelado/pelada: A standard word for "boy" (pelado) or "girl" (pelada) especially in the east of Bolivia.

- El tio de la mina: Most miners in Bolivia worship "El tío de la mina" (Satan) to get more precious stones or help from him.

5 - Common phrases and fun expressions in your native language and their translation in English

Vale un Potosí. Literally "to be worth a Potosí," meaning that something is worth a fortune or someone is really valuable. The city of Potosí was historically renowned for its Cerro Rico ("rich mountain"), as this mountain was said to be "made of silver" and was used to provide silver for Spain during colonial times.

¡Estoy caliente! "I feel so frustrated about it," or "It is driving me crazy!" When someone is angry with someone or something, that person will say this.

¡Hoy hubo una fatal trancadera! "Today there was a terrible traffic jam!" (*trancadera* = traffic jam)

He dicho siempre. Unfortunately most people in Bolivia are never on time for a formal activity. For instance, students who did not study for their test so that they will study harder during the last hour before the test will regret it, saying "He dicho siempre" (I knew I should have studied before).

¡Que pintudo che! An informal way of saying, "This [thing or person] looks terrific, doesn't it?"

¡Ay Tatitu! A way to say: "Oh my god!" Particularly used in the west of Bolivia by those who speak the Aymara language, as well as by other Bolivian people "Tatitu" in Aymara language means God.

Pa' que la vida. When some people are very frustrated about life and apparently there is no a way to overcome a difficulty, then they say this, meaning "My life is full of problems with no solution, why should I continue living?"

Le están haciendo el cuento del tío. This means someone is telling you a tall tale.

6 - Songs and games you remember from your childhood, that are generally passed on to the next generation

- Jugar a las canicas (Playing marbles)
- Jugar al trompo (The spinning top)
- Arroz con leche (A children's song)
- Pesca pesca (Tag)
- Jugar a las escondidas (Hide and seek)

7 - Legends/ stories or famous characters of the Imaginary / Folk tales

Leyenda de la Kantuta. It describes the origin of the kantuta flower, a flower that is one of the most important patriotic symbols of Bolivia.

El Ekeko. This is the name of the Andean god of abundance and every year most Bolivian people worship this god in the hope of receiving more financial support from him.

8 - Products or goods that represent 'the national treasure'

Salteñas. They are savoury pastries with beef, pork or chicken mixed in a sweet, slightly spicy or very spicy sauce and peas, potatoes and other ingredients may also be found in it.

Charango. This is an Andean string instrument. Bolivia has great "charanguistas" (charango players) such as Ernesto Cavour, Donato Espinoza and Pepe Murillo.

Bolivianita. (Other names: ametrine, trystine) A gem that is a naturally occurring variety of quartz. It is a combination of amethyst and citrine with bands of purple and yellow or orange.

***

Bolivia can be described as a country with extensive biodiversity and diverse people. You can see and experience different, amazing landscapes and archaeological sites: Lake Titicaca (the highest lake in the world), the Yungas (tropical valleys), the Altiplano (a region populated by peasant farmers of Aymara origin), the Andean peaks (Illimani, Illampu, Huayna Potosí and others), the Amazon jungle, the salt flats of Uyuni, the Tiwanacu ruins (there you will see impressive sights such as the Bennett and Ponce monoliths, the Kalasasaya temple, the Puerta del Sol and so on) declared as a UNESCO World Herritage Site, the Cerro Rico de Potosí which is also a UNESCO World Herritage Site and much more.

In addition, you can expect to find a friendly atmosphere throughout Bolivia and to meet Aymará, Quechua and Guaraní native communities. Some foreigners have decided to stay in Bolivia and even establish a family because they have discovered the peace and nature that was hard to find in their own countries, and the cost of living is also much cheaper than other countries.

If you travel to South America, you should visit Bolivia. Many tourists and locals say that it is a destination that cannot be missed.

Brazil

FIRST NAME: TATIANA
FAMILY NAME: PERRY
HTTP://WWW.KLTCOMUNICACAO.COM
&
FIRST NAME: MARCOS
FAMILY NAME: MONTEIRO
WWW.MVMONTEIRO.BLOGSPOT.COM

Capital	Brasilia	Population	199,321,000
Government	Federal republic	Currency	Reals (BRL)
Religion(s)	Roman Catholic (nominal), Protestant		
Language(s)	Portuguese (official and most widely spoken language) and a large number of minor Amerindian languages		

Tatiana: I was born in Belo Horizonte, in the southeast of Brazil. I graduated in Social Communication with a specialisation in Journalism. For a while I worked as a journalist for some websites writing about Brazilian football and music, as well as working freelance for magazines. In 2009 I started to translate some short stories on the internet and, after attending some courses in this area, I began translating professionally. At present I am attending a postgraduate course in translation and regularly translate as a freelancer with some agencies in Europe. I am a full member of ABRATES (Brazilian Association of Translators).

In my spare time I write some short stories of my own. Currently, I am writing my first novel.

Marcos: I was born and raised in Rio de Janeiro, one of the greatest – and best-known – cities in Brazil. I lived in a very quiet neighbourhood, however, and spent most of weekends and holidays in a small town by the beach called Rio das Ostras (Portuguese for "Oyster River"; there were no oysters there when I was young, but the river was still a source of fun). I had a very healthy childhood near the beach.

I'm a Biology graduate with a Master's degree in Ecology. My interest in translation began, I think, at university; I would translate almost every article or book chapter I had to read for any course. I already had a University of Cambridge Proficiency Certificate, so I started studying and translating.

I didn't become a full-time translator at that time, however. I started teaching English in private courses, finished my Masters course … and became a police officer for almost a decade.

Only after this enriching, but stressful, experience, I decided to become a fully fledged translator. I specialise in Science and Mechanics, but love to translate Food/Gastronomy and Astrology (I'm a traditional astrology student and practitioner).

1 - A typical conversation – what are the common/universal topics people go for? (weather, politics, etc.) - And some topics that you should avoid discussing with the locals?

- Brazil -

We're a very peculiar people. We can discuss any topic with first-time acquaintances, but it's not really considered polite to disagree, at least before people get to know you better. There is one exception, however: we hate when we're talking about our own problems and people from outside Brazil agree with us. It's okay for me, being a "carioca" (someone born in Rio de Janeiro), to talk about violence in Rio, or the scorching January heat. You should nod, try to play it down, or just smile. Do not be fooled into agreeing with me, or worse, adding other problems to my own litany!

Favourite topics are:

- Soccer. Sports in general, but pay attention to their popularity. Volleyball, F1 and MMA are among the most popular besides soccer. In Brazil, your football team is almost a religious entity and people tend to defend it tooth and nail.

- Elections (it's a competition, like soccer, so we're interested in who's going to win).

- Soap operas: The previous day's episode of a soap-opera is also a recurring subject in most groups. There was a time in which soap-operas were considered a female subject only. In fact, although men discuss soap-operas nowadays, they still tend to deny watching them or being interested in the subject.

- Weather: it's always too hot, too cold, too dry, too wet...

Topics to avoid

It is said that politics and religion are subjects that should not be discussed. However, complaining about politicians and policies adopted by the authorities is something that Brazilians do regularly.

2 - *Events of great significance for the community, deeply stored in everyone's mind*

It is difficult to talk about events that encompass Brazil, both due to method of colonisation and the country's vast dimensions. The North and South are separated not only by many kilometers, but also by their cultures. Some people say that there are several "Brazils" in Brazil.

In the year 1500, the Portuguese navigator Pedro Álvares Cabral and his fleet landed on Brazilian lands and thus began the history of the country. Some years after the country was discovered, to start its process of colonisation, the Portuguese Crown created the General Government and appointed Tomé de Souza as the first Governor. Conflicts between indigenous populations and the Portuguese were constant in the beginning. The Jesuits were the only protectors of the Indians; they prevented slavery, but the application of a rigid and military moral flouted the indigenous traditions and culture.

Brazil has had very few bloody events in its history. The last war we were involved in was the Second World War (we sent troops to aid the allies in Europe). The military dictatorship was a response to a communist coup d'etat that tried to take over the country in the early 60s. Instead, the military rose to power without spilling any blood and left power, almost 30 years later, without much noise (there were people arrested, tortured, and killed for political reasons during the so-called "leaden years," though). Nevertheless, the dictatorship and the start of democracy are a very important part of our collective memory. Since then we are all very proud of "being democratic."

In 2002, Lula's presidential victory can be considered a milestone. For the first time Brazilians elected from the working class as president. Someone who cared about the underprivileged classes and, right or wrong, tried to give them a more dignified life. His popularity has remained high during the eight years of his two terms, culminating in the victory of a candidate supported by him in the 2010 elections, Dilma Roussef. She is not only the first woman to reach this position in Brazil, but also a woman marked by a struggle against the dictatorial period.

3 - Nouns and Figures from the past / present that you use in colloquial expressions

Although we have some noteworthy scientists (Alberto Santos-Dumont, who disputes with the Wright Brothers the distinction of having invented the airplane; Fritz Müller, who was born in Germany but lived and worked in the southern region of Brazil throughout his life; Miguel Nicolelis, a current pioneering neuroscientist; and many others), the names of famous sportspeople and TV actors and actresses are much more vivid in our collective memory. Pelé is the most famous soccer player; Nelson Piquet, Emerson Fittipaldi and the late Ayrton Senna are the biggest names in Formula 1; Vera Fischer, a famous actress, was for several decades synonymous with beauty.

We sometimes use "**Pelé**" as a synonym for "the best in his category," as in "Fulano é o Pelé do time" ("X is the Pelé of the team"), or "Não se preocupe com o jantar. João é o Pelé da cozinha" ("Don't worry about dinner, João is the Pelé of cooking").

In politics, it's common to transform the name of some important politician into a verb, with the meaning that someone became an ally of the former. For example, "**Sarney já lulou faz um tempo**" (Sarney "lulled" a long time ago – that is, Sarney has become Lula's ally).

The Portuguese heritage is still greatly rooted in Brazilian society and it affects even our expressions. Most of them mention biblical characters, and not historical figures. This is the case, for example, for "**onde Judas perdeu as botas**" (there where Judas lost the boots). Legend has it that after betraying Jesus, Judas hanged himself on a tree with bare feet, as he had put the money earned by delivering Jesus inside his boots. When the soldiers saw that Judas was without boots they went in search of them and the betrayal money. No one has ever learned if they found the boots of Judas. From this story sprung the expression, used to designate a distant, unknown place that is hard to access.

Another expression that relates to our roots is "**agora é tarde, Inês é morta**" (now it's late, Inês is dead). Inês de Castro was a Portuguese courtesan born in Castile. At the age of 14 she had been promised to the cousin and heir to the throne of Portugal, Dom Pedro, but she was released from the engagement by King Afonso IV of Portugal, and replaced by Constança, a Spanish Princess. After a few years of marriage, Pedro began to look with fresh eyes at Inês, who was also married by that time. They started a relationship condemned by the Church, an institution with great influence in Portugal. In the end, King Afonso IV, backed by his advisers, ordered the death of Inês de Castro. The executioners took advantage of the absence of Pedro to enter the palace and decapitate her. Upon returning from his trip, Pedro discovered that his beloved Inês was beheaded and decided, as revenge, to take the Kingdom of Portugal by force. When he finally knocked down his father and assumed the throne, Pedro ordered the execution of the murderers of his beloved. Inês de Castro was then proclaimed Queen of Portugal, and her body, already decomposing, was crowned in a formal ceremony. Since then, saying, 'Now it's too late, Inês is dead' means that a situation is hopeless.

4 - Words used to designate a type of person, animal, things

- "Lei de Gerson" (literally, Law of Gerson). Gerson was a soccer player who participated in a TV commercial in which he said something like "I'm a smart guy, I know how to take advantage of every situation." His name was associated with the effort to be right no matter what. This "law" is what some politicians are accused of doing.
- "Filé à Osvaldo Aranha." A very popular meat dish in Rio de Janeiro. It's a grilled filet mignon steak served with sliced garlic, baked potatoes and white rice.
- "Brizolão" ("Big Brizola"). Some state schools in Rio de Janeiro planned and built by the late politician Leonel Brizola.
- "Doutor/Doutora." Officially used for people with doctorates, but it has ended up becoming a form of address for doctors and lawyers. It is also used by poor and illiterate people to refer to anyone who has attended a graduate program or who has a better social status.
- "Trem." A word used in Minas Gerais to designate anything whose name they can't remember at the moment. "Aquele trem ali" (that thing over there).

5 - *Common phrases and fun expressions in your native language and their translation in English*

Assobiar e chupar cana (whistling and sucking sugar cane) - do two things at the same time;

Subir no telhado (climb up on the roof) – to die;

Botar as barbas de molho (put the beards to soak) – take appropriate precautions;

Cão chupando manga (dog sucking mango) – someone very ugly;

Frio de renguear cusco - Very common among the Gaúchos, who suffer with low temperatures during the winter, the term is used when it is so, so cold that even the dog – also called Cusco in Rio Grande do Sul – cringes;

Virado no molho de coentro (Tapped in coriander sauce) - Very common in the Northeast, the sauce is made from a very strong spice, coentro. This expression is used when someone seems to be capable of the highest achievements;

Beber com farinha (Drinking with flour) - Drinking too much alcohol;

Estou num mato sem cachorro (I'm in a bush without a dog) – I'm in a difficult situation.

Ele está no olho da rua (He's in the eye of the street) – He was fired/he is unemployed.

6 - *Songs and games you remember from your childhood, that are generally passed on to the next generation*

Children in big cities grow up and play very much like those from any other place with too many people, buildings, and cars – playing soccer or other team sports, videogames, and going to the beach or to the countryside on weekends. Children from the countryside or city outskirts play more in the open.

There are some games that most children in the country like and play. Hide-and-seek, "cabra-cega" (blind-goat; it's like "Marco Polo," but the blind goat does not ask anything, nor do the other people answer anything, they just run away from that person), "amarelinha" ('little yellow' – a game in which kids are supposed to jump over a specific spot marked on the ground, representing "houses." A stone marks the house they must jump over, instead of onto, in one round), "bafo" ('bad breath' is played with cards, and the kids must turn them over using the vacuum generated by clapping one hand onto them), and "taco" ('bat' – played with two teams of two kids, two bats, two cans and one ball. One team must hit the other team's can away from the base) are among the most popular ones.

As for songs, the advent of political correctness has brought a change to that topic. So it is quite difficult to find a child nowadays singing previously common songs like:

> *Atirei o pau no ga-to-to* / I threw a stick at a cat
>
> *mas o ga-to-to* / but the cat...
>
> *não morreu-rreu-rreu* / Did not die
>
> *dona chica-ca* / Ms Chica...
>
> *admirou-se-se com o berro* / Was astonished with the scream...
>
> *que o gato deu* / That the cat made

miiiiaaaaaaaauuuuuuuu. / Meow.

Some songs still remain and are passed on, like this one, "The House":

Era uma casa muito engraçada / It was a very nice house

Não tinha teto, não tinha nada / It had no roof, had nothing

Ninguém podia entrar nela não / Nobody could get it

Porque na casa não tinha chão / Because the house had no floor

Ninguém podia dormir na rede / Nobody could sleep in the network

Porque na casa não tinha parede / Because the house had no wall

Ninguém podia fazer pipi / Nobody could pee

Porque penico não tinha ali / Because there was no pot

Mas era feita com muito esmero / But it was done with great care

Na rua dos bobos, número zero / The fools in the street, number zero

"Escravos de Jó" (Slaves of Job) goes like this:

Escravos de Jó / jogavam caxangá. / Slaves of Job were playing caxanga.

Tira, bota, deixa o Zé-Pereira ficar! / Put it there, take it away, let Zé Pereira stay!

Guerreiros com guerreiros fazem zigue, zigue, zá! / Warriors with warriors do zig, zig, zá

Guerreiros com guerreiros fazem zigue, zigue, zá!

7 - Legends/ stories or famous characters of the Imaginary / Folk tales

Brazilian folklore is very rich. We mix African, Native Brazilian, and European (mostly Portuguese, but also Italian, Spanish, French, and even Irish) stories and make them our own.

Among the most prominent characters we have is the **Saci**, who looks like a one-legged young black boy. He wears a red hood, smokes a pipe, rides the wind, disappears and appears at will, and is more of a trickster (he hides things from the owner, sours milk, spills salt, etc.), but would grant wishes if trapped or if someone stole his cap.

Another famous character is **Cuca**, an old witch (sometimes depicted with an alligator's face and hawk claws) who kidnaps children and lives in a cave.

Curupira, currupira or caipora is a forest genie who looks like a young white boy with red hair and feet turned backwards. It protects the forest, but may be malicious or evil towards people.

In urban areas, some newer stories have begun to be popularized, such as the Blonde in White (***A Loira de Branco***): a beautiful – but dead – woman that lures men into dating her (according to some versions they either die or go to hell with her).

8 - Products or goods that represent 'the national treasure'

Well, we "export" people (soccer players and MMA fighters, mostly). Apart from that, we are primarily agricultural producers. We plant crops and export bananas, coffee, oranges and sugarcane. Our livestock is also highly appreciated (during the "mad cow" epidemics, our beef – from grass-eating cows, free from the source of the disease – was highly valued in the world market).

Since 2003 we have the Cachaça as our original sugarcane spirit. It can only receive this label if the drink is made from sugar cane, with alcohol content between 38% and 48%, and produced in Brazil.

Brazilian handicrafts are also very rich and demonstrate the cultural diversity of the country. Each region has its raw material to represent its characteristics and qualities.

The Carnival and football cannot be considered national treasures, but are readily associated with the country. People from all over the world travel to Brazil to see the country's Carnival. It includes not only the "Escolas de Samba" parade in the city of Rio de Janeiro, but also parades in the streets of northeastern cities like Recife.

***

From the hot plains of the Northeast to the cold mountains of the South, from the beaches of Rio to the jungles of Amazon, we are a friendly people. We're informal, gossip-spreading, lazy, shallow, and noisy; we're also warmhearted and light-humored. We are also very superstitious, the kind who do not pass under stairs, avoid crossing a black cat on Friday 13, and avoid inviting 13 people for dinners and meetings.

Chile

First name: Andrée
Family name: Goreux
agoreuxb@gmail.com
www.siblings.cl

Capital	Santiago	Population	17,067,000
Government	Republic	Currency	Chilean pesos (CLP)
Religion(s)	Roman Catholic, Evangelical		
Language(s)	Spanish (official), Mapudungun, German, English		

I was born in Belgium and arrived in Chile as a "babe in arms." I learned three languages at the same time, my parents spoke French but my nanny convinced me that I was Chilean and therefore should speak Spanish. However, Spanish was forbidden at the British nursery. After the first day at the Alliance Française Lycée, I returned home speaking French. I won first-class honours in French and English every year.

I continued studying English at the British Council and obtained the Cambridge certificate of Proficiency while working at the Canadian embassy where the secretaries watched me like hawks and taught me all about double meanings and swear words. I did the first translation courses of the University of Chile during 1962-1963 and then worked as translator for several firms.

I emigrated to Argentina in 1970 as most firms in Chile closed due to the socialist government. I worked for Sabena, the Belgian airline, and studied Dutch (required for Belgian civil servants), passing the examinations at the Belgian and Dutch embassies.

Returning to Chile in 1975, I passed the SAT tests and studied Natural Sciences at the Catholic University, specialising in scientific translation. I took minimum credits and continued working as a translator. I had no intention of teaching, but my old school called on me in 1987 as a substitute teacher for three months and I stayed on for fifteen years. The workload was light, so I kept working as a translator.

I won the "Dictée des Amériques" competition in Chile in 2001 and made it to the finals in Canada in 2002. During 2003 I studied for the "Certificate in Translation Studies" at the University of Warwick and obtained the highest marks, acting as a course assistant in 2004.

I am a former vice-president of the Chilean Association of Translators and Interpreters, and received the "Translator of the Year – 2012" award bestowed by the Catholic University and the Chilean Association of Translators and Interpreters for professional and academic achievements.

1 - A typical conversation – what are the common/universal topics people go for? (weather, politics, etc.) - And some topics that you should avoid discussing with the locals?

Weather. Weather in Santiago is usually fine, but the thing to do is to complain that it is too cold or too hot, or complain about the smog – which is dwindling steadily due to pollution fines.

Earthquakes. This is a favourite topic: "Where were you and what were you doing during the last earthquake?" Beware of the answers: Chileans have a somewhat special sense of humour.

Family. You do not discuss your family with strangers, except for saying if you are married (if asked) and that all are doing fine.

Sports. There are huge rivalries between soccer teams; the most enduring have run for decades between Colo-Colo (also known as El Indio) and the Universities of Chile and Católica.

Important topic: The rescue on 23 August 2010 of 33 miners who were buried deep into a mine in the North, the present situation of the miners.

Politics. This can lead to very short discussions, examining which are the worst politicians (adding an insult is okay). The general idea is: a pox on them all!

Topics to avoid

- Religion.
- Sex.
- Financial issues. Your salary and everyone else's is a carefully guarded secret.
- Social status. Everyone believes in knowing what everyone else's status is; but discussing it is definitely no-no. Dress is not a clue and family names are no longer signposts. Do not go where angels fear to tread.

2 - Events of great significance for the community, deeply stored in everyone's mind

1645. A huge earthquake destroyed Santiago on 13 May 1645, killing about a third of the population. The crown of thorns fell around the neck of the Christ in one of the churches and could not be set right again.

1906. A huge earthquake plus tsunami destroyed Valparaíso and other coastal towns. There seems to be a 100 year gap between big earthquakes.

27 February 2010. A huge earthquake followed by a tsunami. Widespread destruction of coastal towns, Valparaíso, Viña del Mar, Concepción (one building fell on its side). Heavy damage was sustained in Santiago.

Politics.

1810 – 1818 The declaration of independence and constitution of an assembly. At the beginning it was a declaration of loyalty to the Spanish King, as Spain had been invaded by the French and there was an impostor on the throne, but due to misunderstandings and overreaction from Spain, it turned into a war.

Chile is a democracy. Presidents during the 19th and 20th centuries (up to 1973) served six year terms.

First Constitution, 26 October 1812. Second Constitution (Liberal Party), 18 September 1925. Third Constitution, 11 March 1981 until now.

Military government from 11 September 1973 to 1989 (voted in by politicians and later disowned by the same, annoyed at not being called back at once) until the referendum of 5 October 1988, called by President Pinochet. First Christian Democrat president Patricio Aylwin assumed office on 11 March 1990. Presidents now serve for four years, with no reelection.

3 - Nouns and Figures from the past / present that you use in colloquial expressions

Teniente Bello. Air Force Lieutenant Alejandro Bello was lost over the Andes on 9 March 1914 and was never found. "Más perdido que el teniente Bello" is said of anyone who does not have a clue about what's going on.

Barros Luco, Barros Jarpa. These are two Chilean politicians who preferred special types of sandwiches.

The Mapuche chief **Galvarino Gallardo** had his hands cut off. This gave rise to the expression "he is a Galvarino," meaning either lazy or tightfisted.

4 - Words used to designate a type of person, animal, things

- Purebred dogs are given noble-sounding names, but street dogs are "quiltros," a native breed that does not bark and is very intelligent. For fun, you may call a street dog "Von quiltro."

- When you are at a loss for a word, you say, "cuestion" which means "a thing." It may be a pair of shoes within a closet, or a dish inside the microwave.

- Compadre, comadre. A godfather and godmother are supposed to take care of your child should you die early. Originally these were the grandparents or uncles and aunts, but now they are your best friends, as they are more likely to survive. The term is also used for very good friends, but in a derogatory manner when speaking of politicians.

- Empolvado. This literally means "full of dust" but is the name of a type of pastry covered by a thick meringue and is extremely sugary. Not recommended for diabetics!

- "Empanadas" – pasties. They are usually made on Fridays and the word also means military cadets who are on leave.
- "Humitas" – parcels of ground corn wrapped in corn leaves.
- We have a bean casserole called porotos con rienda (beans and bridles), which is usually served with spaghetti

5 - Common phrases and fun expressions in your native language and their translation in English

Los viejos. Old ones. This term has two meanings: your grandparents and construction workers. You may only be 18 years old, but if you work in construction you are a "Viejo."

Gallo. Cock. Used to describe any man. The meaning can vary depending on the modifier: "buen gallo" is a nice person, "este gallo" (in an angry tone of voice) is that so-and-so.

Liebre (a hare) - Minibus. Years ago, a bull escaped from a slaughterhouse, and a man (gallo) set out after it in a minibus (liebre). So there was a cock inside a hare going after a bull. It made the front page of every newspaper.

Huevón. Big balls. This insult has become an endearing term, as confirmed by the Spanish Royal Language Academy, but it still depends on the tone of voice. It is usually shortened to "ón" at the end of a spoken sentence. You have been finally accepted as a member of the team when you are called by that name – as I realised when the Head of a university project called me "huevona."

Tu/usted. A minefield for foreigners: you is not always tu. You use "tu" for equals but never to service people. If you are not sure, do like the French and ask permission. Saying tu to maids, taxi drivers or waiters is along the lines of "my good man." Use "usted" instead. Also, if you call a waiter "mozo" he will pretend not to hear, you must say "señor" and waitresses are "señoritas."

Mayoneso. Taken from the dish of abalone (locos - crazy) with mayonnaise, this term is used to brand someone who is wildly insane (not medically, but behaving erratically). It is mostly used for politicians who promote silly or impossible laws.

6 - Songs and games you remember from your childhood, that are generally passed on to the next generation

Sadly enough most of the games played during my childhood have been replaced by stock standard Internet games. I remember "tombo" (a version of baseball), musical chairs and "corre el anillo" (a ring is dropped into one's cupped hands: the others had to guess who had it). A linguist's game "teléfono" where a sentence was whispered by one child to another – coming out as distorted as possible to the great delight of all. There was also "lotería" played using marbles and a shoe box with several holes. You were supposed to make the marble go inside the box and you received one or more marbles as prize; the smaller the hole, the better the prize. Some wise guys glued cellophane on the back of the holes (no plastic in 1950) and had to explain themselves to the school principal.

7 - Legends/ stories or famous characters of the Imaginary / Folk tales

"**El Trauco.**" A legend about an incubus.

La Pincoya. A good spirit of the sea. Beautiful, with long blonde hair, she takes care of the abundance of fish around the Chiloé southern island. She is also the guide of drowned sailors to an eternal life.

The "Caleuche." A beautiful phantom brigantine ship sailing the southern seas said to be seen by vessels about to capsize. The retired naval officer's brotherhood meets at the Caleuche club and restaurant in Santiago.

The "Animitas." These are small shrines on the side of the road, in memory of people who have died in road accidents. Said to be miraculous – they must not be moved – they pose a big problem for road engineers.

8 - Products or goods that represent 'the national treasure'

The "Esmeralda" - a brigantine schooner and Navy training school.

The statue of Virgin Mary - on top of the San Cristóbal Hill in Santiago.

***

Chile's name comes from a little bird that sings sort of "chil chil" and that is how the conquistadors named it. It is a very long and narrow strip of land between the Andes peaks and the deep Pacific trench. Its biodiversity is very great: from the driest desert in the world in the North (astronauts have trained there), where no rain may fall for years, to very rainy forests in the South where yearly rainfall of 3,000 mm is usual. We have salt flats in the desert, icebergs falling into the Laguna San Rafael in the South, as well as the Torres del Paine and ice fields of the Province of Ultima

- Chile -

Esperanza, Magallanes Region.

Further south, we find Patagonian prairies in the Tierra del Fuego ("Fire land") across the Strait of Magellan and then the Antarctic territory. The city of Valparaíso, perched on the hills, and Easter Island have been declared UNESCO World Heritage Sites.

Colombia

First name: Luis Javier
Family name: Otoya
jotoya@gmail.com
www.knowmetry.com

Capital	Bogota	Population	45,239,000
Government	Republic; executive branch dominates government structure	Currency	Colombian pesos (COP)
Religion(s)	Roman Catholic		
Language(s)	Spanish (official)		

A communications professional, I have been involved in marketing communications and market research for more than 20 years. Originally a copywriter, creative director and strategic planner, I became an independent professional translator because of market dynamics: a point was reached when the demand for translations was greater and more rewarding than working as a corporate employee.

- Colombia -

1 - A typical conversation – what are the common/universal topics people go for? (weather, politics, etc.) - And some topics that you should avoid discussing with the locals?

Conversations in Colombia usually begin with a brief questioning about the other person's and their family's state of affairs, but a full answer is not expected, followed by a quick comment on the latest piece of news which is generally about some corruption scandal where a prominent politician, businessman or statesman is involved and there is little chance that justice will ever be done. Then there is a short exchange of opinions on the subject, which usually leads to the devising of a number of solutions to fix the country, are summarized with the expression, "well, if you can't beat them, join them." There is this feeling that things will never change, the proof of which is that the oldest guerrilla forces in the world are still fighting for communist ideals.

Colombians tend to be merciless when it comes to ridiculing people. A good source for their never-ending appetite for others' gaffes are the participants in beauty pageants, who usually give peculiar answers to the judges' questions, as they try to sound interesting and profound, usually with quite the opposite results.

2 - Events of great significance for the community, deeply stored in everyone's mind

Apart from beauty pageants that take place every November in Cartagena, Colombians have grown up with significant sociopolitical events that have shaped the current state of affairs in the country. These include the popular uprising on 9 April 1948, when a Liberal "caudillo" was killed and the city of Bogotá was practically destroyed along with its modern electric tram public transportation system, giving way to the thousands of polluting buses and taxis that cram the Capital today. Other events include the life and death of drug lords such as Pablo Escobar and the stories of the "Violence" the country has experienced most of its independent life to date, with guerrillas destroying any chances of progress, and politicians embezzling whatever is left. Ever since Simón Bolívar and his army of peasants fought for the country's independence from Spain in 1810, Colombia has had a republican life inspired by many of the principles of the French Revolution and the American Declaration of Independence, with a democracy that has traditionally elected representatives from the social, cultural and economic elite.

3 - Nouns and Figures from the past / present that you use in colloquial expressions

Quotes from people in the media quickly become part of the arsenal of connotations that Colombians use in their everyday conversations, like that of Pambelé –a former world champion boxer who said in an interview that, "It's better to be rich than poor," and everyone, from opinion leaders in their newspaper columns to ordinary people quote him all the time.

The word "lagarto" (lizard) is commonly used to designate a person who is always trying to be around powerful, famous people, to be seen with them and then profit from it, whether socially, politically or economically.

And though everybody in Colombia thinks that they are the best drivers around, everybody also thinks that all the other drivers suck and call them "buñuelos," a corn starch and cheese cylindrical fried dough delicacy that also means lousy drivers. This may be because of its tendency to roll around the plate with no sense of direction at all.

Of course, men who are always chasing women are known as "perros" (dogs), and women who fish around to see if they can come up with a tasty "worm" (pardon the unintentional pun) are referred to as "gallinas" (hens).

In Antioquia, a mountainous section of the country where people pride themselves for being very entrepreneurial, they oddly compare brave, determined men or women with boars, or "verracos."

4 - Words used to designate a type of person, animal, things

"**Macondo**," the fictional country of Colombian Nobel Prize winner Gabriel García Márquez, is commonly used as a synonym for Colombia. It is a place where the most incredible, unbelievable things happen, just like in the writer's fantastic realist stories about the Buendía family.

5 - Common phrases and fun expressions in your native language and their translation in English

To refer to a penny-pincher, there is the expression "afloja más que una cauchera de alambre" (yields more than a wire-made slingshot). When it comes to common phrases, Colombians are very creative and new expressions are born whenever groups of people get together to talk about others, so a good number of them have a tinge of cruelty to them. But there are more universally common phrases that are passed from generation to generation, like the following:

- *Más falso que una moneda de cuero* (more fake than a leather coin)
- *No por mucho madrugar, amanece más temprano* (the sun doesn't rise earlier if you wake up earlier)
- *Amor de lejos, amor de pendejos* (love from afar, jerk's love)
- *A veces el remedio es peor que la enfermedad* (sometimes the cure is worse than the disease)
- *Más demorado que despedida de borracho* (takes longer than a drunk's farewell).

6 - Songs and games you remember from your childhood, that are generally passed on to the next generation

Before the advent of the electronic devices that Colombian children from well-off families now grow up with, the most popular games were: jump-rope and "la lleva" (chasing). In preadolescence, there is the bottle game, where kids sit in a circle and spin a bottle, and whoever the bottle points to has to do a challenge, usually of a romantic nature. Hide and seek is also a very traditional childhood game, as well as the usual boy's pranks in the neighbourhood, like ringing the bell and running, and girl's kitchen and dolls games, as well as both gender's knack for stealing the show at family parties with their singing or theatre performances to entertain the adult audience

7 - Legends/ stories or famous characters of the Imaginary / Folk tales

The most famous Colombian legend is that of **El Dorado**, about the incredible gold wealth of pre-Colombian indigenous tribes who would bathe their leader in gold in ceremonies that involved offering gold gifts to the gods. That legend triggered numerous expeditions of Spanish conquistadores to find the treasure, and though they never found the mystical booty, they took along with them in the process boatloads of silver and gold that were shipped to Spain. Many of those shipments were sunk in the Caribbean, and nowadays modern treasure seekers are after them. There are international legal proceedings to determine who owns them, involving American divers, Spanish and Colombian authorities and governments from neighbouring countries that were also a source of gold and silver for those shipments.

Ecuador

First name: Evelyn
Family name: Tinajero
E.TINAJERO@TRADONLINE.FR

Capital	Quito	Population	15,223,500
Government	Republic	Currency	United States dollar
Religion(s)	Roman Catholic		
Language(s)	Spanish (official), indigenous (Quechua, Shuar)		

Hello dear friends. I am Evelyn and I come from Ecuador. I currently live and work in France and I feel very comfortable with a foreign ambiance (indeed I think that I could not live without it…) I have lived in Ireland, Italy, Belgium, Spain, France (and Ecuador of course) and got married to a lovely Indian man, so you see multiculturalism is at the heart of my life.

I have one motto to tell you about who I am and how I see the world: "diversity makes the difference!" Enjoying our diversity (instead of being afraid of it) is the best way to grow up, it helps us overcome our limits.

1 - A typical conversation – what are the common/universal topics people go for? (weather, politics, etc.) – And some topics that you should avoid discussing with the locals?

In Ecuador one of the main topics to first discuss when you meet your friends is family or close friends – you want to make sure that everybody is doing well. It is not surprising if a person opens the discussion with a joke or by making fun of himself. Other topics that are discussed are politics or your professional life (talking about your salary is not a good idea). Weather is not a priority for Ecuadorians, at least not when it comes to "opening" a discussion.

2 - Events of great significance for the community, deeply stored in everyone's mind

We have a few events of great significance for the community. They include the War of Independence from Spain (Batalla de Pichincha), football championships and (Christian) religious celebrations such as the Holy Week (Semana Santa), the Day of the Dead (El día de los Muertos), Christmas (Navidad) and Carnival (Carnaval).

What do we do during these events?

Batalla de Pichincha (24 May 1822): there are military parades as well as exhibitions in museums and concerts at night.

Football: I always say that football is more important than religion for Ecuadorians. People gather in bars or at close friends' or family's apartments to watch football games, eat together and celebrate if their team wins (we celebrate anyway even if the preferred team did not win).

The Holy Week: This celebration takes place before Easter. There are religious parades and when it is Holy Friday, Ecuadorian families gather to prepare a typical soup called 'Fanesca' made with dry-salted fish and different kinds of beans.

The Day of the Dead: Ecuadorians gather to pray for and remember friends and family members who have died; we bake bread and prepare a hot drink made of blackberries, strawberries and blueberries which is called "Colada Morada" (Purple Drink).

Christmas: In some Ecuadorian places Christmas is still celebrated in a religious way and many celebrations are held in churches and schools. Apart from this, Christmas is celebrated in a western way: Christmas trees are set up, the Christmas dinner is prepared and gifts are offered among family and friends.

Carnival: Carnival is one of the happiest celebrations in Ecuador. We play with water, eggs and flour: the one who ends up with more water, eggs and flour over their body loses the game.

3 - Nouns and Figures from the past / present that you use in colloquial expressions

Simón Bolivar is one of the most important personalities from our independence days. Ecuadorian people use this name in different ways, for example to say "yes": the Spanish word for "yes" is "sí" and we often replace it by 'simón.'

4 - Words used to designate a type of person, animal, things

We do not have such a thing in Ecuador but we replace Spanish words with some Quechua (Indian language) words to designate things or sensations:

- Cushqui: money
- Achachay: to feel very cold
- Arraray: to feel (that something is) too hot/burning
- Ayayay: to feel physical pain
- Chuchaqui: hangover

5 - Common phrases and fun expressions in your native language and their translation in English

Indio comido, indio ido

Literal translation: The Indian goes away once he has eaten.

English equivalent: none. We actually say that for ourselves: we are half-Indians so once we have eaten we all go away!

Hierba mala nunca muere

Literal translation: Weeds never die.

English equivalent: A bad penny always turns up.

Salirle el tiro por la culata

Literal translation and English equivalent: To be hoisted by one's own petard.

6 - Songs and games you remember from your childhood, that are generally passed on to the next generation

Among others, we used to play the following games: rayuela (jumping from one place to another according to a drawing made on the floor), escondidas (hiding oneself from your friends) and canicas (marbles).

7 - Legends/ stories or famous characters of the Imaginary / Folk tales

Cantuña

During the colonial period, an Indian builder called Cantuña had agreed to finish the construction of the San Francisco Atrium in Quito (Ecuador's capital) by a certain date. He was not able to meet his deadline and so he was going to be incarcerated. When he was praying and asking for the impossible task of finishing on time, the Devil showed up and offered his help to Cantuña in exchange for his soul. Cantuña agreed on one condition: No single stone had to be missing by daybreak.

When the Devil delivered the finished work, Cantuña realised that he had missed one stone and so Cantuña's soul was saved and he was able to finish his job on time.

On the right side of San Francisco's Square you can see the missing stone from this legend.

8 - Products or goods that represent 'the national treasure'

Ecuadorians are very proud of their flowers, bananas, cacao and Panama hats.

***

Quito is one of the highest cities in the world (1,800 meters above sea level); consequently oxygen levels are lower than in other places. Athletes (mostly runners) go to Ecuador to train by mixing oxygen levels. One example of this is our race walker Jefferson Perez (Olympic and worldwide champion): Jefferson used to train simultaneously at higher altitudes (mountains) and lower altitudes (Guayaquil) so that he could enhance his cardiac resistance and be ready to run in both high and low altitude locations.

- Ecuador -

At one time, official football games were banned in Quito as Ecuadorian players had a slight advantage over other teams who might suffer from a lack of oxygen during the game.

Peru

First name: Erika
Family name: Pacheko
pachecov.erika@gmail.com
http://www.linkedin.com/in/erikapachecovi/en

Capital	Lima	Population	29,549,000
Government	Constitutional republic	Currency	Nuevo sol (PEN)
Religion(s)	Roman Catholic 81,3%, Evangelical		
Language(s)	Spanish (official), Quechua (official)		

I was born in Arequipa, Peru in 1975. My mother tongue is Spanish and since I can remember, I've loved languages. I learned English at school. Then I graduated from the Universidad Femenina Sagrado Corazón 1999 with a degree in translation. To start with, I worked in different areas such as business plans, contracts, economic reports, environmental and social projects for different translation agencies. By 2006 I was being invited to collaborate in technical translations and especially in the localization and telecommunications sector. Since then I have worked with several software developers and web designer professionals.

1 - A typical conversation – what are the common/universal topics people go for? (weather, politics, etc.) - And some topics that you should avoid discussing with the locals?

Common topics:

Cuisine. Peruvian people are proud of their traditional cooking. The menu includes a wide selection of dishes, desserts and drinks. In fact, if you do not know where to start, people will recommend you menus and restaurants to try.

Sports. Soccer is the favourite topic of conversation between males. If you are a big fan, you can enjoy long discussions about World Cups and other tournaments. During the Classics—a match between the best teams from a city —people get together to watch and talk about the game.

Economy. The economic growth of the country is a trendy topic, people are interested in the government's activities to promote the public and private investment in different sectors such us commerce, tourism, construction, fishing, among others.

Travel and tourism. People travel more and more in Peru. Then, they want to share their experiences, like which cities have the most attractive places.

Topics to avoid:

Religion. Although Peruvian people respect different beliefs or opinions, they do not like to be involved in contentious subjects.

Sex. Peruvian people are conservative and they do not like to talk about personal issues.

Politics. Peruvian people are very sensitive on this issue due to the cases of corruption and bribery of past administrations, thus this topic is particularly controversial.

2 - Events of great significance for the community, deeply stored in everyone's mind

15th Century –the Inca Empire was established in Cuzco

1532 Francisco Pizarro and the Spaniards defeated the Inca Empire

1535 Francisco Pizarro founded Lima, the capital of Peru and begun the Viceroyalty of the Spanish Empire

1821 General José de San Martin proclaims the independence of Peru

1879–83 During the Pacific War, Peru lost part of its territory to Chile

1980–90 Peru experienced its worst economic crisis, drug trafficking supported violent rebel movements against the Government; as a result, many atrocities occurred and many innocents died.

1990–2000 Alberto Fujimori was elected President. He introduced changes in the Constitution and established drastic measures reducing the economic crisis in the country, promoted the privatization of several State companies and defeated terrorism. At the end, however, his Administration was involved in scandals and corruption.

2001–Today the economy is growing and the macroeconomic figures are positives, but there is much to do on reducing the social gap between the rich and the poor.

3 - Nouns and Figures from the past / present that you use in colloquial expressions

- Señito. A television hostess, Gisela Valcárcel, in her program Aló Gisela used to say "Hola señitos" to the housewives who watched and participated in her program as a sign of affection. Nowadays, people say "Señito" to an elder woman as a sign of tenderness.

- Chocherita. Lalo Archimbaud was a soccer commentator who had "Primicia Chocherita" as a catch-phrase. Today males used the word "Chocherita" as a warm greeting between close friends.

- Fulano or Fulana. The placeholder noun for a person whose identity is unknown or people do not want to mention it.

- Jugador. This term was coined by Magaly Medina—a television hostess—referring to the soccer players who cheat on their wives, the word "Jugador" in Spanish means player. Now, we say "¡Qué tal jugador o jugadora!" to a person who has sex with different partners.

4 - Words used to designate a type of person, animal, things

- Helena. An informal way to say beer. When you ask for a beer, you say: "Dame una Helena." That means: "Give me a cold beer."

- Villegas. It is a last name but people in casual conversations say "No tengo villegas" when they've run out of money.

- Tío(a). A casual way to address or treat an elder person, but some people would consider this term as disrespectful, it depends on the degree of familiarity.

- Casero. The vendor from whom a customer buys perishables or supplies frequently.

- Choclo. It is a Peruvian word to name the corn.
- Culantro. A popular way to say Cilantro—a condiment frequently used in South America.
- Cancha. This term in Peru refers to toasted corn. In some communities, people say "Canchita" or "Tostado."
- Characato. A colloquial way to name the people who come from Arequipa.
- Doctor. A casual way to name a person who is an expert in one subject but he or she does not have formal studies. For example, a mechanic is called Doctor.
- Lenteja. A small bean like a seed, but if you say a person "Lenteja," it means don't be stupid!

5 - Common phrases and fun expressions in your native language and their translation in English

Caído del palto. You use this expression for a very naive person.

De rompe y raja. It means great, or awesome. For example, if you ask "How was the party last night?", People will answer, "Estuvo del rompe y raja."

Lechero. A person who is too lucky. For instance, a student does not prepare for an exam and the teacher is absent. A classmate would say, "¡Qué lechero eres!" (You are so lucky dude.)

Estirar la pata. A colloquial way to say somebody is dead.

Ni chicha ni limonada. Expression used when a person is always dissatisfied or complaining about everything. In that situation, you would say "Ni chicha ni limonada contigo," that is, "What a piece of work you are!"

Meter floro. A casual way to say a person is trying to impress or convince somebody. For example, during the election campaign,

- *Peru* -

politicians "Meten floro," that is, they try to persuade the electors to vote.

Cabeza de pollo. A funny way to say a person gets drunk easily. People can say—do not give beer to Juan, "Tiene cabeza de pollo."

Una yapita. It refers to a bonus that people ask to the vendor for buying several products. For example, a buyer in the market would say, "Give me two kilos of potatoes, half a kilo of onions and one lemon as Yapita."

6 - Songs and games you remember from your childhood, that are generally passed on to the next generation

Children play many games in the park or during break at school such as:

- Yaces (Jacks)
- Matagente (Dodge ball)
- La gallinita ciega (Blind man's bluff)
- Bata (similar to softball)
- Saltar la soga (jump rope)

And the most popular songs are: La gallina turuleca, En la feria de cepillin, El telefonito, Mi ranchito, A compás del Do, Re, Mi, among others. Yola Polastri has performed all these popular songs and many more.

7 - Legends/ stories or famous characters of the Imaginary / Folk tales

Manco Capac and Mama Ocllo. According to the legend, a long time ago people lived as savages near Lago Titicaca, then the Inti god decided to send their children, Manco Capac and Mama Ocllo, to educate the tribe and to create a prosperous civilization. The Inti god gave to Manco Capac a stick made of gold to find the right place for building the Empire. Manco Capac searched and searched that place, until one day the stick stuck in the land and in that exact place was founded the Inca Empire.

Delfín rosado (the Amazon River dolphin). Once upon a time, there was a young handsome warrior in the Amazonian rainforest. He was so handsome that the gods felt jealousy and decided to transform him into a river dolphin. Since that day, the dolphin has swum by the rivers and lakes of the Amazon. During popular celebrations, the dolphin becomes human again. He visits the town and dances with the young ladies of the town. At the end, he seduces the most beautiful woman and takes her to the depths of the river forever.

8 - Products or goods that represent 'the national treasure'

The Potato. Peru is the main producer of potato in the world with more than 3,000 varieties. This product was cultivated about 8,000 years ago in the Andes. Now it represents 25% of the GDP in the country. Then this food is the base for several Peruvian dishes.

Señor de Sipán. One of the most significant discoveries on the ancient civilizations. He was the highest representative of the Mochica culture. The archeologists are still studying this important figure to learn more about that society and its social organisation, as well as, its advances in agriculture, architecture and working with precious metals.

Pisco. It is the national drink, obtained by the distillation of grape juice. There are four types: Puro, Acholado, Mosto and Italia, this brandy is the base of the Pisco Sour, and many tourists love this cocktail.

Vicuña or vicuna. A South American camel that represents the animal kingdom in the Peruvian coat of arms. The Incas considered this animal to be sacred, because it is delicate and refined. Even today, the wool of Vicuña is very expensive.

***

Peru is considered to be one of the 10 most diverse countries in the world due to the richness of its natural resources, ecosystems, and culture. You will be fascinated to see wonderful and unique landscapes; for instance, the peaceful beaches of the Coast, the amazing mountains in the Andes guarded by the Condor—known as the king of the mountain—and the exuberant nature of the Amazonian rainforest.

It is also the cradle of the largest civilizations known in South America as the Mochica Culture, Chavin Culture and Inca Empire. You will find astonishing monuments, advanced engineering and agriculture techniques, fine metal works and ceramics. Peru also received the influence of the Spanish culture during the colony. For these reasons, Peruvian culture is considered a fusion, which is evidenced in our complex and creative art, music and cuisine.

Peruvian people are friendly with foreigners and they want you feel at home.

Come to Peru... the living legend!

Uruguay

First name: Mónica
Family name: Algazi
PROZ.COM/PROFILE/62856
&
First name: Emiliano
Family name: Bentacur
1ON1TRANSLATION.BLOGSPOT.COM

Capital	Montevideo	Population	3,316,000
Government	Constitutional republic	Currency	Uruguayan pesos (UYU)
Religion(s)	Roman Catholic, non-Catholic Christians and others		
Language(s)	Spanish (official)		

Mónica: I was born and brought up in Montevideo, probably the only capital city in the world that resembles a seaside resort with its fantastic waterfront road along the River Plate. I have had a passion for both music and languages since early childhood. What I find really fascinating is "creative translation," a field that calls for a perfect blend of expertise and creativity often associated with 'how things sound' to the target audience.

Emiliano: Hi everyone! I'm Emiliano Bentancur, from Uruguay. Even though I earn my living in an import company, it's been my dream since the age of 8 to become a successful freelance translator. Pretty young, right? I was lucky to stumble upon English as an extracurricular activity at an early age and totally loved it! So much so that I decided then and there I wanted to dedicate my life to it. So far I'm only halfway there, working at Widd Media in my free time as a subtitler and project manager and as an independent interpreter, all of this while getting my degree as a Sworn Translator at Universidad de la República.

1 - A typical conversation – what are the common/universal topics people go for? (weather, politics, etc.) - And some topics that you should avoid discussing with the locals?

Uruguayan people are quite old-fashioned in almost every aspect of their lives, so they are very careful with their conversational topics. Surely the weather is a universal topic of conversation with the remarkable advantage that it generates no controversies of any kind. Politics, on the other hand, tend to kindle heated arguments as Uruguay is virtually divided into two halves with radically opposing political views. Stay away from sports; the rivalry between teams in both football and basketball is rather harsh, and serious disagreements may arise, even among best friends! Another topic that is gaining momentum is technology – from LED TV sets to the latest mobile phone or tablet.

There is also increasing awareness of multinational investment projects that entail devastating environmental impacts, especially considering that we are particularly proud of our pristine beaches and blue skies.

2 - Events of great significance for the community,

deeply stored in everyone's mind

A milestone in the history of Uruguay is the Éxodo del Pueblo Oriental, when people from every corner of the country decided to follow their leader, National hero José Artigas, by cart, on horseback or even on foot.

Being a South-American territory close to Brazil, Uruguay was under alternate Portuguese and Spanish dominance from early 17th century until August 25, 1825, when independence from the Portuguese Empire was declared. Uruguay then became part of the Provincias Unidas del Río de la Plata (United Provinces of the River Plate) and gained sovereign territory status in 1828, consolidated by the creation of its first Constitution on July 18, 1830.

As far as sports are concerned, we are proud to say Uruguay was the first world football champion in history, and we still remember our national team's resounding victory over giant Brazil twenty years later.

3 - Nouns and Figures from the past / present that you use in colloquial expressions

When Uruguay was searching for independence, slavery hadn't been abolished, and our national hero José Gervasio Artigas came across a black slave called **Ansina**, whom he proceeded to buy and then free. Ansina had lost his family, so he stayed with Artigas as his personal helper, as well as a high-ranking officer in the liberation army against the foreign powers.

The Mate was a key part of society back then too, so Ansina is always portrayed as making it for Artigas, as a symbol of their unconditional bond. Consequently, the phrase "Hacer de

Ansina" ("playing Ansina") is used in reference to the person in charge of making mate and pouring the water; nowadays, a thermos is used to pour water several times, and usually the owner of the thermos and mate will be the one to do the job, since pouring the water in the wrong way can ruin the drink, and the owner is supposed to know his tools well enough to prevent that from happening.

4 - Words used to designate a type of person, animal, things

Carlos Gardel, a legendary tango singer born in Tacuarembó, a town in northern Uruguay, is still present in a widely used saying. Whenever someone is really good at something, we say: *¡Es Gardel!* or "He or she is Gardel." Ironically, El Rey del Tango is also a reason for rivalry between Argentina and Uruguay, since his place of birth remains a mystery to this day and both countries struggle for the privilege to call him theirs.

5 - Common phrases/funny expressions in your native language and their translation in English

Probably one of the most recent catch phrases used among young people today would be "salado," which literally just means "salty." It's virtually impossible to pinpoint exactly what "salado" means, because it is used in an incredibly wide arrange of situations. For example, it can express agreement, such as when you say "It's really hot today," the other person could say "salado, I can barely breathe"; another meaning could refer to something outstanding or impressive, much in the way "awesome" is used in English.

Es más viejo que el agujero del mate. It's as old as the hole in the mate. (Very old.)

Está más contento que perro con dos colas. He is as happy as a dog with two tails. (Very happy.)

Por donde el diablo perdió el poncho. It's where the devil lost his poncho. (Far, far away.)

6 - Songs and games you remember from your childhood, that are generally passed on to the next generation

Truco. This is a card game that calls for a certain degree of craftiness. Players make secret grimaces to their partners, to let them know which cards they have. It's fun to play!

Nearly every country in Latin-America has among its cultural heritage a dessert called "**arroz con leche**," which is to say "milk and rice." On top of the two obvious ingredients, people also add sugar and a variety of spices, most typically vanilla, cinnamon or clove. This particular dish got its own children's song a long time ago, and children today still sing it, sometimes in the context of a recreational activity, and sometimes just for the sake of singing a simple, easy song.

An emblematic tango is *La Cumparsita*, by Matos Rodríguez.

People also sing songs by contemporary popular music composers Jorge Drexler ("Frontera"), Jaime Roos ("La Calle Convención") and Rubén Rada ("Cuando yo me muera"). Here's a link to Uruguayan composer Jorge Drexler's song Sea (Let it be).[1]

7 - Legends/ stories or famous characters of the Imaginary / Folk tales

---

[1] http://www.youtube.com/watch?v=cr2LlTtm_6c

A typical fantasy story, especially in the countryside, is that of the *Lobizón*. Similar to the Werewolf, the Lobizón is a man who becomes partly animal during the night, although it's a large wild dog instead of a wolf, and it has different requirements to meet to be able to transform. According to the legend, the Lobizón is a couple's 7th son, who will turn into this half-dog only on a Friday's or Tuesday's full moon. This legend also has Christian implications, for example, saying the Lord's Prayer or sprinkling holy water on it will drive the beast away from you.

8 - Products or goods that represent 'the national treasure'

Natural and tender, Uruguayan beef is our flagship export product.

People who visit Uruguay are eager to eat asado (barbecue), drink our tannat (wine), and have dulce de leche (custard cream) or Martín Fierro (jam and cheese) for desert. Last, but not least, they always try our national drink mate.

***

While there are differences between the people in urban and rural areas, Uruguayans have traditionally been known for their high level of education and friendliness. They are always ready to help and give a hand, perhaps because their own grandparents once needed a hand when they first came from across the ocean to settle in "the new land."

Another feature (weakness?) of Uruguayans is that, because Uruguay is a little tear-shaped wedge between South American giants Argentina and Brazil, we feel small and find it hard to "think big," like Argentineans, Brazilians and even Chileans do.

Venezuela

FIRST NAME: MARY
FAMILY NAME: OLSEN
MARYLOLSEN@GMAIL.COM
&
FIRST NAME: JUAN PABLO
FAMILY NAME: SANS PALACIOS
HTTP://HABLEMOSDETRADUCIRYDIVERTIRNOS.COM/

Capital	Caracas	Population	28,047,900
Government	Federal republic	Currency	Bolivars (VEB)
Religion(s)	Roman Catholic		
Language(s)	Spanish (official), numerous indigenous dialects		

Mary: I was born in Caracas, Venezuela, however, thanks to my father, an American citizen, I learned English. My professional Translation activity began in 1992. I went to live on the Island of Margarita, located in the State of Nueva Esparta, and there I obtained a Certificate as a Tour Guide. That gave me the opportunity to meet people from many countries and we would exchange cultures. Nowadays I live in Florida, U.S.A., working also as a tour guide and translator. My father used to call me a "mixed up kid" as on my father's side my grandfather was Norwegian and my grandmother was born in Brooklyn, New York, like my Father. On the other side, my mother was born in Caracas, Venezuela and

- Venezuela -

her parents in Spain.

Juan Pablo: I was born in Caracas on June 21, 1987, to Juan Francisco Sans and Mariantonia Palacios. My childhood dream was to become a soccer player and work with video games. I suppose now that I translate those topics, it must be frustration-avoidance.

I am also an English-Spanish Italian-Spanish translator and localizer who works in many fields. Video game localization, medicine, legal, tourism, engineering, sports, ecology, politics, finances are my favourite ones.

I have never been a "no-I-can't"-type person, but rather a "yes-I-can" one. Actually, at 24, I became the pioneer of video game localization in Venezuela, just because I said to myself: "I can do this stuff," with my only video game localization training being a brief webinar with Pablo Muñoz in August 2011, who has since become a guide and a tutor to me.

Among my hobbies, video games, reading and playing soccer are the top three.

1 - A typical conversation – what are the common/universal topics people go for? (weather, politics, etc.) - And some topics that you should avoid discussing with the locals?

Venezuelans are very friendly, happy people, even though they are going through tough times nowadays due to the government led by Hugo Chavez. They make jokes about the political situation and are always smiling. When they say hello or goodbye there is of course always a hug and a kiss on the cheek. Being Latin people, they spend more time saying goodbye than they spend talking at a family reunion. They usually talk a lot about the government, they talk about the family and like to get together and celebrate birthday parties. In Venezuela, politics is THE hot topic: ever since the Hugo Chavez' victory in 1998, population has been divided between "escualidos" (opposition) and "chavistas" (pro-government groups) to the point that many families have split over political issues. Basically, each group exists in a bubble, and a group member does not talk about politics with another, thereby creating a situation where no bridges connect the two sides, where no understanding is possible, putting peace and security in Venezuela at stake in more than one way, and thwarting the country's development. You can talk about politics only if you are within your "political social bubble," lest you be rejected and insulted by the other.

On Sundays, after going to church, family and friends get together at one of the family's home and they cook a barbecue and have a couple of word-famous Venezuelan "Polar" beers. They also like to talk about the European football games as well as American baseball.

2 - Events of great significance for the community, deeply stored in everyone's mind

There is a saying in Venezuela that Saint Peter asked God, "Why do you put so many riches in Venezuela such as gold, diamonds, oil, the wonderful climate, beautiful beaches, and so many other wonders?" And God replied, "Just wait and see the Presidents the country will have and you will see that they do not care about the country nor the people." Venezuela has gone through Democracy as well as Dictatorship. First we had Perez Jimenez, a dictator, who had to flee the country, and now we have a fake democracy ruled by Hugo Chavez, since 2000. We have the right to vote but who knows how he wins the elections when he never keeps his promises about helping the poor people. When he wins, people do not go out on the streets to celebrate his victory. Many people have left Venezuela to live in other countries as there is no safety. Parents send their children to study in other countries so they may be safe.

June 24 1821: This is the day when Venezuela's independence was achieved. Simon Bolivar led the patriot army into victory over the Spanish Empire in Carabobo State. Although not the last battle during the Independence War, the Carabobo Battle is deemed to mark the birth of Venezuela and liberation from the Spanish Empire.

3 - *Figures from the past / present*

Christopher Columbus discovered Venezuela in 1492 when he was supposed to have gone to India, but he ended up going west instead of east, and, believing that he was in India, he named the inhabitants of Venezuela Indians. Most of the jewels that the Queen of Spain had were gifts that Christopher Columbus brought her from Venezuela, such as gold, diamonds and pearls.

Simon Bolivar, the "Libertador," came from a wealthy family but he decided to get on a horse and with a small army he liberated six countries from the Spaniards. He liberated Colombia, Venezuela, Panama, Ecuador, Peru and Bolivia. Our local currency is the Bolivar.

One of the wonders of the world, "The Angel Falls" was discovered by **Jimmy Angel**. While he was on a flight, his aircraft was having some mechanical problems and he landed close to the falls.

4 - Words used to designate a type of person, animal, things

- "Chamo" and "Chama" are colloquial words which mean boys and girls.
- "Chevere" is also a colloquial word meaning that everything is great. It came from a car advertisement that said "que chevere, que chevere mi Chevrolet."
- "Pana" colloquial for friend.
- "Birra" colloquial for beer.

5 - Common phrases and fun expressions in your native language and their translation in English

Dame la cola: (give me a tail) give me a ride;

Cachicamo diciéndole a morrocoy conchu'o: the pot calling the kettle black;

Entre bomberos no se pisan la manguera: you don't pick holes in your own clothes;

Éramos muchos y parió la abuela: things started to get complicated and then Grandma gave birth;

6 - Songs and games you remember from your childhood, that are generally passed on to the next generation

Venezuelan children play hide and seek, and "la ere," which consists of children running to catch each other. Baseball and football are also popular. They love to swim at the warm beaches. Surfing is one of the most popular sports. Nowadays they go on the internet and play digital games.

During festivals it is common to see the Diablos danzantes del

Yare, a traditional parade, or listen to Gaitas, a set of modern Christmas rhythms and Villancicos, the traditional Christmas carols.

7 - Legends/ stories or famous characters of the Imaginary / Folk tales

Stories told by previous generations still live on, for example the tooth fairy comes when a child loses a tooth. The child puts it under the pillow and when he or she is asleep the tooth fairy takes the tooth away and leaves a present or some money.

Also **"La Sayona"** was supposed to be a woman who was going to get married and her boyfriend left her. Many people say that they have seen her on roads asking for a ride, and when she is in the person's car, she suddenly disappears. The legend also describes a roaming soul who lost her children and now frightens people in Venezuela's Llanos.

8 - Products or goods that represent 'the national treasure'

Arepa: Venezuela's traditional food, a dish made of ground corn dough or cooked flour. You can eat it at any time of day. Stuff it with cheese, ham, meat, or whatever you want!

Pabellon: another traditional dish, rice, meat, fried plantain slices and beans were never as tasty as in the Venezuelan traditional meal!

During Christmas, to celebrate the festivities, they make the "Hallaca" (similar to a Tamale) plus chicken salad and "pan de jamon" (a special bread that inside it has ham, olives and raisins).

***

Venezuela is like Franklin's glasses: on the upper part you have a wonderful and fantastic country, full of natural resources, and literally swimming in oil, with beautiful beaches and breathtaking waterfalls and views that could be used by the tourist industry, while on the bottom part you have a country with great social inequity, which is increasingly oil-dependent. On one hand you have a country with everything you need to be happy, which offers its people every opportunity for good quality of life, while on the other hand you see a country with increasing levels of violence (over 120,000 fatalities in the last 14 years!), poverty, and corruption, with an almighty State that, along with ever-increasing inflation, has made "fishing up" something from the oil revenues easier than trying to achieve good quality of life through work and education.

I would like to say everything is fantastic in Venezuela and all aspects on the right track, but they are not! Sadly, my country is a rich poor country, where oil has become both a curse and a blessing, paradoxically helping a part of the population to ascend the social scale, while forcing the other part deeper into poverty, leading to a split country with two different realities and two different Venezuelas, just as you would see through Franklin's glasses.

NORTHERN & EASTERN AFRICA

- Algeria
- Ethiopia
- Kenya
- Uganda

Algeria

First name: Nesrine
Family name: Benahbib
Benhabib.nesrine@gmail.com

Capital	Algiers	Population	37,367,000
Government	Republic	Currency	Algerian dinars (DZD)
Religion(s)	Muslim – state religion		
Language(s)	Arabic (official), French (lingua franca), Berber dialects		

I was born in Temcen, in Northwestern Algeria in June 1984. I've lived in Oran since my childhood, it's a very beautiful city known for its gorgeous seascapes.

Passionate about languages, I decided to studying translation at university. I graduated in 2006. At this point it wasn't easy making the right choice for my future. How can a young student guess what she might be good at, if she hasn't tested a bit of everything?

At first I expected to be either a teacher or a translator, but it wasn't possible at the beginning of my path. So I started by working as secretary in a small company, then a call center advisor agent, and as interpreter at Liquefied Natural Gas exhibitions (LNG16) organised in Oran by the biggest Algerian oil company,

Sonatrach. These experiences taught me my main qualities, how creative I was, leadership, and how to be responsible, objective, flexible, communicative and open to worldwide experiences.

However, I was looking for opportunities to expand my knowledge and boost my interaction skills. As soon as I found out that a competitive examination to designate sworn translators was published by the Ministry of Justice, I took part in the national exam for sworn translators, and I passed it.

Currently, I'm a sworn and certified translator & interpreter for Algerian courts. I just started my business and I expect to build up a successful career in the field of translation and interpreting, because it was my precious dream. Every day, all of us recognise how important it is to master foreign languages and I think acquiring working knowledge of several languages in contemporary society is vital.

1 - A typical conversation – what are the common/universal topics people go for? (weather, politics, etc.) - And some topics that you should avoid discussing with the locals?

Common topics:

Family: The family is the most important unit of the Algerian social system, for instance when you shake hands with someone, you also ask about family, work, parents' health, or children.

Religion: Islam is practiced by the majority of Algerians.

Sports: The most popular and beloved sport in Algeria is football; it's the favourite conversation topic of young Algerians. Some of our football clubs are: MCO (Oran) – USMA (Algiers) – WAT

(Tlemcen)

Politics: it's a large and interesting subject of discussion; everyone tries to give his or her point of view and illustrate it with convincing arguments.

Music: The main topic of conversation in a group of teenagers is often a new singer or a new song, and exchanging music.

Food: Algerians are generous and hospitable people; they usually receive guests at home for lunch, or for coffee with tasty cakes, or for dinners; visitors appreciate delicious meals and speak about recipes and different ways of cooking that vary from one region to another in Algeria.

Topics to avoid:

Sex: Algerians are conservative people and usually they avoid speaking about sexuality in a discussion.

Alcohol: because it's forbidden in Islamic religion.

Financial Issues

2 - *Events of great significance for the community, deeply stored in everyone's mind*

1517: Algeria was made part of the Ottoman Empire by Hayreddin Barbarossa and his brother

1830: The conquest of Algeria by the French was long and resulted in considerable bloodshed. A combination of violence and disease epidemics hit the indigenous Algerian population.

1954: the Front de Libération Nationale or FLN launched the Algerian War of Independence which was a revolutionary movement

1962: the independence of Algeria.

3 - *Figures from the past / present*

Abd al-Qadir ibn Muhieddine - (عبد القادر ابن محيي الدين) 1808 – 1883), known as Emīr Abd al-Qādir great leader, who fought with incredible skill and valor against the French invasion in the mid-19th century.

Abdelhamid Ben Badis - (عبد الحميد بن باديس) 1889-1940) He was an intellectual and a representative figure of the Islamic Reform movement in Algeria. He founded the Association of Muslim Algerian in 1931; this was a national consortium of many Islamic scholars in Algeria.

Mohammed Dib - (محمد ديب) 1920–2003) A talented Algerian novelist and poet, he had plenty of novels and short stories, poems, and children's literature, his works are written in French language, the most famous ones are "The Algerian Trilogy", and "An African Summer." His works were influenced by Algerian history, focusing on Algeria's fight for independence.

4 - *Words used to designate a type of person, animal, things*

- Minoucha: A way to name a cat. When we see a cat we automatically call it Minoucha. It's also used sometimes as a term of endearment for little girls.
- El Sheikh: A gentle way to say "dad," for elderly people.
- El ajouze: A gentle way to say "mum," for elderly people.
- El hadj for men or El hadja for women: a respectful title given to an elder.
- The true signification of El hadj or El hadja is the person

who visits the holy Mecca but in Algerian culture we use it for all aged people.

- Doro: The name of an ancient currency that we use always in our discussions when someone says "I don't have money" or "I don't have doro."
- Si: this world is a diminutive for the word in Arabic « El Sayid » translated in English as Mister: 'Si Omar'-'Mister Omar' it is a respectful manner to call somebody, only for men.
- Lala: A polite way to call women translated in English as Lady: 'Lala Khadidja' or 'Lady Khadidja.'

5 - Common phrases and fun expressions in your native language and their translation in English

Hna Aghniya wa nhabou lahdiya "أحنا أغنياء و نحب الهدية" (Algerian dialect). It's translated in English as "We are wealthy but we like receiving gifts" which meaning is: gift-giving is used to strengthen relationships, and the gesture of giving in Algerian culture is more important than the gift.

Soltan Bdatou w Tahkam Fih Mratou "السلطان بذاتو و تحكم فيه امراتو" (Algerian dialect). It's translated in English as "The king himself can be manipulated by his wife." This saying refers to the power of a woman in influencing others, and her big role in society

El Sadik wakta el dik "الصديق وقت الضيق" (classical Arabic saying). It's translated in English as "A friend in need is a friend indeed"

"To live in Cartagena." It's the name of a Spanish city. People from the west of Algeria (Oran) use it to express distance. If someone tells you: "I have to go right now, I live in Cartagena," the meaning is that his home is very far.

6 - Songs and games you remember from your childhood, that are generally passed on to the next generation

- 'Ghoumayda.' Hide and seek
- 'Pitchak.' A rubber ball that little boys play with in the street
- Ami Mansour el Najar: Children's song

7 - Legends/ stories or famous characters of the Imaginary / Folk tales

"**Ain Bent Essoltane**" or "The King's Daughter's Fountain." According to popular belief, this source is inhabited by the benevolent spirit of a princess, and her water has the extraordinary trait of being both fresh and salty.

"**Hammam Messkhoutine**" or "The Legend of the Cursed Bath."

It is not without reason that this place is called "el-Hammam Meskoutine" or "Cursed Bath," it witnessed a terrible punishment to a community of sinners who were changed into stones.

8 - Products or goods that represent 'the national treasure'

Kalb el-louz قلب اللوز is a typical Algerian pastry, from Constantine city, prepared with semolina, almonds, orange flowers water and served with an abundance of honey syrup or ('cherbette' in Algerian dialect). It is also called Chamia in western Algeria and H'rissa in eastern Algeria. This pastry is today one of the most popular in the country, is widely consumed during the evenings of the holy month of Ramadan with a mint tea or coffee.

Chorba الشوربة is a kind of soup cooked with meat and vegetable and different added spices. A very tasty dish, we can serve it with bourak, or with delicious home-cooked bread

El Kuwitra الكويترة (kouitra or quitra) is a musical instrument from Northern Africa. It is part of the Lute family of instruments, used in Arabo-andalouse music.

El Bournous البرنوس or typical North African Berber clothing: a coat, topped with a cap, and worn in travels.

***

The rich history, and the elegant blend of Islamic, Berber, Andalusian and French culture made Algeria the home of many ancient civilizations and a beautiful mix of cultures and customs which characterise Algerian personality.

That's it my friends, I tried to show you an insight into my beloved country, I hope you will visit us soon.

You're welcome and warmly received, come to discover Algeria and enjoy it.

Ethiopia

FIRST NAME: EYOB
FAMILY NAME: FITWI
EYOB.FITWI@GMAIL.COM

Capital	Addis Ababa	Population	91,195,000
Government	Federal republic	Currency	Birr (ETB)
Religion(s)	Orthodox, Muslim, Protestant		
Language(s)	Amarigna (Amharic) (official), Oromigna (official regional), English (official) (major foreign language taught in schools), Arabic (official) and others		

I was born in Jeddah, Saudi Arabia, where I lived until I was ten. Then my family moved to Addis Ababa, Ethiopia, to get a better education, and I've been living there ever since. It was after I moved to Addis that I learned Amharic, which wasn't that difficult because the fact that my original language (Tigrinya) is related to Amharic and they basically use the same written script, which I learned from my father, made the transition easier. Now, Amharic is my native language, though I still understand Tigrinya. In Addis, I continued from fourth grade and went on to get my LLB in Law from Addis Ababa University. Then I started working as a reporter for the English daily newspaper Ethiopian Herald, where I worked for three years. Working at the Herald involved translation tasks from Amharic to English, and hence it was during my stay here that I started translating with my friends and expanded my translation activity. As I started getting more into translations for foreign clients I started enjoying the nature of the job as well, i.e. the relative sophistication of my relationships with my clients and the educative nature of the translation jobs. Best of all, I enjoyed localizing software as I have a passion for technology and related fields. Currently, I'm involved in the localization of products for a major tech company.

1 - A typical conversation – what are the common/universal topics people go for? (weather, politics, etc.) - And some topics that you should avoid discussing with the locals?

At first, Ethiopians may appear to leave foreigners alone, either out of respect for privacy or due to language problems. However, if an Ethiopian is befriended he or she is very helpful in helping that person find his or her way in the country. Sometimes this may appear a little *too* friendly for the outsider. This culture of hospitality is prevalent in Ethiopia. You will notice a sense of modesty in people. There is a term, "yilugnta," which explains when a person seemingly refrains from doing something out of consideration for others' feelings. This is in contrast to when they are challenged or disrespected, in which case they can be confrontational or aggressive.

Ethiopians are capable of discussing a variety of issues. With acquaintances, people are expected to show cordial respect to each other and what's theirs and be civil to each other. Once familiarity is developed, they discuss freely about "deeper" things or topics they would normally avoid. We sometimes make humorous self-criticisms about our country or society; usually it goes something like *ay Abesha...* ("Oh, Abeshas..."), a term used by Ethiopians to refer to themselves, but unless one is friendly with them, or raises this issue in a neutral manner, freely indulging in this may be considered disrespectful.

Ethiopians do not like it when they or their country are presented in a very negative light. For example, they resent the way some foreign media represent Ethiopia as an example of a famine stricken country. They consider this portrayal currently outdated and unfair. Also, there may be cases of extreme differences of culture between Ethiopia and other countries, like acceptance of homosexuality. If people are sensitive to the issue they may have a light conversation on these topics, but they are best avoided.

2 - *Events of great significance for the community, deeply stored in everyone's mind*

Ethiopians are a proud people. They point to their three thousand-year history and especially to the fact that they have never been conquered. Aksum was a powerful kingdom that existed a few centuries after the birth of Christ, and many Ethiopians see the Aksumite obelisks that are standing today as monuments to their ancient heritage. The fact that it was the second country to accept Christianity also adds weight to the country's legacy. The people also consider the peaceful coexistence between Christians and Muslims as exemplary.

The most notable historical moment is the Battle of Adwa in which Ethiopia defeated the Italians in 1896 and maintained its independence. Ethiopians view this historical moment as a key example of Ethiopians' fierce defense of their country (Italy did occupy the country during World War II, but Ethiopians would be quick to point out that it was only a five-year occupation and not colonisation by any means, which is true).

When the current government came to power it ushered in a new era of equality and respect for all nations, nationalities and peoples. Previously Ethiopians had to conform to a unitary identity, which led to the suppression of some people's languages and their culture. Now, Ethiopians are evolving a new self-image which accommodates all people and their cultures as their own. It is very common now to see multilingual songs, dances and events.

There is currently rapid economic growth which is radically adjusting the way people lead their lives by pushing them to be more economically active. Despite the inflation, people are perhaps expecting a changed and not-so-poor Ethiopia for the next generation.

3 - *Figures from the past / present*

Perhaps the most influential person on the Ethiopian scene and beyond is **Emperor Haile Selassie I**. He introduced many reforms to the country during his reign. He is also revered in Africa for his strong Pan-African and anti-colonialist stance. Unfortunately, he is also considered responsible for the many problems that plagued the country including feudalism, a covered-up famine and the repression of the diversity of the multicultural Ethiopian people. His failure to adapt eventually led to his overthrow.

Another famous historical person is **Emperor Menelik II**, a predecessor who established the modern nation of Ethiopia through conquest and diplomacy, and is very famous for his enthusiasm for bringing in modern technology to the country. It was he who began most of the basic modern services like telecommunications, postal, electricity and water services, automobiles, etc. He was also renowned for his liberal and diplomatic demeanor, which was quite uncommon considering the people that surrounded him. Some however accuse him of causing the repression of multiethnic people that was to explode a century later.

In literature, **Hadis Alemayehu** is famous for his book "Fikir eske Meqaber" (Love till the Grave). It is considered a classic and has been translated into other languages. Another famous writer is Bealu Girma for his book "Oromay," a story that revolved around the situation of the country in the 1980s.

Another recent well-known figurehead is the late Prime Minister **Meles Zenawi**. Though he has his detractors, many now consider him as prominent in driving the country towards economic growth and an irreplaceable advocate for Africa. His skillful statesmanship and oratory mean he is considered one of the most influential people in the country's history.

5 - Common phrases and fun expressions in your native language and their translation in English

- "Tamo kememaqeq asqedmo metenqeq" (Be careful first rather than get sick and languish): Used as a warning.
- "Abayn yalaye mintch yamesegnal" (He who did not see Abay [Nile] will thank the stream): Someone who will settle easily for small things if he or she doesn't have a wider outlook.
- "Yene tolo tolo bet gidgida senbelet" (Roughly "The walls in the house of 'Fast' are straw"): Used to explain that something made hastily will be of poor quality.
- "Mikerew mikerew embi kale mekera yimkerew" (Advise him advise him, if he refuses let hardship advise him):

Used when someone refuses advice from others, he's better off learning from his mistakes.

6 - Songs and games you remember from your childhood, that are generally passed on to the next generation

Ethiopians have a vibrant social life, and thus I feel that many of the songs sung by children reflect various aspects of social lives and culture. "Ete Mite Yelomi Shita," a song about a woman being asked about her suitor, "Bezia Bebega" (During that Summer), a song about a tragic love affair, "Wondime Yacob" (Brother Yacob) a song about a sleepy brother being woken up to go to school, and others point to various themes about people's lives. There are also songs that originated from religious events. "Hoya Hoye," a song by boys during a minor holiday commemorating the revelation of Moses and Elijah to Jesus Christ, and "Abebayehosh," a song sung by girls during the Ethiopian New Year.

It is very common for children to rush out to open fields in their neighborhood and play after they come from school or are done with their chores. Football is a favourite game for boys until late adolescence and even continues as a pastime into adulthood for some. Another well-known one is "Abarosh" (roughly "chasing"), a sort of run-and-tag game which involves a lot of running; girls also play this game sometimes along with boys. Girls play "Si," a game in which they form two groups and one tries to avoid being hit by a small plastic ball by the other while laying six bottle caps on top of each other. Girls also play games that reflect social life; a particular one is called "eqa eqa," in which they copy and replay various social activities performed by the adults they observe.

7 - Legends/ stories or famous characters of the Imaginary / Folk tales

"**Aleqa Gebrehanna**" (Sir Gebrehanna) was a real life historical deacon who lived through the reign of three Emperors. He was said to be so witty that even today his name is usually used as the main character in jokes.

Other common characters in children's stories are "**Aya Jibo**" (Mr. Hyena), a character used usually to represent an evil children should be wary of, and "Mamo Qilo," a foolish person whose follies are used to teach children to avoid them. There are also other stories that are told to children. One example is "Aba Qorit," a monster or demon that dwells in rivers and lures children that swim in them. This is used to teach about the danger of drowning and to discourage unsupervised swimming.

8 - Products or goods that represent 'the national treasure'

The single most important product and national treasure of Ethiopia is its coffee. Not only is it renowned for the production of its high-quality coffee, but it is also its birthplace. This is reflected in the status it is accorded in people's lives. Ethiopian coffee-making is a mini-ceremony that exists in every house where mostly women take between 30 minutes and an hour to make coffee with a small stove like cooker and some other utensils when meeting with people socially, or even while sitting alone to relax, and this occurs almost every day.

Kenya

FIRST NAME: BONFACE
FAMILY NAME: ANDENGA
ANDENGAB@YAHOO.COM

Capital	Nairobi	Population	43,013,000
Government	Republic	Currency	Kenyan shillings (KES)
Religion(s)	Protestant, Roman Catholic, Muslim, indigenous beliefs		
Language(s)	English (official), Kiswahili (official), numerous indigenous languages		

I was born in the Republic of Kenya in 1986. I studied Journalism and Mass Communication. I work in the field of translation as a Swahili translator.

I have over five years of experience as Swahili tutor and translator. I have taught high school students and tutored more than a hundred foreigners in the beautiful Swahili language. In 2008, I was one of the Swahili translators who translated Microsoft Windows 7 Office Note 14 from English to Swahili.

I have had the opportunity of participating in live Swahili Radio programs. I was a radio teacher at Kenya Institute of Education and I am also on the forefront of developing a Swahili syllabus for foreigners at Consolata Language Centre. Together with other team members, we researched, wrote, and narrated fascinating African stories and transcribed them.

In 2011, I joined a team of interpreters that travelled to Arusha, Tanzania, as an English-Swahili interpreter. To this day, I still contribute to our local Swahili newspaper Taifa Leo, in the letters to the editor column. Due to my passion for the Swahili language, I decided to start my own blog where I write and post articles on different topics.

I believe that language is a very key tool of communication and that people need to understand languages much better and converse with the world. This is why I decided to use my language abilities to speak to the world through writing, translating, and transcribing. My aim is to use the language fluently and become a mentor to those I communicate with.

1 - A typical conversation – what are the common/universal topics people go for? (weather, politics, etc.) - And some topics that you should avoid discussing with the locals?

When one begins an average conversation in an African country, it's advised that they start by greeting the other parties, asking them how their life is, how their families are, and what they are currently doing. After this, the other parties might ask something too. You can respond by telling them how you are and what you are up to. Also, one must pay attention to greetings before a conversation begins. Greetings are used for every rank and age of individuals in a society. This custom must be carefully observed, as it shows respect.

Topics to discuss:

- Politics, Elections, Corruption
- Weather
- Food prices, Hunger, Diseases
- Land, Employment/Unemployment, Insecurity

Topics to avoid:

- Tribalism (talking badly about other tribes)
- Conversations about albinos
- Illegal sects, people with HIV/AIDS, drug peddlers

2 - *Events of great significance for the community, deeply stored in everyone's mind*

December 1963 - Kenya gained independence from colonial rule.

In 1978, the first president of Kenya passed away after falling ill for a short time.

October 20th - Kenya observes Mashujaa Day (formerly Kenyatta Day) to celebrate and remember our freedom fighters.

July 5, 1969 - the assassination of Tom Mboya, a prominent politician in the Kenyatta government. He was shot dead along Moi Avenue in Nairobi. His killing caused chaos in different parts of the country with people wanting to know who was behind it and why.

December 2002 - the defeat of the long-serving president, Daniel Arap Moi, and the political party that had been popular since independence, KANU (Kenya African National Union).

In January 2003, the new NARC government introduced free primary education in public schools. This resulted in many children and adults enrolling in schools. The person who took many by surprise was Mr. Kimani Ng'ang'a Maruge (may God rest his soul in peace), who holds the Guinness World Record for being the oldest person to start primary school — he enrolled in the first grade on January 12, 2004, at age 84. Although there was nothing to prove his age, Maruge believed he was born in 1920.

In December 2007-2008, Kenya witnessed a civil war that brought the country to its knees after the announcement of the presidential election results. More than 1,000 people were killed, property was destroyed and more than 300,000 people were left homeless.

June 2010, Kenyans voted on a new constitution.

In September 2011, the Nobel Peace Prize Winner, environmentalist and a political activist, Professor Wangari Maathai died.

In 2012, the Kenya Defense Forces captured Southern Somalia and chased away the Al-Shabaab soldiers.

3 - Nouns and Figures from the past / present that you use in colloquial expressions

Many people in African traditional society believe that when a child is born, it should be named after someone in society. According to them, this helps or helped to continue the person's lineage. This perception is dwindling due the increase in education, though a few still practice it. Some names are for famous people in society: politicians, musicians, actors or actresses, preachers, athletes, footballers, and many more.

For example:

- Nabongo Mumia: This was king of the Luhya community. Mumia is said to have been derived from the word

Mumias, which is a name of a place in Western Kenya. He was believed to be a very strong leader. Many people have named their sons after him.

- Daniel Arap Moi: He was the second president of Kenya after Jomo Kenyatta. Many criticised his leadership style as being dictatorial. Still, many parents have named their sons Moi.

- Tom Mboya: This is a common name in Kenyan society. He was a politician said to be eloquent and who spoke fluent English and Swahili (the official languages of Kenya). Some parents used both names for their sons.

- Jomo Kenyatta: The first president of Kenya. He fought for Kenya's independence. He spoke boldly against those who he believed were his rivals or enemies. Many people today have his name (either Kenyatta or Jomo).

4 - *Words used to designate a type of person, animal, things*

- Bwana: Refers to Mr. It's also used in other contexts to refer to God or husband.

- Wafula: Refers to a male. It's a name given to a male child who was born during a rainy season.

- Mheshimiwa: Means honourable. When this noun is used, it refers to a man or woman who is a guest of honour, legislature, minister, judge, or president.

- Bi/Bibi: a noun used to refer to a woman in a respectful way. It could mean wife, Mrs./Miss/Madam, depending on the context.

- Mzee: a noun used to address old people in a respectful manner. Though it refers to both genders, people tend to associate it with an old man as opposed to a woman. For instance, Mzee Jomo Kenyatta.

- Bahati: This is a male or female name. It means luck. A

child is given this name to symbolize success in their family or in their life.
- Tajiri: It's a noun used to mean a rich person. But nowadays people use it to refer to their boss in the workplace. It can be used for both males and females.

5 - Common phrases and fun expressions in your native language and their translation in English

Kata tamaa (To give up)

Haraka haraka haina baraka. (Haste makes waste)

Asiyefunzwa na mamaye hufunzwa na ulimwengu. (Literally: He or she who is not taught by his or her mother, is taught by the world. He or she who does not heed a mother's advice, suffers most)

Umoja ni nguvu, utengano ni udhaifu. (Together we stand, divided we fall.)

Damu ni nzito kuliko maji. (Blood is thicker than water.)

Kidogo kidogo hujaza kibaba. (Little by little fills up the measure.)

Fimbo ya mbali haiui nyoka. (A bird in the hand is worth two in the bush.)

Kidole kimoja hakivunji chawa. (It takes two to tango.)

Mtoto akililia wembe mpe. (A burnt child dreads fire.)

Usipoziba ufa utajenga ukuta. (A stitch in time saves nine.)

Siasa mbaya, maisha mabaya. (Bad politics, bad life)

Ufisadi ni adui wa maendeleo. (Corruption is an enemy of progress.)

Wengi wape. (Literally, "Give to many." Listen to the people's cry.)

6 - Songs and games you remember from your childhood, that are generally passed on to the next generation

Songs:

Naskia sauti (I can hear the voice). This song is sung by pupils in lower classes just a few minutes before lunch. They claim to be hearing their mother's voice and they bid their teacher goodbye as they break for lunch.

Marobo Tandoroba: (Swahili folk song)

Mama Nipe Mayai (Mama give me eggs): A song sung by children in school asking their mothers to feed them eggs because they are tired of eating ugali with cabbage.

Games:

- Kibemasa (Hide and Seek)
- Gololi (Marbles)
- Merry-Go-Round
- Karata (Cards)
- Kuruka kamba (Jump rope)
- Jugwe (Tag of war)
- Kati: A game played by three or more people, especially girls in primary school. One girl stands aside while the other is on the other side. The third one stands in the middle and becomes the target of the other two girls standing to the side. When she is hit by a small ball made of plastic bags (thrown by the girls), she steps aside for another person's turn.

7 - Legends/ stories or famous characters of the Imaginary / Folk tales

Lwanda Magere: A folk legend from the Luo community in Nyanza, Kenya. He was believed to be unable to die and feared by many.

Fumo Liyongo: A Swahili legend, poet and warrior who is believed to have existed between the 9th and 13th centuries.

Koitalel Arap Samoei: He was a Nandi legend born in 1860; he died in 1905. He led the Nandi people of Kenya against British colonial rule.

Wangu wa Makeri: She was a very powerful chief in the 19th century among the Gikuyu people in Kenya. It is believed that she would order men to kneel on all fours to sit on their backs.

8 - *Products or goods that represent 'the national treasure'*

Mahindi (maize): This is a very important product in the country. It's grown largely in Kitale, in the western province of Kenya. Serves as a staple food. Many use it to produce maize flour for cooking ugali (gruel or porridge), a common food in Kenya.

Majanichai (tea): Tea is grown in Kericho in the Rift Valley province.

Sukari ya Mumias (Mumias Sugar): Sugarcane is largely grown in Mumias in the western part of Kenya.

Kahawa (coffee): A product largely grown in Central Kenya and exported to other countries around the globe.

Maua (flower): It's largely grown in Naivasha Rift Valley province and exported to other countries around the globe.

Samaki (fish): Fish are found largely in the Nyanza province in

Lake Victoria and the coastal provinces as well.

Mchele wa Pishori (Pishori rice): Largely grown in the central and Nyanza provinces.

Ngano (wheat): Largely grown in Narok in the Rift Valley province.

9 - *Tribes*

Kenya has more than 42 tribes. Each tribe has its own culture and tradition. This is a source of diversity: something that everyone is proud of and cherishes above all. The following (common) tribes are known for their own traditional foods:

- Kikuyu: Githeri (mixture of maize and beans)
- Kamba: Mukimo (mixture of maize, potatoes and pumpkin leaves)
- Kalenjin: Mursik (traditional fermented milk)
- Luo: Fish
- Coastal people: Wali/Pilau (Cooked rice with other delicacies like meat)

Uganda

First name: Moses
Family name: Wobusobozi
mwobusobozi@gmail.com

Capital	Kampala	Population	33,640,000
Government	Republic	Currency	Ugandan shillings (UGX)
Religion(s)	Roman Catholic, Protestant, Muslim		
Language(s)	English (official national language, used in courts of law and by most newspapers and some radio broadcasts), Ganda or Luganda (most widely used of the Niger-Congo languages, preferred for native language publications in the capital and may be taught in school)		

I was born in Hoima, 200 miles from Kampala city, located in the heart of Uganda in 1982. I finished my studies at the Balma College of Commerce, Technology and Studies - the most accredited institution in my town (2003), and then I started to work for a company called Nabors Drilling for 2 years. It's a company from England drilling oil in Uganda; I worked as a safety officer. Afterwards I joined Goal Uganda for 3 year as security manager- working with people of HIV/AIDS, I also worked for KOLIN construction company as safety manager for one year, and currently I am employed at Balma College, as Tutor in ICT/Business Law; I also volunteer with other organisations. Because of my experience, I worked for different, important local and international organisations.

Later, in 2008, I developed an idea together with my wife, for a small orphanage home school ten miles from my town, deep in the village. The project now has 200+ children, it has really grown. In short, our aim is to empower orphans and immediate members of affected families, as well as community members, to engage in self-help hence education, health, and agricultural production for improved food security, nutrition and income. We think that through primary education, vocational training, the OVCs will have the skills that enable them to engage in decent, meaningful and gainful economic activities. The educational, medical care and business skills given to the OVCs and to community members will also enable them to live a more hopeful, productive and dignified life. In all these, HIV prevention will be a cross-cutting issue, in a bid to prevent further spread of the pandemic. I have now gained experience in NGO and community work, which has enabled me to meet a great number of people from different countries, of various ages, races, social statuses.

I am married to Kugonza Joyce, a teacher by profession. She teaches in a public school in Uganda. We are blessed with three children: one boy, Businge Moses, and two girls: Bainamugisa Keren and Asigunza Jemimah.

1 - A typical conversation – what are the common/universal topics people go for? (weather, politics, etc.) - And some topics that you should avoid discussing with the locals?

- Uganda -

Common topics:

*Weather. - Here we have two seasons, with dry and cold weather respectively. During the rainy season, farmer are happy because they are able to cultivate crops, though when it's sunny and dry, food prices are high. The seasons are divided in two: from March to June and from August to November. Uganda is blessed with oil, which is in the process of being drilled, so we wish it best in its development, because we have hope as Ugandans for the oil to be a blessing to all Africans and Ugandans, especially when thinking of our children's futures.

Uganda has good touristy sites, like Lake Albert in Western Uganda, Lake Kyoga, Victoria which is the source of the River Nile. Other places to see are: Machision Fall National Park, Queen Elizabeth National Park, Kidepo National Park, the Bwindi reserve.

*Family. Families are important in the life of Ugandans, and even if you have an extended family, the home is made of: the children, mama and papa. Parents are sometimes as young as 18, but it's not too late even if you're 35! Children are given responsibilities, like collecting water in nearby well, digging in plantations, hunting animals, girls helping their parents in the kitchen

*Sports. Here sports aren't well developed in schools, so it's still a challenge. Our national soccer team is dubbed "The Ugandan Cranes," who recently lost a game that would have got them qualified for the 2013 African Nations Cup. Stephen Kiprotich is our world-renowned long-distance runner, and the 2012 Olympics marathon champion. We consider him to be our national "miracle," as it's been 40 years since Uganda has won a Gold

medal.

*Politics. It can lead to various hours of discussion, and every person will take the time to defend his or her political party. We have the NRM, or the National Resistance Movement, which went against the Obote II regime. Kaguta Yoweri Museveni has been our president since 1986, and his party replaced a brutal government.

2 - Events of great significance for the community, deeply stored in everyone's mind

Where I come from, everyone remembers Kabalega of Bunyoro. He fought the colonial rule in Bunyoro Kingdom. Claiming our independence in 1962 is also one of the great events, a few months ago Uganda celebrated 50 years of unhindered development.

We're laying down roads, promoting tourism, and developing oil production.

3 - Figures from the past / present

In 1960-1970, we were ruled by a dictator called Idi Amin. He commited a series of crimes and offences, including consorting with underage girls, and was generally an extreme nationalist. He executed many, sent others out of the country (especially Asians). Before dying, he asked for the Ugandans' forgiveness, but he was not forgiven.

4 - Words used to designate a type of person, animal, things

Sete. This word is used to talk about "money," you usually can hear this phrase "Tinyina sete" (In English: I don't have money).

- Uganda -

Abazare Bange. A tender way to say "my parents"

Ebwa yange. A general way to say "dog." You can usually hear "Itanhemu? Toina Ebwa, Oina?" (May I come in? You don't have a dog, do you?)

Ekiro kiri kita? A respectful way to say to "how is your day?"

Omwonjo/Omwisiki. A usual way to name to a "boy" (Omwonjo) or a "girl" (Omwisiki) specially in the western Uganda part.

5 - *Common phrases and fun expressions in your native language and their translation in English*

Oburugi bwekitu. "good" meaning that something is valuable.

Obugaiga buruga omukukora namani, Tinkubaire munaku kuba nyasomere. "Riches come from working hard, I wouldn't be poor if I had studied."

Mukazi wange mugoza muno, nkekimuli kya Rosa. "I love my wife a lot, like a Rose Flower."

Uganda ekukurakurana ko rubunga rwamafuta, twesimire. "Uganda is developing as an oil-rich country, we are blessed."

6 - *Songs and games you remember from your childhood, that are generally passed on to the next generation*

- Okuguruka omuguha (Rope skipping)
- Wakame na wajojo (The Rabbit and The Elephant)
- Enbizina bya baina (A children's song)
- Kwesereka no kuzorwa (Hide and seek)

Wakame na wajojo (The Rabbit and The Elephant)

There was famine in the area where these two animals lived. The rabbit had two young rabbits, and the elephant had three little elephants, so the small rabbit came up to the big elephant and said, well, we should eat these young animals of ours, and we shall give birth to others. So the sneaky rabbit said, "We shall eat yours first because you have many, and they are big compared to mine." They ate all the elephant's young animals, and when they were finished, the rabbit said: "I will go to the hole where I keep my small children..." But when it entered inside it said to the elephant: "You are a fool, how can you eat your own children, I couldn't possibly eat mine!" By then, big as the elephant was, he couldn't get into the small hole, and that's how the elephant lost its children.

7 - Legends/ stories or famous characters of the Imaginary / Folk tales

Omukama wa Bunyoro no bukama bwe. (The king of Bunyoro and his kingdom)

8 - Products or goods that represent 'the national treasure'

We have many different products, like beans, sweet potato, rice, bananas, cassava, caw meat, fish, handmade pots and drums.

CENTRAL, SOUTHERN & WESTERN AFRICA

- Cameroon
- South Africa
- Mali
- Senegal

Cameroon

FIRST NAME: CLEMENTINE
FAMILY NAME: AYAMBA AGBOR
CLEMIE.02@GMAIL.COM
&
FIRST NAME: CARLOS
FAMILY NAME: DJOMO TIOKOU
WWW.CARLOSDJOMO.TK

Capital	Yaounde	Population	20,129,800
Government	Republic; multiparty presidential regime	Currency	Central African Franc (XAF)
Religion(s)	Indigenous beliefs, Christian, Muslim		
Language(s)	English (official), French (official), 24 major African language groups		

Carlos: I was born in 1983 in Douala, the country's economic capital, and lived there until I recently moved to Yaoundé. I hold a Bachelor's Degree in Bilingual Studies with a minor in Communications, obtained at the University of Douala, and a Master of Arts in Translation, obtained at the Advanced School of Translators & Interpreters (ASTI), University of Buea.

My six-year diverse work experience covers the media (newspaper, print & advertising), and the field of language and art services. I have been using my natural art talents (drawing, painting, graphic design) to supplement my linguistic services (translation, editing-proofreading) which I provide to a range of clients around the world – from individuals to translation companies, NGOs and international charities (Plan Cameroon, Biteng Program Unit Cameroon, etc.).

Clementine: I was born in 1985 and I hail from the South West Region of Cameroon. I attended the University of Buea, where I read English and French (Combined Honours) and graduated with honours. After graduating with a BA Degree, I worked as an English language teacher for six months in a vocational training school in the nation's economic capital, Douala.

From 2009 to 2011, I studied Translation at Institut Supérieur de Traduction et d'Interpétation (ISTI), Yaoundé. Various domains have fascinated me in the world of translation because they gave me knowledge in many fields, and I get to meet a great number and variety of people from different countries and of various ages, races, social status.

As a freelance Translator and Communicator, I do my own little best to contribute to the development of my country.

1 - A typical conversation – what are the common/universal topics people go for? (weather, politics, etc.) – And some topics that you should avoid discussing with the locals?

Weather: Rainy days are the most discussed weather topic.

TV shows: South American TV series are also suitable as the starting point of a normal conversation. People (mostly women) discuss missed episodes and actors' performances.

Football matches: This is a favourite topic among men, and they can happily discuss football for hours.

Social events: These cover local celebrations, upcoming public holidays, etc.

Latest news: The latest news – whether local, regional or international – is generally discussed and enjoyed by many people, especially when there is an event that is subject to controversy.

Topics to be avoided include:

Sex-related topics are scarcely discussed in public or with strangers.

Politics: This subject creates so much passion that people prefer to keep their views for themselves, and only expose them or criticise other political parties when they are with their relatives.

Occultism and homosexuality: Homosexuality and lesbianism are seen as practices of occultism. People who practice this habit are said to be doing it to fulfill their duties to their spiritual deities.

Social status: Some people cannot really define their social status and they hate to have it defined for them especially if the definition is demeaning.

2 - *Events of great significance for the community, deeply stored in everyone's mind*

January 1, 1960 – The independence of Cameroon and reunification between the East (French Cameroon, also called the La République du Cameroun) and West (English-speaking Cameroon, at the time called Southern Cameroons) with El Hadj. Ahmadou Ahidjo was the first president of the Federal Republic of Cameroon, as it was called at the time.

1986: Discharge of poisonous gases from Lake Nyos kills nearly 2,000 people.

2008 (February): A nationwide transport strike in protest at fuel costs turns into a series of anti-government demonstrations in the capital, Yaoundé, leaving many dead.

2011 (June): The Government bans all buses and taxis from using the roads at night to reduce Cameroon's high number of fatal traffic accidents.

3 - *Nouns and Figures from the past / present that you use in colloquial expressions*

- Roger Milla & Samuel Eto'o – They are used to refer to young, skillful football players (e.g. This boy is a Milla). The names are positive acknowledgement of the talent showcased by budding football players.

- Bam's – Shorter version of Bamileke, an ethnic group from the western part of the country. The term is often used to refer to somebody who thrives at business and the meaning may be either positive (when praising the person's efforts) or negative (if the individual's dynamism is considered a form of domination).

- Calixthe Beyala – The name of the famous France-based Cameroonian writer is used to recognise the outstanding writing skills of a lady. E.g. She writes like Calixthe Beyala.

- Ndem. A general name for a fool or someone who has acted stupidly. For example "le vieux type est un vrais ndem" (The old man is really "stupid")

4 - *Words used to designate a type of person, animal, things*

- Mbengusit (e) is used to refer to Cameroonians and

generally people who live abroad, be it in an African or Western country.

- Mokwanye/Nyongo. These two terms are used to refer to cultists or people who kill others for financial gains especially if the killing is not physical.
- Kmer – From or related to Cameroon (neutral) (e.g. The Kmer attitude or lifestyle).
- Bamenda – It is the main town of the NW Region, but the name is negatively used by some French-speaking Cameroonians to refer to their English-speaking fellow compatriots.
- Thomas – The name is a negative reference to an individual who always requires evidence before accepting something.
- John Book – (negative) designates somebody whose activities almost exclusively focused on academics. The term is most used in the English-speaking area of the country

5 - *Common phrases and fun expressions in your native language and their translation in English*

Je wanda. This literally means "I wonder" and it is a mixture of Pidgin English and French. It is used especially when something is surprising or unexpected. The group Bantu Posy even has a song on it entitled "Moi je wanda."

Come nhyeh. Meaning "join us (me)," depending on whether it is a person or group saying it.

Nnanga Mboko. Used to refer to someone who sleeps away from home. Generally, it is used for people who spend nights with their lovers away from home.

God no fit forget ei pikin. God never forgets his children

(Expression of faith and trust in God, the Almighty, who looks after his creatures).

Afrique en miniature. Cameroon is Africa in miniature, since it gathers the main features found elsewhere in Africa.

6 - Songs and games you remember from your childhood, that are generally passed on to the next generation

- Tabala (skipping squares drawn on the ground)
- Bam-bampe (a children's song)
- Ma pikin dem o (a chasing game where children try to get to their 'mother' on the other side, with a 'satan' in the way. If you are caught, you get to play "satan" in the next round of the game)
- Football (enjoyed by most populations)
- Ndochi (girl's game whereby one person leaps over a rubber rope being swung by two friends)
- Songho (the game is based on a model whereby nuts should be moved from a specific hole and redistributed to other neighbouring holes)
- Fap Fap (a card game very popular among teenagers)

Due to recent technological developments, children from wealthy families usually prefer video games (PC, PlayStation, Xbox or Wii) and tend to be ignorant of the above-mentioned ones.

7 - Legends/ stories or famous characters of the Imaginary / Folk tales

The Story of the Bamilekes – And their long journey from Low Egypt (the cradle of people and "The 13th Tribe of Israel");

The Story of the Betis – Who supposedly crossed the Sanaga River carried by their Great snake totem ancestor;

Magical stories of the Maquis resistance – The amazing tales of resistance leaders who could fly or disappear whenever they wanted.

Kirikou describes the story of a talking foetus who starts walking on the same day he is born and his wisdom and strength help the villagers to overcome the wicked witch of the village.

8 - Products or goods that represent 'the national treasure'

Eru and Water fufu. The traditional meal of the Manyu people in the Southwest region. The food is a combination of sliced leaves, cooked using palm oil, pepper, meat and smoked fish, and fufu, which is soaked cassava that is drained and the paste cooked until it becomes hard.

Ndole. This is the traditional meal of the Sawa people of the Littoral Region. The dish is vegetables cooked with a lot of groundnuts, meat or smoked fish and other spices.

The traditional regalia is symbolic of the Cameroon culture regarding clothing within and outside of the country.

Local ceremonial meals: nkui (West), eru (Southwest), sanga, nkwem (Centre)

Great monuments: Douala Statue of Liberty, Reunification Monument (Ydé), the Edea Bridge

***

Cameroon is known to be a multilingual country with over 250 national languages and two foreign official languages. However, there is little knowledge about the "Camfranglais," which, as the name infers, is a mixture of Pidgin English, French and some Cameroonian expressions. Cameroon has been called "Miniature Africa" due to its cultural richness. At least one aspect in the culture of every African and even some European countries can be found in Cameroon, be it names, meals, dances, traditional attire, etc. The country is also rich in biodiversity, providing amazing experiences. There are also amazing touristic sites like the Waza Park, Mount Cameroon (which is one of the highest in Africa and where the yearly mountain race takes place), the Bamoun palaces and more. There are also archaeological sites such as Lake Nyos and the twin lakes of Kupe Muanenguba as well as the Pigmy region (a region populated by peasant farmers).

South Africa

First name: Thabani
Family name: Ngwane
TSNGWANE@GMAIL.COM
&
First name: Shirley
Family name: Finkel-Hall
SFINX7@VODAMAIL.CO.ZA

Capital	Pretoria (administrative), Cape Town (legislative)	Population	48,810,000
Government	Republic	Currency	Rand (ZAR)
Religion(s)	Protestant, Catholic and other		
Language(s)	IsiZulu, Afrikaans (official), IsiXhosa (official), English (official)		

Thabani: It was in the fall of 1985 on the 15th of March that I came into existence. My mother named me Thabani which means Rejoice in isiZulu my native language. I live in the coastal city of Durban, in a township called KwaMashu. I am a language practitioner, translating from English to isiZulu.

Shirley: I am a translator and linguist from Cape Town, South Africa; specialised in translation services from Spanish (most varieties) into English (most varieties), in several technical and general areas of translation specialisations as well as experienced in proofreading a vast array of documents.

Founder of ¡Traducido! Translation and Language Services, with emphasis on translation, proofreading and editing from Spanish > English and English, respectively. Clients include major and minor translation companies, independent entities and various private individuals from across the globe (US, UK, Europe and South Africa).

1 - A typical conversation – what are the common/universal topics people go for? (weather, politics, etc.) - And some topics that you should avoid discussing with the locals?

In South Africa, it is polite to ask someone how they are, how their work is going, how their week is progressing and how their family is.

Some of the greatest friendships which have stood the test of time began with these simple words, "Ngisacela ungipha isikhathi," which when translated means, "can I please have the time" or "what time is it?" The response to this request is often followed by another conversation starter, "Kwaze kwashisa namuhla (IsiZulu-Language)," "Namhla kushushu (IsiXhosa-Language)," "Go mogote gompieno (Setswana-Language)," "Namusi hu khou fhisa nga maanda (Venda-Language)," just in case you are wondering what this statement means, wonder no more because I will tell you: "Today is a hot day." After this ice breaker, conversations range from last night's soccer game to the latest news headlines. Everyone is a "soccer or political analyst," hence it is not surprising to hear a person who has never played professional football express his dissatisfaction with his soccer team's performance, and how he thinks the only solution is to the "fire the coach."

Music is another favourite topic of discussion especially amongst the youth of South Africa. Conversations about this topic usually go along the following lines, "Have you heard the latest BIG NUZ song, Umlilo, it is a killer track you have to hear it!" Music is a part of us, when we are sad we sing, when we are happy we sing, when we are frustrated we sing and funnily enough, even when we protest against poor service delivery, we would have placards with our list of demands but just in case the government doesn't get it, yes we sing.

We are a very religious society hence it is not surprising to find the CEO of a major company swap his business attire for his green and white Zionist Church uniform. Talking about religion is not considered a taboo, except when you express doubt.

Topics to avoid:

- Religion
- Past Politics such as Apartheid
- Xenophobia
- HIV – Aids
- National/provincial sports team losing a game badly

2 - Events of great significance for the community, deeply stored in everyone's mind

South Africa is a melting pot full of interesting and significant – some sad and others joyous – past events and experiences, with our unique and diverse cultural background being a springboard for this.

- South Africa -

Before the "Rainbow" we were once a society filled with misery and sorrow, enveloped by a dark cloud, a society which seemed doomed. Whilst many feared going to hell after death, we feared it not for we, the black majority, were already in hell under Apartheid Rule, which officially ended before the birth of the Rainbow Nation in 1994. Though we are no longer under Apartheid Rule there past events which will forever be in our minds as a nation.

June 16, 1976 is one day that will never be forgotten; in fact it has been designated as a public holiday in this country, Youth Day. On that cold winter morning, young people from Soweto marched in protest against the use of Afrikaans as a medium of instruction in black schools. It was supposed to be a peaceful protest, 12 year old Hector Pieterson was supposed to return home after the march but it was not to be. Many young people died that day, Hector Pieterson being the first to die at the hands of a white policeman. It has been over 30 years since that those tragic events, but South Africans still remember.

February 11, 1990, this was the day that many of us got to see for the first time the man who would become the first democratically elected president of South Africa. This was the day that Nelson Mandela was released from prison after spending 27 years behind bars. He was to be the father of this "Rainbow Nation." The image of him and his former wife, Winnie Madikizela Mandela walking hand in hand out of Victor Verster Prison, symbolized the end of Apartheid.

It seemed like a dream, the storm had finally gone away and the rainbow had finally conquered the once dark sky. The nightmare was finally over! As a kid at the time I feared the coming of that day for I didn't know what it really meant. While playing in the street we would often say, "Uyeza u-April 27," or "April 27 is coming." This is the day South Africa had its first democratic elections. On this day, black South Africans got to choose who they wanted to be led by. Many spent long hours waiting to cast their vote. They came wide and far, some being pushed in wheelbarrows and some were carried to the voting stations. This was the day that the Rainbow Nation was born. It has been 18 years since the events of April 27, 1994, but till this day, people still remember the day the Rainbow Nation was born.

In May of 2004, The president of FIFA, Seth Blatter, announces that South Africa will host the 2010 FIFA World Cup event.

In 2006 South Africa becomes the first African country and fifth in the world to legalise same-sex marriages.

3 - *Figures from the past / present*

John Langalibalele Dube (1871-1946) is the founding member and first president of what is now known as the ANC or African National Congress which is the ruling South African political party. He also founded the isiZulu newspaper called "Ilanga," which has existed for over a century. He is noted for being a scholar and leader at a time when not much was expected from a Black South African. His influence is still felt up to this day, as many places have been named after this great giant of a soul.

At a time when medical technology was still in its infancy, he did the seemingly impossible. When people said it was impossible, he knew it was possible. So who was this great pioneer in the medical field? It was **Christiaan Barnard** (1922-2001) a South African cardiac surgeon who performed the world's first successful human to human heart transplant in Cape Town. His work led to a medical revolution which has helped people everywhere.

And most importantly South Africa would not be a Rainbow Nation if it weren't for **Nelson Mandela** (July 18, 1918). This larger than life South African political icon is a Noble Prize Winner and the first democratically elected South African president who brought about a bloodless transition. Despite spending 27 years in prison, when he was released from prison in 1990, he was determined not to let his enemies get the best of him and most importantly not to let hate conquer him. He is a symbol of what we can all be if we search for the good in ourselves and others.

4 - Words used to designate a type of person, animal, things

- Bafana Bafana – the name of the national football team
- Barnie – a fight or punch-up
- Bunny Chow – curry in a dug-out loaf
- China – friend, buddy, pal, used all over the country
- Robot – traffic lights
- "The Cape Doctor" – the southeastern wind that howls across the Cape Peninsula in summer, it can last for up to a week. This wind blows the pollution away so that the air is clear and crisp- like a doctor remedying the Cape of its pollution.

5 - Common phrases and fun expressions in your native language and their translation in English

- "Eita"- means hello
- "Just now"- one of the most amusing phrases for foreigners when they are in South Africa, meaning in a little while,

very soon or in the near future.
- "Howzit bru"– how are you doing my brother or my friend (only used when talking to men)
- "Let's gooi a braai"– let's have a braai
- "A dop 'n a chop"– when going to a braai, this is what most people take along – drink and meat
- "It's ayoba time"– it's time to have some fun
- "Diski dance"– soccer dance
- "I'm kished"- I'm exhausted
- "Usewu-Bill Gates yini?" "Is he now Bill Gates?" This expression is often used to describe someone who made it financially, or who's a geek.
- "Induku enhle igawulwa ezizweni" (a beautiful stick if found in the nations), this expression simply means that to find a beautiful wife, one has to search far away, in a distant land.
- "Zofa izinsizwa kuyosala izibongo" (young men will die but their surnames will remain), this expression means that a young man might die but his legacy will live on.
- "Indlela ibuzwa kwabaphambili" (those at the forefront know the path), this expression simply means that to find your way in life or to get wisdom, you need to ask those who are older or who have walked the path you want to walk.

6 - Songs and games you remember from your childhood, that are generally passed on to the next generation

Growing up in the township in the 90s we never had the luxury of parks or computer games, so the streets were our only playground. Soccer games were played in the street with a plastic ball we would all share, bricks or shoes were used as goal posts. This still happens even in our day. We would play for money, back then R1.00 was worth a lot, you could get 10 ice blocks at 10 cents each with that amount of money, so often fists would fly if one team felt they had been robbed of that R1.00. Coming from poor families we often played soccer without any shoes on that tar road, playing with shoes was for the fortunate few, but we never complained, we loved it. Hide and seek was also a hot favourite, it gave us boys an opportunity to steal a kiss or two from our childhood crush, it was sweet.

Since girls couldn't play soccer with us, games like "three tin," "sprite," "donkey," and "ushumpu" made up for that. These were very competitive games which often have forged friendships which last a life time. Climbing mango trees and making kites out of plastic bags was also another favourite past time we enjoyed.

7 - Legends/ stories or famous characters of the Imaginary / Folk tales

Tokoloshe, from Zulu mythology, is a dwarf-like creature considered mischievous and evil.

In Cape Town, legend has it that a Dutch pirate, **Jan van Hunks**, took part in a smoking competition with a stranger who turned up to be the devil and when he had almost beaten the devil in this competition, thunder suddenly roared and Van Hunks disappeared, with smoke left behind that became the table cloth spills over the mountain when the strong South Easter wind blows.

The story of **Shaka Zulu** is probably one of best stories ever told, because it tells how we the Zulu nation came into being. It's about a brave young man who experienced hardship with his mother while growing up. That young man would change military strategies; he would late conquer tribes and later be killed by his own brothers. Most of us heard stories about this brave Zulu warrior, who was supposedly not a fan of short people.

8 - Products or goods that represent 'the national treasure'

Because of our "rainbow-nation" diversity, and with 11 official languages, there is a large array of goods that represent "The National Treasure" or our heritage, culture and traditions. Below are examples of those I believe are central to this:

- The Springbok Rugby Team – When South Africa was re-accepted into international rugby, the 1995 Rugby World Cup was held and won in South Africa; we will never forget how our precious Madiba held the trophy high up in the midst of our newborn democracy.

- Braai – as mentioned in a previous section, this flame-inspired tradition is the heart and soul of many South Africans when it comes to cooking meat, boerewors, chicken, fish, potatoes and some vegetables throughout the year. Heritage Day (a public holiday) on 24 September is also fondly known as national "Braai Day."

- The vuvuzela – a plastic horn that produces a very loud monotone sound, made famous during the 2010 FIFA World Cup held here.

- Biltong – a type of cured meat made from various types of meats.

- Makoya Makaraba – the hand-painted fan helmet worn by many South Africans and tourists during the 2010 FIFA World Cup.

- Handcrafts - The country's people produce an exceptional

array of arts and crafts. Styles include tribal designs, Afro-French wirework, wood carvings, beautiful pottery and bronze casting, stained glass, basket weaving, beading, clay and stone sculpting, paper from elephant dung and ornaments made from recycled waste.

- Kwaito – the youth culture is discovering its own voice and style of music known as Kwaito and creating a new, lucrative industry. Kwaito is not merely music; it is an expression and demonstration of a way of life. It is comparable to hip hop in the streets of New York and California. Kwaito is likened to the musical voice of young, black urban South Africa. It is a mixture of SA disco, hip hop, R&B and a lot of American and British house music.

- Sakkie-Sakkie dance – a dance style unique to the Afrikaans peoples of South Africa also known as "langarm," literally translated as "longarm."

- The Big 5: The lion, leopard, elephant, buffalo and rhinoceros encompass the big 5 of Africa. Unfortunately the rhino is almost extinct as poachers continue to hunt this magnificent creature down. There are numerous game parks, some small, others large, where these big 5 can be viewed together with the other animals that usually roam alongside them. Many consider a trip as incomplete if these animals have not been spotted.

***

I wanted to add a section on a very special place that I have visited:

Paternoster is a "dorpie" or tiny town situated on the West Coast about 150 km out of Cape Town. This is perhaps the most picturesque and adorable quaint town I have ever visited. It is a fisherman's village with many arty people who have moved here from Cape Town and other parts of the country. The pristine beaches stretch for many kilometres and 10 months of the year, whales and dolphins can be seen playing in the water very close to the beach. There is so much to do for nature lovers with hundreds of bird species and millions of indigenous flowers carpeting the area with an array of colours, quite striking against the white buildings, homes and beaches. Walking, diving and fishing are some of the outdoor activities. Paternoster is my favourite weekend getaway for a peaceful, relaxing and down-to-earth experience. It is a truly tranquil and magical place with Mother Nature at her simple best!

Mali

First name: Brahima
Family name: Ouologuem
BrahimOuologuem@gmail.com

Capital	Bamako	Population	15,490,000
Government	Republic	Currency	West African Franc CFA (XOF)
Religion(s)	Muslim, indigenous beliefs		
Language(s)	French (official), Bambara, numerous African languages		

I was born in Bandiagara, which is located in the southwestern part of Mali. Bandiagara is a medium-size city by Malian standards with about 70,000 inhabitants. The people are mainly farmers and they grow millet and lots of starchy foods.

My main qualifications are:

- Major in English (Ecole Normale Secondaire de Bamako)
- Master of English Language (University of Bamako)
- Human resources and finance (Institut de productivité et de gestion prévisionnelle de Bamako)

After spending over 20 years in organisations like Plan International, DHL International, Peace Corps and other companies, I am currently working as consultant in many organisations with a role of translator and interpreter. I also devote some of my time to tourism as a guide and cultural advisor.

1 - A typical conversation – what are the common/universal topics people go for? (weather, politics, etc.) - And some topics that you should avoid discussing with the locals?

Malians talk and laugh a lot. The topics of conversation depend on age groups and gender.

Women generally walk in groups to the market for their daily supplies. Most of the time they talk about their households and co-wives, such as how the co-wife behaves or how much she is worth. They also worry a lot about the cost of living and family expenses, as it is well-known that they pay a large part of household expenses. A Malian woman's day starts at 5 am. She fetches water from the well, cooks the meals, collects firewood, looks after the children and provides for many needs.

Men are busy during the rainy season that runs from June to October. They grow crops for the family. Once the field work is over, men will sit by the market road gossiping. They talk about people who went abroad and became wealthy and famous, or political issues, or the increasing prices of goods.

2 - Events of great significance for the community, deeply stored in everyone's mind

From Mali's independence until 1968, the country was socialist. The early days of independence were years of unfulfilled dreams. School attendance was free of cost. All types of commodities were available and prices were affordable. All the songs of that time were about what Mali had achieved; they praised socialism and condemned all other paths that opposed socialism.

In February 1968 the first president, Modibo Keita, was overthrown by the military. Our intelligentsia, who mostly graduated from universities in Cuba, Soviet Union, China and other socialist countries, could not stand the new regime. They were often arrested and jailed for minor offenses because they openly showed their refusal to support the regime. The dictatorship under President Moussa Traore lasted over 20 years. During his regime all the state-run enterprises started to go bankrupt. People's freedoms were restricted. Men, women, children, and students: no one could dare speak out lest he go to jail.

Moussa was overthrown in 1992 and this event is celebrated every year in commemoration of the end of dictatorship, nepotism, and monopartism. Since then, March 26 has been instituted as a national holiday and joyfully celebrated throughout Mali. Malians have not allowed our democracy to be stepped on since that time.

3 - Nouns and Figures from the past / present that you use in colloquial expressions

To say 1 man in Bambara, we say Cè kelen (1)

11 = tan ni kele, which literally means 10 and one

The griots (historians and musicians in charge of keeping and sharing our history) of Mali always sing and praise our former kings, fighters, and exemplary people. Their goal is to perpetuate the braveness and good deeds of these individuals and encourage people to not take the easy way out. Three big empires have existed in Mali. Each of them has left its mark on Mali's past. The empire of Mali, the empire of Ghana and the Songhai empires have all had glorious moments and exemplary chiefs that are sung about during every historical event and celebration.

4 - Words used to designate a type of person, animal, things

To refer to people:

- Muso means a lady
- Cè means a man
- Den means a child
- De+muso = denmuso, or daughter and den+Cè = dencè means son
- Sunguru means young girl
- Kamalen means young man

For animals:

- Surugu means hyena (refers to stupidity)
- Sonsan means hare and rabbit (refers to smartness)
- Sama means elephant (refers to power)
- Waraba means lion (refers to strength)

5 - Common phrases and fun expressions in your native language and their translation in English

Don o don tulo bè taa kalanso means, every day your ears go to school

Yiri kuru mèn o mèn ji la a tè sé ka kè bamba yé means that no matter how long a log stays in water, it can't became a crocodile.

Kalanbaliya yé dibi yé means ignorance is darkness

6 - Songs and games you remember from your childhood, that are generally passed on to the next generation

In Mali there are many songs passed on over the years from one generation to another. Among them are songs related to love and fidelity, farming and hardworking; there are also songs related to wisdom. This song refers to loyalty and honesty. Sanata is a poor lady from a poor family who never cheated or betrayed.

Sanata tè son suniyani ma/ Sanata does not agree to steal

Sanata tè son Janfan ma/ Sanata does not accept to betray

Sanata tè son Nambara ma/ Sanata does not agree to cheat

Sanata tè son wali cè la/ Sanata does not accept another woman's husband

Sanata tè son wali nafolo la/ Sanata does not accept another person's goods

Sanata yé ladiri yé/ Sanata is honest

Sanata yé horon yé/ Sanata is noble.

Today, during a time when many of our good virtues tend to disappear, kids often will meet in public places where they sing and dance to the refrain of this song. The song perpetuates our dying values.

7 - Legends/ stories or famous characters of the Imaginary / Folk tales

In rural areas, after every hard day of field work and after a late dinner, parents and elders often gather the kids by the fire and tell fascinating legends and stories. The sessions may sometimes last until very late at night because of how fascinated the kids can be.

People fast the whole month of Ramadan. Starting with the 15th, kids go from door to door singing, dancing and begging. They are offered many things like food, money, and candies. During the last week they pool money together and cook a very big meal that they offer to **Bafaro**. Bafaro is a mermaid. Her head and trunk are human and the lower part is fish. Bafaro lives in the water and she is said to be the queen of all our rivers and ponds. She often comes out late in the night to eat eggplants and vegetables. Few people have ever had the chance to see her. It is said that if you happen to see Bafaro, and if you don't panic and approach her and request something, the request will be fulfilled. Thanks to Bafaro, the rivers and water sources never dry out. Thanks to her, fish are always plentiful. Thanks to her, neighbouring villages are safe and quiet. No one drowns in the rivers.

They sing and praise her all the way to the river. Once they reach the bank, they beat drums, blow on flutes, and clap hands while saying the following to Bafaro:

"We have brought you a little food in recognition of your assistance to the village. We know, we are sure that as long as you are here we won't starve and we won't get thirsty. Our villages and our parents are in your hands, please take care of them. We beg you, we invoke you, please! Please!"

8 - *Products or goods that represent 'the national treasure'*

Mali is a large country and there are a variety of goods from one region to another. However, one thing they have in common is that all Malians are farmers, fishers and animal-farmers. Mali produces millet, sorghum, corn, beans and many other products. Farming can be performed mainly during the rainy season, but villages and cities located by the rivers and water sources can garden all year long if enough water remains.

Mali is the second-largest cotton-producing country in Africa and the third-largest producer of gold after South Africa and Ghana. Mali's mangoes and watermelons have the reputation of being among the best.

Mali was a major tourist destination until the recent invasion of the country by rebels and drug dealers. Tourists would visit the dogon country and famous places that are UNESCO world heritage sites, such as Timbuktu and Djenné.

***

Last Friday we celebrated tabaski. It is a feast in commemoration of Abraham's sacrifice. In the morning we put on our best clothes and go to the mosque for prayers. We then slaughter our rams for the large day-long meals. Then we visit neighbours, families and friends to ask for their forgiveness for all our mistakes and faults. Kids go to different houses and ask for gifts. They get lots of presents and gifts. By 4 pm, people come out in their nicest outfits and dance in public squares to the sounds of jembe, cora and xylophones. It an unforgettable event in our communities and we consider it to be a month of sharing and love.

Senegal

First name: Eric
Family name: Lamine
lamineric@gmail.com
twitter.com/Lamineric

Capital	Dakar	Population	12,969,000
Government	Republic	Currency	CFA franc
Religion(s)	Muslim		
Language(s)	French (official), Wolof, Pulaar, Jola, Mandinka		

I am Lamine Eric Mbaye, an African citizen from Senegal. I live in Dakar, the capital city, and I'd like to achieve my goals by contributing towards the development of my community. In 2003 I participated at the 2nd Model United Nations (MUN) held in Dakar. I represented Senegal in the sustainable development committee, and since then I've been interested in world affairs and in political sciences.

During the last 5 years I've been involved in many youth organisations worldwide such as THIMUN and Student World Assembly to give the African perspective of the world, and to act in a way that can make this world a better one.

I am from a country where the majority of the population consists of young people. They are involved in all areas of the country. However, for an effective participation of these people, they must be competent and that means good training and experience. I'm a Panafricanist as well; to tell you the truth, I "fell into" the translation business by accident.

I remember when I was preparing my bachelor degree at Cheikh Anta Diop University, in the English department's hall I saw a notice calling for translators from a private agency. When I approached the board to write it down, my seniors stared at me because it was posted on the master's field- so I felt offended. I asked myself "Why not me?" and rose up to the challenge. I decided to apply. I was called to an interview that I passed easily. The job consisted in transcribing audio about market research into English. After that brief experience, I focused on my M.A in Arts, and as a Panafricanist I'd like to write about "Africa Must Unite" by Dr. Kwamé Nkrumah.

My real experience regarding translations started with a French agency that has an affiliate in Dakar, where I'd worked for 7 months. This experience opened up my mind towards the translation industry. The thing I like the most about translation is that you don't have time to be bored! At any given time you have something to do, and after each project you have another one waiting for you, from another field totally different compared to your previous one. After a full 3 years' experience I can now "pretend" to be a translator, while pursuing my studies to and getting a degree in translation and interpretation. My full profile can be found at linkedin: http://www.linkedin.com/pub/lamine-eric-mbaye/32/909/159 and viadeo: http://viadeo.com/en/profile/lamine.mbaye7

1 - A typical conversation – what are the common/universal topics people go for? (weather, politics, etc.) - And some topics that you should avoid discussing with the locals?

Sports: Unlike on the subway or other public transportation in Western countries, in Senegal people can easily talk to a stranger, for instance about sports, especially football or wrestling. The type of wrestling competitions in Senegal are unique and drive crowds to stadiums where giants fight for hundreds of millions of francs CFA. It's a full-on business for sponsors, promoters, television broadcasting, and for the wrestlers who have a huge fanbase.

Politics: Senegal is known in Africa for its democratic behaviour, mainly at presidential elections. Since 2000 the people have become aware of their power, and changed the ruling party of over 40 years, The Labor Party (Parti socialiste) with the PDS (Parti Démocratique Sénégalais), who remained in power for 12 years, it too has been changed to a newcomer party, APR (Alliance pour la République), in the presidential elections of March 2012. These changes show a profound desire for better life conditions. When supporters of these different parties meet, they openly show who they side with, and begin a 4 hours' argument!

Weather: We have two main seasons in Senegal commonly called: the dry season and the rainy season. The latter has caused many damages these last 12 years by provoking floods in the suburbs of Dakar mainly. At these times, many families are affected directly or indirectly by the catastrophes.

Sex: Considered as taboo, it's tending to change because of the media. Between people of the same age it's "permitted" to talk about it. We avoid talking about sex with our elders, as well as publicly.

Salary: People start choking when they're asked about their salary. You have to very careful when addressing this topic.

2 - Events of great significance for the community, deeply stored in everyone's mind

1960: Independence of Senegal

After centuries of direct administration by France, Senegal gained its independence in presence of Leopold Sedar Senghor, the father of the nation, at the symbolic Place de l'indépendence of Dakar.

1986: The conflict in Casamance. A conflict between MFDC (Mouvement des Forces Démocratiques de la Casamance) and the Senegalese Army, ended up killing hundreds of people; it is also considered as one of the indirect causes of the Joola's tragedy (see below).

2000: Political Alternance. The arrival of the PDS. This change gave the youth great hope in finally getting jobs and living decently, after a 40 years' rule by PS.

September 26, 2002: Joola's shipwreck. With almost 1865 deaths, Joola's sinking is known as "the African Titanic." Many people have been killed because of this tragedy. The boat was the preferred and safer way to travel from Dakar to Ziguinchor in the South. Due to the conflict in Casamance, passengers prefer the sea instead of the road, to avoid attacks of the rebels. This played a crucial part of the overloading of the boat that was designed to carry 500 passengers in all, but 2000 passengers are believed to have been on board. Each year at the commemoration of this mourning day we can feel sadness of the families and nation solidarity.

June 23, 2011: A spontaneous movement arose, with people going straight to the national assembly to fight against the law proposed by former president Abdoulaye Wade to the MPs, who were mainly from his party. That law once voted would have established the quart blocking- that is to say, the president could be elected by ¼ of the total of voters. A tremendous day when anyone and everyone stood up and demonstrated, until president Wade was forced to ask the MPs to cancel the vote. This gave rise to the M23 movement, a civil society association working for good governance and for democracy.

3 - Nouns and Figures from the past / present that you use in colloquial expressions

Kocc Barma: A wise man with 4 tufts of hair, each with a different meaning, that are still used today: the first tuft means *Buur du Mbok* (A king is not a relative), the second means *Jigeen sopal te bul wolu* (Love a woman but never trust her), the third- *Mag matna bayi si reew* (An old man is always useful in any country) and the last one *Domu jitle dou doom* (A son-in-law is not a son but an inner struggle).

4 - Words used to designate a type of person, animal, things

- **Kilifa** is a noun derived from Arabic *califa,* it means a leader and respected person; commonly used for the head of the family (*Kilifa keurgui*)

- **Awo** is the first wife: as Senegal consists of almost 95% of Muslims, it is quite normal to see a family of one husband and 4 wives, as Islam permits it. Niarel for the second wife, nietel for the third, and nientel is for the fourth wife.

- **Taaw** is a noun used for the first son and the elder among the siblings - I am the Taaw of my family :)
- **Keur gu mag,** literally "the big house," as in where Grandpa and Grandma live with uncles and aunts, nephews, cousins. Generally people choose to celebrate big events like weddings or christenings there, where everyone will get together for sure.
- **Tabaski.** Called *Aid* in Arab countries, it is the feast of sheep. Apart from the religious act, it is commonly used by people as a time of forgiveness regarding hurtful words they may have said, or unintentionally hurtful actions. A fresh start. Muslims also give a part of that meat to poor people and to non-Muslims, to share the joy together, a great moment of popular fervor.

5 - *Common phrases and fun expressions in your native language and their translation in English*

Lu wank di doh nor: similiar in meaning to "One swallow does not make a summer." Literally it says that someone (a friend or relative) you haven't seen for a while, suddenly comes to you without calling.

Ku nbobine reye sa maam, fo seene lu gnul daw: Someone whose grandfather was killed by a raven, will run away whenever they see something black.

Goor gna xa goor nga, jigeen yi ci jiigen yi: can be "Boys will be boys, girls will be girls." Literally it means: boys must go with boys and the same for the girls.

6 - Songs and games you remember from your childhood, that are generally passed on to the next generation

Ayo néné: a popular lullaby, it goes like this: *ayo nene nene tuti nene nene tuti tuti tuti Saloum Saloum niari neg la; nietel bi negu buur la.* "Nene" means "baby": Ayo baby little baby, baby baby little, little little Saloum[1], Saloum has two bedrooms. The third is the king's bedroom. This king is the king of Saloum.

7 - Legends/ stories or famous characters of the Imaginary / Folk tales

Leuk Darou: a horse with one leg that trots around every Thursday night, to prevent people from hanging out at late hours.

Njol weh: literally "tall and white", a "thing" that hides in dark places at night and that follows people walking alone.

Mere maraté: an old woman who carries a heavy pan, and when she sees a young boy hides it to ask for help. While helping her, she tries to find your neck to bite you, just like a vampire. Mere maraté means the old biting woman.

Abdou Jambar: meaning "Abdou The Brave." A great angel which balances your good and bad deeds when you die.

8 - Products or goods that represent 'the national treasure'

Tiebu jene: "rice and fish," the famous Senegalese dish composed of red rice with fish and vegetables- delicious, and appreciated by anyone who has once tasted it.

Dibiterie: meat cooked on wood that gives it a special taste, with

---

[1] Saloum is a kingdom from the past

onions, spices, and mustard.

Guerrier Ceedo: literally "Warrior Ceddo." A ceddo is a knight at the service of the king in the past, in the Senegal of kingdoms. He was famous for his courage during wars. Also known for his love of beautiful women and wine. It was also said that before each battle they partied like there was no tomorrow, just meaning that they'd never think about coming back. The most famous of them was Birima. Youssou Ndour dedicated a very nice song to him, and his statue stands in front of the presidential palace in Dakar.

***

Senegal is the country of "teranga," meaning hospitality. It's a country where people live peacefully, independent of their individual religions and ethnicities. The diversity of the population can be seen every single day. For instance, in the streets you can see people with traditional clothes hand with hand with people wearing jeans and T-shirts. Many families are composed of both Muslims and Christians. This common will of living together is most visible during national holidays like Christmas, New Year's Eve, Korité, and Tabaski (Aid el Kebir).

A place not to miss, if you come visit Senegal, is Gorée Island; it's a former trading post for slaves and goods, now a historic and symbolic place. The keeper of the house of slaves from the middle of the island could tell you a very sad and true story, almost like an eyewitness. The Niokolo Koba reserve in the South, with its virgin forest and its wild animals, is a very popular destination, without forgetting Ndindifero Falls in Kedougou.

What else? Dakar Sunshine come visit!

EUROPE

- Armenia
- Belgium
- Bulgaria
- Denmark
- Estonia
- France
- Italy
- Portugal
- Romania
- Spain
- Sweden
- Ukraine
- United Kingdom

Armenia

First name: Shushanik
Family name: Melik-Adamyan
SHMELIK_ADAMYAN@YAHOO.COM

Capital	Yerevan	Population	2,970,490
Government	Republic	Currency	Dram
Religion(s)	Armenian Apostolic		
Language(s)	Armenian		

I am Shushan, a name that means 'lily' in Armenian. I live in Yerevan, Armenia. My mother tongue is Armenian, but I went to a Russian university here, that's why my Russian is as good as my native language. I am a linguist, a specialist in English and French, and I have also learned Italian, Spanish and a little Turkish. I have always dreamt of being a linguist and this is an essential part of who I am. I graduated from university this year and currently I'm enrolled in translation/interpreting, and doing private tutoring. I translate and interpret four languages: Armenian, Russian, English and French. I strongly believe languages open up an entirely new and wonderful world for their learners. It is no surprise that one of my cherished dreams is to learn as many languages as possible. In addition, I plan to do a PhD in linguistics, because that is my one true love.

I very much like living in Armenia, and I believe that even if we are facing some hardships now, things are changing and a beautiful future lies ahead for the country.

1 - A typical conversation – what are the common/universal topics people go for? (weather, politics, etc.) - And some topics that you should avoid discussing with the locals?

One of the stereotypes about Armenia is that people are very hospitable. And this is (unlike many stereotypes) the truth. We are a very warm and open nation welcoming anyone from anywhere. This is especially true of remote Armenian villages. I myself live in the capital city which is quite hospitable, but when I was travelling to some villages this summer I discovered that the further the village, the more hospitable the people are. In remote areas you can easily stay overnight at a stranger's house, and they will treat you to so much food that you will immediately gain weight.

Because of this hospitality and openness, we tend to speak about anything and everything. In addition, we gesticulate a lot, which makes people from other countries sometimes think we're quarrelling, whereas we are just having a pleasant chat. For many Europeans who open up about their personal life to only a few people, we may seem a little rude. In Armenia they can ask you about your salary, your personal life, and your problems as well as your ideas about politics, religion, etc. Concerning religion, it is important to know that most people are Christian and we have our own branch of Christianity, the Apostolic Church. More than 90% of Apostolics are Armenian; that is why there is little religious or cultural diversity. We are a reasonably homogeneous nation.

2 - Events of great significance for the community, deeply stored in everyone's mind

Our history is full of events every Armenian knows. Among these are the adoption of Christianity as a state religion in 301 A.D. and the creation of the Armenian alphabet in 405 A.D. We are especially proud of those two events, as we were the first country in the world to officially adopt Christianity and we are one of the few with an alphabet of our own. The alphabet was created by Mesrop Mashtots, and we believe that Christianity and an alphabet of our own are two major reasons why we managed to survive as a nation.

Alongside these historical events we have had tragic moments in our history. In 1915 a massacre of Armenians took place in Turkey. More than one and a half million Armenians were tortured and killed, and it was the first genocide of the 20th century, which is, unfortunately, still not recognized by Turkey.

We have a very long history, but, surprisingly, we have had few years of independence. We used to be a kingdom, but we lost our sovereignty about 1500 years ago. We regained our independence in 1918 only when the first Armenian Republic was officially announced. It lasted for two years. Then came the second Armenian Republic as a part of the USSR, and only after 1991 did we become finally independent. The Third Republic of Armenia is as old as I am: 21.

3 - Figures from the past / present

I might start with Tigran the Great, a king under whose reign Armenia was called 'tsovits tsov Hayastan' (Ծովից Ծով Հայաստան), Armenia from sea to sea, because his kingdom was large and occupied the territory from the Caspian Sea to the Black Sea. He lived from 140 to 55 BC. Mesrop Mashots created the Armenian alphabet in 405 AD. Anania Shirakatsi, a world renowned mathematician and medieval scientist, lived and worked in Armenia in the 7th century. He compiled a geographic atlas of the world, and he was the first to thoroughly study the hard sciences in Armenia. Grigor Narekatsi was a poet in the 10th-11th centuries. His poems are usually addressed to God. In the Middle Ages people used to put a volume of his writings under their pillow when sick, and many claimed to have recovered overnight. Aram Khachatryan, our talented composer, is known all over the world for his Sabre Dance (Suserov Par – Սուսերով Պար), though he created many other wonderful pieces of art as well. Martiros Saryan, a renowned painter, Victor Hambardzumyan, a world-famous astronomer, and many other outstanding sons and daughters of Armenia are our pride and joy; and our crown jewel: a wonderful female soprano voice, that of a prominent opera singer, Gohar Gasparyan.

4 - Words used to designate a type of person, animal, things

- Kikos (Կիկոս) – a fairy tale hero who always dreaded something long before it happened. It is used to designate the same personality type.

- Nazar (Նազար) – another fairy tale hero, who boasted he was afraid of nothing, but was afraid of everything, even his wife's shadow. It is used to refer to people who boast a lot but are very cowardly on the inside.

- Ustian (Ուստիան) – Nazar's wife. It is used to refer to powerful women, pejoratively.

- Huri-peri (Հուրի-փերի) – Not a proper noun in the strict sense of the word, though she is also a fairy tale heroine. It is used to designate beautiful, eloquent and mysterious ladies whose beauty is indescribable.

- Akhtamar (Ախթամար) – She is the heroine of an Armenian legend. It is the story of a young girl and a boy who fell in love. To see his love, the boy swam across a lake every night while she waited on the shore with a lit torch to show him the way. Once she could not come, and the boy drowned and died. While dying he pronounced the words 'Akh Tamar,' which means 'Oh, Tamar,' Tamar being an Armenian female name. It is used to refer to girls who cannot be with their true love.

- Khachatur Abovyan (Խաչատուր Աբովյան) – He is one of our most famous writers who contributed a lot to the development of our language. He lived in the 1800s and was also known for climbing Mount Ararat. Once he left his home and never returned. To this day, no one knows the real reason for his death. So the name is used for someone who doesn't come back for a long time and gives no information about their whereabouts.

5 - Common phrases and fun expressions in your native language and their translation in English

Jan (ջան) – this is probably the most common word in Armenian. It is roughly translated as 'dear,' but its peculiarity in Armenian is that it is used very often and with virtually everyone, you just say someone's name or his profession or position, then add 'jan.' That is the reason that many people address me as 'Shushan jan.'

Inch ka chka? (Ի՞նչ կա չկա) – Literally it means 'What is there and what is not'. An equivalent to the English 'What's up?'

Ban chka (Բան չկա) - The rough translation would be 'There is nothing,' which is the same as 'never mind' in English.

Tsavd tanem (Ցավդ տանեմ) – The literal translation would be 'Let me take away your pain.' It also means 'dear.' It is usually used by elderly people when they speak to the young.

Apres (Ապրես) – A synonym for thank you (shnorhakalutyun) which literally means 'let you live.' Everyone says these words when someone has been kind to them, but in an official situation.

6 - Songs and games you remember from your childhood, that are generally passed on to the next generation

Children in Armenia are just like children from anywhere else. They used to play outside and with their friends more often, but now they are more addicted to computer games. Nonetheless, there still are some games that are passed on from ancient times and that our grandparents played when they were young.

One of them is pakhkvoci (պախկվոցի). The rough translation would be something like 'game of hiding,' similar to the English game 'hide-and-seek'.

When it comes to songs, we have lovely ones. My grandmother and mother used to sing 'Close your eyes and sleep calmly,' a traditional Armenian song, to me when I was little.

There are also mixtures of games and songs that are used with very young children, such as this one: the mother or grandmother puts the child on her lap and sings a song about matsun (մածուն), a traditional Armenian yogurt. While singing they rock the child back and forth. The meaning of the song is that food is divided equally between all the members of the family, and the grandmother and the child share the matsun.

7 - Legends/ stories or famous characters of the Imaginary / Folk tales

Armenia is blessed with a wonderful cultural heritage. One part of our heritage is that we have our own epos, or epic poem. It's called **The Daredevils of Sassoun** /Սասնա Ծռեր/ (Sasun is the name of a town in ancient Armenia). The epos is at least 1000 years old. It was revised to its current form in the 8th and 9th centuries. Many say that it is up to 5000 years old. This epic poem has four parts, and the most famous one is called David of Sassoun (Սասունցի Դավիթ). It tells the story of a brave man who was very powerful and who managed to keep his motherland safe and sound. It is very interesting to observe how he, a national hero, is both naïve and brave. As with any epic poem, The Daredevils of Sassoun does not have just one single author. The author, as we like to say, is the Armenian people.

Ghazaros Aghayan wrote volumes of fairy tales which are much loved in Armenia. The next bedtime stories I would like to tell you about are Hovhannes Tumanyan's fairy tales. Tumanyan wrote not only fairy tales but also poems, novels, etc. He's known as the all-Armenian Poet. He was one of the authors who paid attention to the fairy tale genre. Many children in Armenia go to bed listening to his fairy tales in which, no matter the hardships, kindness always defeats evil. The phrase 'kindness always defeats evil' is the most common phrase in our fairy tales. In the long run it's true, isn't it?

8 - *Products or goods that represent 'the national treasure'*

There are several: one of our national foods is dolma, minced meat surrounded by grape leaves. Every Armenian family has it once in a while. Matsun (our national yoghurt) is another food that is purely Armenian. And we also have a special style of barbecue. We call it khorovats (meaning roasted).

Then we have khachkars (cross-stones) which are unique as you can only find them in Armenia. They are typically found on graves, and they can also stand as a monument by themselves. No decoration on a cross-stone is ever repeated. In the Middle Ages, it was considered a shame for a master of cross-stones not to have his own style of decoration. That is why it was often used instead of a signature to refer to the master craftsman who made it. The pomegranate is considered to be a symbol of Armenia. Every tourist gift shop offers a large variety of both pomegranates and little crosses used for necklaces and other jewelry. When it comes to images, we tend to depict Mount Ararat for our national symbol. This mountain is unfortunately not in our territory nowadays, but in Turkey. I own a bag whose fabric and decorations come from traditional Armenian carpets. There is also the 'taraz,' our traditional garment, which can be seen during national dances.

***

I will write a separate passage on the Armenian alphabet because of a simple linguistic fact: there are over 6000 languages in the world and only a dozen or so alphabets. Armenian has an alphabet of its own. It has 39 letters and each letter represents a sound. It was created in 405 by Mesrop Mashtots who travelled a lot with his students to create an alphabet for a language that existed long before (Armenian). He succeeded in his work and returned to Armenia, where the King and the people greeted him warmly. His alphabet had 36 letters, however. Only after, during the Middle Ages, were three more letters added. In Yerevan, the capital city of Armenia, there is now a museum of manuscripts called the Matenadaran (which literally means "place to keep writings"). Thousands of ancient manuscripts are kept and examined in this museum, which is also a scientific institution. In front of it you can see a monument to the creator of the Armenian alphabet with his student kneeling before him as a sign of respect.

Being a linguist, I am especially proud of being Armenian. Armenian is an ancient language with its own alphabet. It belongs to the Indo-European family of languages, but has no siblings, for it is rather unique in its construction and form. Thus, there aren't any languages that are close to Armenian. We don't have the pronouns he and she. Instead we have one: na (նա). There is no gender either. The word "table" in Armenian has no gender, just as in modern English. Nevertheless, the language is considered complex. There are declensions and a different conjugation system to learn. The language is quite flexible in terms of syntax. What comes to the lexicon, we tend to translate almost every word into Armenian. So the word international has become mijazgayin (միջազգային), unlike in many other languages which adopt international words (like the world international itself).

Colloquial Armenian is rather different from literary Armenian.

The World in Words

There are also more than 40 dialects in our small country, some of which are mutually unintelligible. However, this linguistic diversity doesn't hinder the cultural unification of our wonderful country.

Belgium

FIRST NAME: KARLA
FAMILY NAME: BRONSELAER
HTTP://WWW.KARLABRONSELAER.BE
&
FIRST NAME: GERT
FAMILY NAME: GEYSELS
HTTP://WWW.AEETOS.BE

Capital	Brussels	Population	10,438,000
Government	Federal parliamentary democracy under a constitutional monarchy	Currency	Euro (EUR)
Religion(s)	Roman Catholic and other		
Language(s)	Dutch and French (official) legally bilingual, German (official)		

Karla: I was born in the city of Geraardsbergen, about 50 km west of Brussels, in the Dutch speaking part of Belgium where I have lived ever since. I was planning on studying engineering, but chose languages instead. I hold a master degree in translation studies. At Vlekho Brussels I studied Dutch, English and Spanish. I did an additional year in Media & Communications at Ghent University. I am full time translator and web editor for Wallonia-

Brussels Tourism; I also work part-time as a freelance (certified) translator and proofreader. My working languages are English, French and Spanish.

Gert: I was born in 1973 in Turnhout-Belgium, the capital of the Campine, a region in the north-east of Belgium. When I finished my Bachelor studies in 1994, I started working for a large pharmaceutical company, Organon.

In 1995, my father, a university college English teacher, started working as a freelance translator. Eight years later, I was thrilled when he asked me to join his company. So my career as a (part-time) translator started back in 2003. The year 2006 was a very special year for me; a lot of things happened. My father was ready to start enjoying his well-deserved retirement, so I took over his translation business, I started working for General Electric Company, and I met my lovely wife. Last year, I decided to quit my job at GE and go for a full-time career in the linguistic services business.

I am married to Veronique and we have three wonderful children: two sons, Simon, aged 7 and Marniq, aged 5 and a daughter, Anne-Laura, aged 3.

1 - *A typical conversation – what are the common/universal topics people go for? (weather, politics, etc.) - And some topics that you should avoid discussing with the locals?*

Common topics:

- Weather: As in any country, I guess, we tend to start conversations with a remark about the weather, which, in most cases, is not that sunny in Belgium.

- Family/children: When picking up the kids from school, conversations with other parents are mostly about our children; how well and what they are doing.
- Sports: A common topic amongst men is sports, especially soccer and cycling, two of the most popular sports in Belgium.
- Politics: As Belgium has a very complicated political environment, this topic is very common, often leading to heated, but friendly, discussions.

Topics to avoid:

What I really love about my country is that we all have a very open mind and very few taboos. Belgians prefer not to discuss personal subjects except with close friends. A topic that is avoided in a common conversation is money.

2 - Events of great significance for the community, deeply stored in everyone's mind

Belgium has experienced two world wars in the 20th century. We suffered enormously during World War I. World War II caused a rupture in the government. After the war, King Leopold III had to abdicate in favour of his son Baudouin I because he had capitulated to the Germans after 18 days. This shaped our political system with a strong focus on consensus.

As one of the six founding members of the European community in 1957, Belgium has always played an important role in the development of the European Union.

In 1958 the World Expo was organised in Belgium and a building was erected especially for the occasion: the Atomium. It symbolized an optimistic vision of the future. It has become one of the most, if not the most, famous buildings in Belgium.

In 1996, our country was shaken up by the Dutroux scandal. From 1995 to 1996, Marc Dutroux kidnapped and tortured at least six girls, four of whom were murdered. He was arrested in 1996; about 300,000 Belgians marched in Brussels ("White March": "Witte Mars" in Dutch) to express their discontent with the criminal justice system. This scandal led to a large-scale police reform.

3 - *Nouns and Figures from the past / present that you use in colloquial expressions*

The Dutch language does not have any connotations derived from real people; Belgium does however have a very long list of famous people. Here are a few:

- Baekeland, Leo Hendrik, inventor of the synthetic resin or "Bakelite"
- Sax, Adolphe, inventor of the saxophone
- Clijsters, Kim & Henin, Justine, world-class tennis players
- Merckx, Eddy, cyclist and 5-time winner of the Tour de France
- Mercator, Gerardus, cartographer, mathematician and geographer
- Hepburn, Audrey, Hollywood actress
- Remi, George Prosper (Hergé), author of Tintin

An expression that very recently been gaining traction on the internet is "een Letermeke doen" ("doing a Leterme") which means accidentally sending a private message to many people. Our former Prime Minister Yves Leterme sent private Twitter messages to *all* of his followers on several occasions.

4 - Words used to designate a type of person, animal, things

- In Dutch there are several words derived from people or places to designate an object or a thing:
- Duffel, a town in the Belgian province of Antwerp gave its name to the duffel bag and duffel coat (duffeljas) and the material from which it is made: duffel (thick woollen cloth).
- Bakelite (bakeliet in Dutch) is a type of plastic that was developed by the Belgian chemist Leo Baekelandt in the early 20th century.
- Another famous Belgian who gave his name to an object was Adolphe Sax. This Dinant-born musical instrument designer and musician invented the Saxophone ('Saxofoon').
- The Walloon city of Spa with its healing hot mineral springs gave its name to the word "spa," also known as balneotherapy.

We also have expressions that carry names, biblical or other, to designate a type of person or a situation:

- *Een Alexander zijn* (to be an Alexander): to be a very selfish person. Used in the expression: Mijn naam is Alexander, alles voor mij en niks voor een ander (everything for me, and nothing for another person)
- *Zo arm als Job zijn* (to be as poor as Job): to be very poor
- *Een boezemvriend* (a soul mate) – Used to designate a person that is extremely close and important to you
- *Een uil* (An owl) - Used to designate a dumb person

5 - Common phrases and fun expressions in your native language and their translation in English

- *Een baksteen in de maag hebben* is a widespread expression in Belgium. It literally means to have a brick in the stomach. Many Belgians prefer to build a house of their own rather than buying an existing property.

- *Het regent pijpenstelen* (it's raining pipe stems): It's pouring => it's raining cats and dogs
- *Blaffende honden bijten niet* (Barking dogs don't bite): When someone talks tough but really isn't => all bark and no bite
- *Oude koeien uit de gracht halen* (Getting old cows out of the ditch): bringing up old issues in a new argument => rake over old coals
- *Een vreemde eend in de bijt* (a strange duck in the hole in the ice): refers to someone who is a stranger in a group => the odd one out
- *De bloemetjes buiten zetten* (putting the flowers out): celebrating, having a party => paint the town red
- *Beter één vogel in de hand dan tien in de lucht* (better one bird in the hand than ten in the air): a bird in the hand is worth two in the bush
- *Zo zat zijn als een kanon* (literally: As drunk as a cannon) – To be very drunk

6 - Songs and games you remember from your childhood, that are generally passed on to the next generation

Every year on 6 December, Sinterklaas or Sint-Nicolaas is celebrated. The figure that Americans know as Santa Claus is derived from our Sinterklaas. He usually arrives mid-November by steamboat. On the occasion of his arrival, children put their shoes in front of the chimney with a carrot and sugar as a gift for the horse of Sinterklaas. They also sing Sinterklaas songs: *Zie ginds komt de stoomboot, Sinterklaas kapoentje*.

As in other countries, electronic games are becoming increasingly popular, and it's hard to find a household without an Xbox, Wii or PlayStation. However, lots of children go to youth groups where many songs and games are taught. Children not only go to youth groups, but they often practice sports as well. One of the most popular sports in Belgium is soccer and thousands of boys and girls are affiliated to a local club.

Other games:

- Bikkelen: Game (play at dibs, five stones)
- Tikkertje: Game (playing tag)
- Verstoppertje: Game (Hide and seek)
- Klein klein kleutertje: Song (literally: Little, little toddler)
- Handjes draaien: Song (literally: Twirling hands)
- Slaap kindje slaap: Song (literally: Sleep little child sleep)

7 - Legends/ stories or famous characters of the Imaginary / Folk tales

In Belgium, the fairy tales collected by the Brothers Grimm are very popular as bedtime stories. They tell the classic story of good versus evil. Queen Fabiola, the widow of the late king Baudouin I, also wrote a series of fairy tales.

In addition, every geographical region has its own legends and folk stories, like the famous legend of the horse Bayard, which appears in an Old French twelfth century *chanson de geste*. A large procession is organised every ten years, in towns in Belgium. The horse was capable of carrying Rinaldo and his three brothers ("the four sons of Aymon") all at the same time. Near the end of the story, Renaud is forced to cede Bayard to Charlemagne who, as punishment for the horse's exploits, has a large stone tied to Bayard's neck and the horse pushed into the river; Bayard however smashes the stone with his hooves and escapes to live forever more in the woods. Nowadays, outside the town of Dinant in Belgium stands "Bayard rock," a large cleft rock formation that was said to have been split by Bayard's mighty hooves.

8 - Products or goods that represent 'the national treasure'

Belgian art covers everything from the Flemish primitives with Jan Van Eyck to the surrealism of René Magritte. Turn of the 19th century Belgium, and more specifically Brussels, was the home of the Art Nouveau movement. Important architects were Victor Horta, Paul Hankar and Henri van de Velde.

Comics are an integral part of our culture. We have dozens of comic strip authors; listing all our comic strip heroes is a next to impossible task, but among them we count some world famous comics: Tintin, Lucky Luke and the Smurfs.

Belgium is also known for its wide variety of beers. We have about 200 breweries and 1,000 different beers. It is not just a drink; it is an important part of our social life, culture and tradition. Another Belgian delight is chocolate and more specifically "pralines."

We must not forget to mention our famous fries: irregularly shaped potato slices that are crispy on the outside and soft on the inside. They are preferably eaten in a cardboard cone with a large variety of sauces and eaten either on their own or with other snacks.

Bulgaria

FIRST NAME: EVELINA
FAMILY NAME: SHARAPANOVA
EVELINA.SHARAPANOVA@GMAIL.COM

Capital	Sofia	Population	7,037,900
Government	Parliamentary democracy	Currency	Leva (BGN)
Religion(s)	Eastern Orthodox and others		
Language(s)	Bulgarian (official)		

I hope that after reading these lines I will not be seen just as a freelance translator from Bulgaria, but as a combination of all these things I want to tell you about – about two different ethnicities that united to create Bulgaria, about the existence of heroic kings and brave subjects who fought enemies and, against all odds, preserved the integrity of the Bulgarian people, its culture, values and traditions up to the present day.

1 - A typical conversation – what are the common/ universal topics people go for? (weather, politics, etc.) - And some topics that you should avoid discussing with the locals?

It is not uncommon to talk about politics in Bulgaria in everyday conversations, but cautiously, because you can never be certain whether what others are saying is really true or whether they are trying to test you. Politics in Bulgaria doesn't mean the same thing to everyone. That is why really heated conversations about politics can only be tolerated by supporters of the same party. A topic understood by everyone, though, is the state of current world affairs, which Bulgaria is dependent on. It is probably a better choice of conversation than politics. Now that many Bulgarians live and work abroad and nearly every family in Bulgaria has a member living abroad, Bulgarians are not only interested in world affairs, but in the economic status of other countries as well. A large percentage of Bulgarians abroad live in Spain, Greece, the UK, and Germany. The immigration policies of these countries are as important for some Bulgarians as government policies in Bulgaria. That is why comparisons between similar activities in different countries (shopping, sightseeing) are often made. Something men in Bulgaria are always chatting about is football – football in Europe, on one hand (especially in clubs that have Bulgarian footballers), and football in Bulgaria on the other. Football is a question of pride for Bulgarian men. As for topics to avoid, you're good as long as no lines are crossed and other people's views are respected.

2 - Events of great significance for the community, deeply stored in everyone's mind

Perhaps the two most memorable dates in Bulgarian history are that of the creation of the first Bulgarian State (681 A.D.) and the day of Bulgaria's liberation from the Turks on March 3rd, 1878. On this day Bulgaria became an independent country again after 500 years of Turkish oppression. Opinions are usually divided on important dates in more recent Bulgarian history. That's why it is impossible to say with certainty whether the day on which Bulgaria's government became socialist (September 9th, 1944) after the end of WWII was a socialist revolution or a military coup d'état, or whether November 10th, 1989, was the end of socialism and beginning of a transition to democracy. Historical dates from the more recent past don't have the same meaning for everyone. Nevertheless, all Bulgarians are proud of Bulgaria's survival up to the present day.

3 - Nouns and Figures from the past / present that you use in colloquial expressions

Bulgarians identify others with real individuals from the past and these comparisons are used to express approval or disapproval of other people's deeds. For example, a quality appreciated by everyone in Bulgaria is a good work ethic. Bulgarians call women who don't like to work Bogdana, after a heroine from folk tales and songs, who didn't work and instead sat and did nothing. On the contrary, the image of the good girl or maiden (there are a number of such images in folk stories), who has some of the most common female names in Bulgaria like Gergana, Kalina and Elena, is always an example of neatness and diligence.

A negative character from Bulgarian literature (from a novel by author Aleko Konstantinov) is Bay Ganyo. Bay Ganyo is a Bulgarian pseudo-merchant who takes advantage of others who want to exchange ideas with him and doesn't have much regard for culture. Though ironic and humorous, Bay Ganyo's character represents attitudes viewed as highly negative by others. In short, Bay Ganyo is the anti-hero in Bulgaria. Bay-Ganyovshtina is behavior Bulgarians detest and point out. There are also historical figures who are associated with good and heroic deeds. These include big, strong men who pushed back attackers. There are a number of such characters in Bulgarian history and folklore; they include Borimechkata (someone so strong that he could fight bears) and the leaders of Bulgarian resistance against Turks during the Bulgarian national revival, including voyvods (leaders), Hristo Botev, Vasil Levski and many others. Anyone who uses their bare hands to stop thieves and criminals in Bulgaria is associated with these heroes. These deeds are hyperbolised and it is more a belief than a fact that such people really exist, but it helps people in their everyday lives.

4 - Words used to designate a type of person, animal, things

The qualities of the above heroes and anti-heroes are often attributed to people in Bulgaria, which is why it is not uncommon to hear someone being called by these names depending on the occasion. If the person is not present, instead of the name of the character, proper nouns are used to describe him or her. For example a person having excelled in something is "юнак" (a brave man). This word, though it has a positive meaning, can be used ironically as well to describe a person pretending to be heroic. Similar nouns are "хайдути" and "комита," used in various versions with the two different meanings, because these characters are ambivalent – besides being heroes they are known for having engaged in not-so-noble deeds. One very popular noun with ever newer and newer meanings is "чорбаджия," initially wealthier Bulgarians who didn't oppose the Turks, and today used to refer to rich and powerful businessmen.

5 - Common phrases and fun expressions in your native language and their translation in English

The Bulgarian language is very rich in proverbs and sayings that convey wit and wisdom. Most of them teach a lesson and, though funny and original, deal with old pangs and pains. Just as traditional medicine is sometimes more useful than the latest drugs invented, proverbs can heal your mind better than the most learned scientist. Thus various aches can be treated, such as lack of unity "Сговорна дружина, планина повдига" – "When united, men can lift a mountain" or "Сития на гладния не вярва" – "The satiated one doesn't believe the hungry"; poverty "Роди ме мамо с късмет, па ме хвърли на смет." – "Mother, give birth to me as a lucky man, then you can throw me in the waste" or "Сиромах човек – жив дявол" – "The poor man is the devil alive"; lack of common sense "Ум царува, ум робува, ум патки пасе." – "The mind reigns, the mind is a slave, the mind looks after the ducks" or "Докато мъдрите се намъдруват, лудите се налудуват." – "The crazy do their crazy deeds while the wise think their wise thoughts."; people's vices: "Не е луд който яде баницата, а който му я дава" – "The one offering the treat is to blame and not the one eating it."

6 - Songs and games you remember from your childhood, that are generally passed on to the next generation

The songs and games children play in Bulgaria today are different from those their parents and grandparents used to play. To be honest I'm not sure children today realise the purpose of the games they play, because playing on the computer and watching games on TV is not the same as getting together with other children and interacting. So it's almost certain that games no longer have the educational impact on children that they used to have in the past. Still, some of the most popular and easiest games to play are "Криеница," or hide and seek, "Гоненица" (chase) (children chase each other and when somebody is caught the chase starts over), "Дама" (Jump Over) which is like hopscotch.

7 - Legends/ stories or famous characters of the Imaginary / Folk tales

Bulgarian folklore is rich in legends telling of people's lives and troubles and what they did to overcome them. Legends have been largely exploited in literature and art in modern times, but they haven't lost their original wisdom and appeal. Among the many legends, one is hard to forget – that of the serpent's wedding.

When the richest and most beautiful girl in a village was getting ready to marry, a serpent living in the mountains stole her and wanted her to become his wife. The girl agreed to be his wife in exchange for the serpent's protection for the village. This legend has been created to reaffirm faith in all that is good and to defeat what is bad. The serpent kept his promise and instead of doing evil things to the village, he proved his love for the girl.

Another character mentioned very often is that of the king's daughter. According to the tale of the poor lad and the king's daughter, there was a king who had a daughter and the daughter wore out a new pair of slippers every night without anyone understanding how. The king announced a reward for the man who could tell him where his daughter was going. However none of the candidates succeeded because they all fell asleep in the night. Only one poor lad woke up when a serpent came in the night and took the king's daughter to his castle to a ball, where she danced so much that wore her slippers out. The lad followed them and told the king what he saw on the next day. The king gave him half of the kingdom and his daughter to be his wife as agreed before. Just as the serpent is often used to depict evil, the king's daughter is used as a symbol for the meaning of life and rewards for effort.

8 - Products or goods that represent 'the national treasure'

Bulgaria does have a real treasure, bequeathed to it by Thracian nobility who lived on Bulgarian land during ancient Greek and Roman times. There's still a geographical area known as Thracia in modern Bulgaria. These include plates and cups with original designs made of gold and silver. That's why, besides modern goods produced and exported for their unique value, this physical treasure is proof of the existence of an ancient culture on Bulgarian land even before Bulgaria was founded. Nevertheless, Bulgaria is now known for food products like wine, banitza (traditional pastry), lyutenitza (appetiser), yoghurt, meat delicacies, etc., as well as cultural phenomena like Bulgarian folk singing.

Denmark

First name: Steen Poul
Family name: Johnsen
steen.poul@gmail.com
&
First name: Lisa
Family name: Hersild
lisa@pregotranslation.com

Capital	Copenhagen	Population	5,543,400
Government	Constitutional monarchy	Currency	Danish kroner (DKK)
Religion(s)	Evangelical Lutheran		
Language(s)	Danish (official)		

Steen: I was born on August 14, 1965 in Copenhagen, Denmark. After finishing high school I spent two years in Louisiana, Alabama and Mississippi as a missionary for The Church of Jesus Christ of Latter Day Saints. When I returned to Denmark I served 9 months in the Danish military as a medic. I studied Market Economy at Niels Brock Copenhagen Business College and started working in sales and marketing shortly after I graduated. I consider myself a happy, easy-going, curious person with a great appetite for traveling and meeting new people. I am married to

Karina and we have two wonderful daughters, Alice and Helena. At present I live in Sao Paulo, Brazil which is my wife's hometown, and I am employed full-time as a freelance translator.

Lisa: I was born in Denmark in 1973 in a small town just west of Copenhagen. From when I was about 8 years old I always wanted to become a translator and interpreter, quite amusing as all my friends at that same age wanted to be circus princesses or movie stars! So the way forward was always quite clear to me, and as my second and third languages I later chose Italian and English.

I consider myself very fortunate in my job as a translator; every day I get presented with new subjects to translate which range from the highly technical texts to complicated legal matters. To keep myself up to date with my second language, I also combine translation work with a job as a travel guide in Tuscany, Sicily and Campania which brings me to Italy two-three months every year.

1 - A typical conversation – what are the common/ universal topics people go for? (weather, politics, etc.) - And some topics that you should avoid discussing with the locals?

When you meet a Dane for the first time, the first question will almost always be: "Where do you come from?" and "What do you do for a living?" I have learned that it can seem a little strange in some cultures that we define ourselves, and others, by what we, or they, do for a living. It's a matter of finding a connection to continue the conversation. Danish people consider it to work well as an ice breaker. I think that compared to some cultures the Danes are a little reserved at first but this is soon overcome, revealing that we are an open-minded culture with a good sense of humour. Danes master sarcasm very well which can confuse foreigners, who can't tell whether we mean something seriously or not.

Something typically Danish is 'hygge,' which best translates into coziness. Danes loves to 'hygge sig,' that is, have a good time together with friends and family while enjoying good food and drinks. Danes are very protective about their private lives and they are, at first, very reserved people.

Common topics

Headlines from the newspapers, teletext, the Internet – last night's football match, foreign and domestic politics, popular TV series, reality shows, etc.

Sports in general – Results, rankings, tournaments

The weather – Danes always complain about the weather: it's either too warm or too cold. This is a good subject where everybody normally agrees.

Topics to avoid

As there are very few taboo subjects (if any), religion is something most people are a little uncomfortable talking about because they consider this something very personal. Also you should avoid asking questions about how ethnic Danes feel towards the growing number of foreign immigrants in Denmark, as this is a topic that very much divides the population.

Among the Danes it is not very popular to admit that you vote for the political party called Dansk Folkeparti (Danish People's Party) which is frequently described as a right-wing populist party and is considered a bit extreme and nationalistic - that said, they managed to get 12% of the vote at the last election for parliament. Do not worry about mentioning the famous Muhammad cartoons, as Danes will generally defend them and the freedom of speech.

2 - Events of great significance for the community, deeply stored in everyone's mind

15th of June 1219: According to legend the Danish flag - Dannebrog - fell from the sky during a battle in Estonia. Today the day is called Valdemar's Day (from Valdemar who participated in the battle). Even though this day is not celebrated in any particular way, the Danes are very proud of their national flag and use all occasions (birthdays, holidays and national sports) to celebrate a particular event.

5th of June (1849): Constitution Day. The signing of the Danish constitution. Public holiday.

5th of May (1945): Liberation Day. This was the day when German forces surrendered in Denmark during World War II.

16th of April (1940): The Danish queen Margrethe II's birthday. This day is celebrated at the royal castle every year where she appears on her balcony.

3 - Figures from the past / present that you use in colloquial expressions

Den går ikke, Granberg (that won't work, Granberg): This expression derives from 1857 when a Swedish balloonist failed to ascend the balloon and had to jump down to a rooftop. Today the expression and his name are still widely used to describe a "failure."

4 - Words used to designate a type of person, animal, things

Brian / a Brian: A name that has become synonymous with a loser.

Tudemarie (crymary / crybaby): Said about a person who is easily moved to tears or is a bit wimpy. The name derives from a series of three books from the 1930s and 1940s about a working class girl from Copenhagen who is known to cry all the time during her childhood and adult years.

Rasmus Modsat (Rasmus Opposite): Said about a person who argues for the opposite of what others say, or who doesn't accept an idea.

5 - Common phrases and fun expressions in your native language and their translation in English

- "Tak for kaffe" (literally meaning "thanks for coffee") which is used as an exclamation to express surprise like "oh my God," "my goodness."

- Man skal ikke kaste med sten hvis man selv bor i glashus - (literal translation: Don't throw rocks if you live in a greenhouse). Meaning: Don't be a hypocrite!

- At tage benene på nakken - (literal translation: Put your legs on your neck) Meaning: To hurry up.

- Strissere, pansere (cop, copper), salatfad (salad bowl): These expressions are commonly used to describe the police. The latter is a slang term for the police vans used to transport prisoners. In 1880 the police vans were "salad green," and the story goes that a man who got arrested said: "Just because the van is green like salad, you gentlemen don't have to be "as sour as vinegar."

6 - Songs and games you remember from your childhood, that are generally passed on to the next generation

- Lille Peter edderkop (children's song): Itsy Bitsy Spider
- Jens Hansen havde en bondegård (children's song): Old McDonald had a farm
- Åh abe - (children's song): Monkey song
- Tag den ring og lad den vandre (children's game)
- Rundbold (children's game often played in school yards): A game similar to soft ball
- Høvdingebold (children's game): two teams compete by throwing a ball at each other. The last person to be hit wins the game.

7 - Legends/ stories or famous characters of the Imaginary / Folk tales

Thor: In Nordic mythology, the god of thunder and lightning. Today, when there is a thunderstorm, we tell the children that it is Thor passing in the sky in his carriage with his hammer.

The Little Mermaid: The national symbol of Denmark and the popular fairy tale by Hans Christian Andersen. In Copenhagen there is a small bronze statue of her, and she remains one of the main tourist attractions in the city. She has had quite a turbulent life with at least eight vandalism attacks where she has had both arms and her head amputated but she's still standing today on her little boulder in the water.

Holger Danske: In the catacombs of the Kronborg castle in Elsinore, Denmark, you'll find the ancient Viking warrior Holger Danske. Legend says that whenever Denmark is faced with a threat by a foreign enemy, Holger Danske will rise from his seat and defend the country against its enemies.

8 - Products or goods that represent 'the national treasure'

LEGO - The name 'LEGO' is an abbreviation of the two Danish words "leg godt," meaning "play well." Based on the world-famous LEGO brick, the company today provides toys, experiences and teaching materials for children in more than 130 countries.

Danish beer: Danes love beer, especially Tuborg and Carlsberg, home-grown beers which have become world-renowned brands. There are also a lot of micro-breweries in all of Denmark producing very tasty local beers.

***

Watch out for the bicycles. It is estimated that 50% of all citizens in Copenhagen commute to work every day by bike. Another curiosity is that 63% of all members of the Danish Parliament also commute daily by bike and hence setting a great example.

Learn the queuing culture: All Danes have a great sense of queuing culture and master this discipline very well, often with number systems. Good advice to all visitors would be to learn to stand in a line properly i.e. never try to squeeze in, and don't stand too close to the person in front or behind you.

Be punctual: Or even better, be there before the agreed time. It is very much considered a waste of other people's time if you are not punctual.

Estonia

First name: Kersti
Family name: Skovard
KERSTISKOVGAARD@HOTMAIL.COM

Capital	Tallinn	Population	1,274,700
Government	Parliamentary republic	Currency	Kroon (EEK)
Religion(s)	Evangelical Lutheran, Orthodox and others		
Language(s)	Estonian (official), Russian		

Becoming a translator was a dream come true for me– that's what I was training for in university, but it didn't really happen until Estonia became a part of the European Union. Being a freelance translator gives me much flexibility, while also requiring quite a bit of discipline. Translating various texts gives me insight into many different and interesting areas, and calls for constant learning.

1 - A typical conversation – what are the common/universal topics people go for? (weather, politics, etc.) - And some topics that you should avoid discussing with the locals?

When starting a common conversation, be prepared for Estonians to be rather cold with strangers. As the conversation carries on, they warm up, and by the end of the conversation, you may be best friends forever. Ask questions about the country (many foreigners do not know much about Estonia) and the person you are speaking with. Estonians are pleased when a foreigner knows something about Estonia; they like to discuss politics and learn about you and your country.

Topics to avoid: none really; or rather, you'll have to find out on a case-by-case basis.

2 - Events of great significance for the community, deeply stored in everyone's mind

1343 – St. George's Night uprising (**Jüriöö ülestõus**) – an unsuccessful attempt by Estonians to rid themselves of the Danish and German rulers who had occupied the country in the 13th century. The date on which it started – April 23rd (St. George's Day) – is still an important date in the traditional calendar.

1561 – Northern Estonia submitted to Swedish control, southern Estonia formed the Duchy of Livonia under Polish-Lithuanian Commonwealth. The period until the Great Northern War is referred to as "the Good Old Swedish Time."

1632 – University of Tartu (Dorpat) was founded by Swedish king Gustav II Adolf.

1700-1721 - the Great Northern War; the Swedish empire lost Estonia to Russia.

February 24th, 1918 – **Estonian independence** was declared.

1940 – Estonia was occupied by the Soviet Union.

1941, 1949 – Mass deportations of Estonians to Siberia by the Soviets.

August 23rd, 1989 – **The Baltic Way**: a peaceful political demonstration against the Soviet occupation. Approximately 2 million people from Estonia, Latvia and Lithuania joined their hands to form a human chain spanning over 600 km across the 3 Baltic states, connecting the three Baltic capitals: Tallinn, Riga and Vilnius.

August 20th, 1991 – restoration of the Republic of Estonia.

May 1st, 2004 – Estonia joined the European Union.

February 24th – **Independence Day.**

June 24th - **Jaanipäev** (Midsummer Day). On Midsummer Night's eve, bonfires are lit all over the country and people celebrate the shortest and brightest night of the year. It's a night of romance.

3 - Nouns and Figures from the past / present that you use in colloquial expressions

For Estonians, artists (especially writers) seem to be more popular than politicians. Quotes from Estonian classical works (A. H. Tammsaare, O. Luts, J. Kross) are used more often than quotes from the Bible. Probably the most popular quote is from Oskar Luts' book "Kevade" ("Spring"): "Kui Arno isaga koolimajja jõudis, olid tunnid juba alanud" ("When Arno and his father arrived at school, the classes had already started"). Lydia Koidula (1843-1886) and her poems are considered a national treasure, along with legendary choir conductor Gustav Ernesaks and opera singer Georg Ots. Contemporary artists include composer Arvo Pärt, symphony orchestra conductor Neeme Järvi, as well as ballet dancers Age Oks (Agnes Oaks) and Thomas Edur, who were the leading ballet couple in the English National Ballet for nearly 20 years and are now back at the Estonian National Opera and Ballet Theatre.

4 - Words used to designate a type of person, animal, things

These come and go. At the moment some of them refer to political parties, e.g. "oravad" (squirrels) for the ruling Reform Party, "kampsunid" (sweaters) for one wing of the IRL party, "ninasarvik" (rhino) for the leader of the Center Party. During Soviet times, "valge laev" (white ship) symbolised the hope that the West would help liberate Estonia.

"Kutsu" (doggie) – for a dog whose name you don't know, "kiisu" (kitty) for a cat whose name you don't know, and interestingly, taxi drivers call taxi call ladies "kiisu"; you also have "jänes" (rabbit) for a coward, or even "jänes püksis" (rabbit in the pants), "rebane" (fox) for a cunning person, "vene karu" (Russian bear) refers to Russia, Finns are often colloquially called "põder" (elk), Swedes are "svenssons," all in a friendly way.

5 - Common phrases and fun expressions in your native language and their translation in English

Proverbs are popular and often used:

Kes ei tööta, see ei söö (whoever does not work shall not eat)

Nälg on kõige parem kokk (hunger is the best cook).

Parem karta kui kahetseda (better to be afraid than sorry).

And there is a whole book[1] full of them – 624 pages!

---

[1] http://www.folklore.ee/~kriku/VSR/FRAMEST.HTM

In Estonian, instead of putting shoes on, you put them INTO your foot ("Pane kingad jalga"), you put a hat INTO your head ("Pane müts pähe") and you put clothes ONTO your back ("Pane riided selga"). We are so used to this that we don't notice the nonsense but foreigners who learn the Estonian language are baffled.

A word that you may hear whenever something goes wrong or just as a 'parasite word' is "Kurat!" ("Devil"), meaning "Dammit!"

Expressions from the past 20 years:

Ämbrisse astuma (step into the bucket) – for people who do something improper or stupid, especially politicians

JOKK ("juriidiliselt on kõik korrektne" – legally everything is correct) – used for actions that are legally, but not necessarily ethically, correct.

6 - Songs and games you remember from your childhood, that are generally passed on to the next generation

- Kes aias (Who's in the Garden) - a song and a game
- Peitus (hide and seek)
- Mädamuna (Rotten Egg) - a ball game
- Mutionu (Uncle Mole) – a popular children's song
- Põdra maja (Elk's house) – a popular children's song
- Õllepruulija (Brewer) – a song sung at parties

And many other songs – Estonians like to sing not only during the famous Song Festivals but also at family events.

7 - Legends/ stories or famous characters of the Imaginary / Folk tales

Kalevipoeg – a hero from the national epic story.

Valge Daam (The White Lady) appears in the window of a church in the coastal town of Haapsalu on full moon nights in August. This shape is a combination of moonlight and branches. Legend says it's the soul of a girl trapped in the wall of the chapel because of her forbidden love. For centuries she has appeared in the window of the local church to prove the immortality of love. Many people come to watch it, and every year Haapsalu hosts the White Lady music festival during the full moon in August.

8 - Products or goods that represent 'the national treasure'

We are still looking for it. Oh! Skype was developed by three Estonian programmers. It also seems that cyber defense is becoming one of our strong points.

About food, perhaps Baltic *sprat* should be mentioned, and our many kinds of dairy products as well as black bread – these are the things Estonians miss most when abroad. Apart from their home country, that is.

Sauna – that's something that no Estonian can live without. And we have many forests, even though the country is tiny.

***

The first known human settlement in Estonia is about 11,000 years old.

Estonia has seen many rulers of different nationalities: Danes, Swedes, Poles, Germans, Russians. They all have left their own mark. In 1216, to justify the crusade in Estonia, Pope Innocent III confirmed the name that Bishop Albert had given to Estonia:

"Maarjamaa" (Terra Mariae). Since the 20th century, "Maarjamaa" has been used as a literary name for Estonia.

There is a legend that Danes got their Dannebrog flag in Estonia on June 15th, 1219, when it fell from the sky during a battle under Lyndanise (Tallinn). Nowadays the silver cross on a red background is also found on the coat-of-arms of Estonia's capital city (Tallinn).

The oldest records of written Estonian date from the 13th century. The first book written in Estonian is from 1525.

Estonia is known for its song-loving people and the song festivals that take place every 5 years. Song Festivals are some of the largest choral events in the world. The joint choir usually has 25,000 – 30,000 singers, performing for an audience of 80,000 – 100,000 people. The singers and many of the listeners wear colourful national costumes.

Even though Estonia is a very small country, you can drive tens of kilometres without seeing any houses. Local people value homegrown food and many people still prefer homegrown fruit and vegetables to the imported food in supermarkets.

France

First name: Stéphanie
Family name: Taif
frenchconnectiontraductions@gmail.com
&
First name: Elodie
Family name: Saliceto
Elodie.Saliceto@wanadoo.fr
&
First name: Eva
Family name: Seris
eva.seris@gmail.com

Capital	Paris	Population	65,630,000
Government	Republic	Currency	Euro (EUR)
Religion(s)	Roman Catholic and others		
Language(s)	French		

Eva: Hi, I'm Eva! I live in the lovely city of Annecy, near the Swiss border, with my 2 year old son and my husband. I studied business and worked in the HR field for 4 years before I realised my dream of becoming a translator, almost two years ago. I love being told stories, from as far as I can remember, so I have always been a book worm. I have a sweet tooth, and I love to experiment in my kitchen. I like to think people enjoy what I cook. I am slightly addicted to my smartphone.

- France -

Elodie: I am a French girl in her thirties, with a passion for culture (s), languages and travelling!

I was born in Antibes, on the French Riviera, in 1980.

I have worked as a teacher and researcher in college (in France and Italy), and then created my own company as a freelance translator, proofreader, and researcher. I am currently working for a French "packager" on two magazines (as a translator from Italian to French and as an author). I am also working on a few publishing projects, including a book based on my thesis (about neoclassicism in French travel narrative on Italy in the nineteenth century).

I have lived in many places, in France (Nice, Brest, Lyon, metropolitan Paris) as well as abroad: in Madrid, Spain (1988-1991); Rome, Pisa and Milan, Italy (1998-2005); West Palm Beach, Florida, USA (from 2009 until now). These stays and travels introduced me to different cultures, which has further developed my appreciation of all sorts of cultural exchanges, arts, and cultural institutions.

Stéphanie: I have always had a passion for foreign languages, since I was a kid. I studied English, Spanish and Italian at school. I originally studied International Business and Marketing and transferred to the University of Florida, U.S.A. for one exchange semester. After graduating with a Bachelor's degree in Business in France, I moved back to the USA to work in marketing. I started translating as a hobby at first. I worked as a freelance part-time translator for 5 years until it became clear that I wanted to dedicate my career to translation and I was willing to put aside my marketing career for it. Today I live in the south of France, and I work as a full-time translator. You can find more information on my Proz profile at: www.proz.com/translator/849944

1 - A typical conversation – what are the common/universal topics people go for? (weather, politics, etc.) - And some topics that you should avoid discussing with the locals?

When meeting a French person, always greet them before anything else. Even a simple "hello, how are you?" will be appreciated. It is not a matter of discussing each other's health and feelings thoroughly, rather a way to be polite, and even filling the void when you don't know what to say.

What happened in the "journal télé" (TV news): French people are very interested in the news program, which is twice a day, once at 1pm and once at 8pm on the main TV channels. This half-hour program is really part of the popular culture. So French people are aware of what is going on, nationally and internationally and they will want to talk about what they saw on TV lately. Asking them what they think of the latest news is a good way to start a conversation.

Sports: men will likely talk about the latest achievements of their favourite football team ("PSG" team for Paris or "OM" team for Marseille trigger the most enthusiasm among their fans)

The French like a good debate, or even a small controversy. We can have passionate conversations about politics and all things related to the Republic: secularism, public services, the welfare State… However, be aware that religion, racism and immigration are touchy subjects.

2 - *Events of great significance for the community, deeply stored in everyone's mind*

Everyone will remember the year 1789 as the beginning of the **French Revolution**, with the famous and symbolic storming of the Bastille on the 14th of July.

The Dreyfus Affair (1894-1906) is probably one of the origins of France's culture of debate. People were really passionate for or against Jewish officer Alfred Dreyfus, (falsely) accused of being a traitor. To support him and to denounce the true guilty party, Émile Zola wrote his well-known "J'accuse…!" (1898).

World War I and II are still pretty fresh in everyone's memories, even among young people. It is a subject widely covered in History classes from primary school to high school. The older citizens remember it vividly and they used to share stories during family events, about scarcity of food or curfews during the war.

During WWII, certain regions of France used to be occupied by Germany and the older generation still remembers the occupation. There are a lot of popular French comedies set during the war, actors Louis de Funès and Bourvil played in popular comedy movies.

May 1968: The symbol of youth protests and aspiration for more freedom, and the beginning of broad social movements and recurrent strikes in the country. Even more than the importance of the movement, it is the tone that still resonates today. It was the time of sexual revolution, of the hippie movement, people were craving for freedom, and the movement was deeply utopian: people were not only standing for their rights, they wanted to build a better world.

1981: The abolition of the death penalty by President François Mitterrand.

3 - Nouns and Figures from the past / present that you use in colloquial expressions

Jeanne d'Arc, "the Maid of Orléans" (in French "la Pucelle d'Orléans"), is a symbol of loyalty, nationalism, Catholicism and fighting against England, France's traditional enemy. This figure has been almost exclusively appropriated by the extreme right-wing.

Napoléon Bonaparte, initially a general, he became consul and then emperor (1804-1815). Despite his despotism, he gave the country great spirit and remains an inspiration for energy and leadership.

Le Général de Gaulle is admired for his active role in the French Resistance against the Nazis, and for the strong opinion he voiced about French independence and greatness. But he was also criticised for his actions during the Algerian War (and May 1968). Still, he is a major reference in politics.

4 - Words used to designate a type of person, animal, things

- Tanguy is the name of a character in the eponymous movie, released in 2001. In this movie, a grown man, named Tanguy still lives at his parents' home and does not want to leave the nest. His parents do everything they can to make him leave the house. Nowadays, an adult who still lives at mom and dad, is often called a "tanguy."

- Un chateaubriand: It is a beefsteak cut from the tenderloin, a recipe especially created for the famous author François-René de Chateaubriand (1768-1848). Sometimes it is written "châteaubriant" (like the city).

- Une poubelle: A trash can. Eugène-René Poubelle (1831-1907), "préfet" of the Seine region, introduced this object to Paris in 1884, for hygiene reasons.
- Un Paris-Brest: A dessert made of choux pastry and praline cream. It is wheel-shaped because it commemorates the first bicycle race between the cities of Paris and Brest (Brittany) in 1891.
- L'Arlésienne designates something people talk about but never see, and comes from the character of the young girl from Arles (a city in Provence) in Alphonse Daudet's short story and play L'Arlésienne – because the girl never appears on stage.

5 - Common phrases and fun expressions in your native language and their translation in English

Avoir de la bouteille: It means "to have a lot of experience," but "bouteille" (bottle) refers to wine… a very French image!

Poser un lapin: literally, it means "to put down a rabbit"! When someone made an appointment but didn't show up, "il/elle m'a posé un lapin!"

Aimable comme une porte de prison: "kind as a prison door"… quite easy to understand!

Il vaut mieux l'avoir en photo qu'en pension: "it is better to have a picture of him or her than to take him or her as a lodger." When a person eats a lot and is expensive to feed!

Occupe-toi de tes oignons: "go take care of your onions," meaning "mind your own business," "don't put your nose in my business."

6 - Songs and games you remember from your childhood, that are generally passed on to the next generation

Songs for children (and sometimes adults):

- "Alouette"
- "Au clair de la lune"
- "Il pleut bergère"
- "Une souris verte"
- "Frère Jacques"
- "Il était un petit navire"
- "Petit Papa Noël"… and many others!

Popular games, at school or elsewhere (they may also be popular in other countries):

- Cache-cache and "1, 2, 3… soleil!" (Hide and seek)
- La marelle (Hopscotch)
- Jouer aux billes (playing marbles)
- Sauter à la corde (to jump rope)
- Je te tiens par la barbichette (both a song and game: two people hold each other's chins while singing the song, at the end of the song they are supposed to look directly into each other's eyes and the first one to laugh loses).

7 - Legends/ stories or famous characters of the Imaginary / Folk tales

La Dame blanche (the White Lady) is a scary legend! It is a ghost who supposedly jumps in front of drivers when they approach a dangerous bend… a sort of hitchhiker!

An imaginary character not coming from religious sources is **la petite souris** (Tooth fairy or literally "the little mouse") - he brings a coin to a young kid in exchange for a baby tooth, that is put under the pillow at night.

In the late seventeenth century, Charles Perrault created tales, and most especially princesses, that have been a part of the imaginary, not only in France, but also all over the world, like Cinderella or the Sleeping Beauty. But my favourite princess, **Peau d'Âne** (Donkey Skin) was never brought to the screen by Walt Disney.

8 - Products or goods that represent 'the national treasure'

I know French people are called froggies, but you rarely see frogs in restaurant menus. Nor snails, for that matter. I never tasted snails, by the way (I did taste frog… during an Asian meal).

However, we do love our smelly cheese. There hardly ever are frogs at the restaurant, but there is almost always a plate of cheese you can order instead of a dessert. I grew up in Normandy, land of the camembert, and I now live near the Swiss border, land of fondue, so I feel like cheese is a part of my destiny…!

French pastries and "baguettes" are a huge part of the French culture. Many are those who cannot eat a meal without bread on the side. "Pâtisseries" and "Boulangeries" are a staple in the French landscape in any town.

Popular Haute-Couture designers like Chanel and Jean-Paul Gauthier create fragrances which are now part of the French culture.

France has countless great wines and French people usually know a great deal about wine. At what temperature it should be stored or drunk, with what type of food (meat/fish/dessert) it should be served etc. The stores have entire aisles dedicated to different types of wines. When people are invited to dinner at someone else's house, the common custom is to bring a good bottle of wine.

***

You're having a passionate conversation, but you just can't make your point. And as soon as you've left, you have an epiphany: "Gosh, I should have said that!" It happens to me all the time.

In France, we have an expression for that: "l'esprit de l'escalier" ("the staircase wit"). It was first described in the 18th century, during the Enlightenment, by philosopher Denis Diderot in his *Paradoxe sur le comédien* ("The Paradox of Acting"), where he relates how speechless he once was left during a dinner: "l'homme sensible, comme moi, tout entier à ce qu'on lui objecte, perd la tête et ne se retrouve qu'au bas de l'escalier" ("a sensitive man, such as myself, overwhelmed by the argument levelled against him, becomes confused and can only think clearly again when he reaches the bottom of the stairs").

Italy

First name: Claudia
Family name: Salamone
www.translationfactory.it
cla.salamone@gmail.com

Capital	Rome	Population	61,261,000
Government	Republic	Currency	Euro (EUR)
Religion(s)	Christian		
Language(s)	Italian		

Born in Germany to a Spanish mother and an Italian father, I soon developed a passion for foreign languages and multiculturalism thanks to my European family, as I like to define it.

The idea of becoming an interpreter and translator initially came up when I was 16 and while at university (BA in Translation and Business Interpreting + MA in Conference Interpreting at SSLMIT Scuola Superiore di Lingue Moderne per Interpreti e Traduttori, Università di Bologna), I realised that this was exactly what I wanted to do with my life: to facilitate communication between people.

I started working as an interpreter for business meetings and trade shows in Italy and abroad, and so far I have been working as a freelancer from the end of 2007. Over the years I have had the chance to collaborate with clients from different industries, with diverse needs, which proved to be the ideal condition to improve my knowledge and specialisation in a wide range of fields like fashion (textile), beauty and cosmetics, tourism, art and design, to mention just a few. What I like most about this job is the opportunity to discover lots of different topics and to meet people and cultures. Besides being a curious person loving languages and words, I am a teaholic, book-lover, belly dancer and football fan.

To learn more about my professional profile, please visit my website www.translationfactory.it/en. You can also follow me on twitter @Tra_factory.

1 - A typical conversation – what are the common/universal topics people go for? (weather, politics, etc.) - And some topics that you should avoid discussing with the locals?

Weather. The weather is certainly a common topic for small-talk while you are sitting at the doctor or when you meet someone you are very familiar or close with. A nice sentence most people would say, especially when the weather is hot one day and cold another, would be "non si sa più come vestirsi" (you wouldn't know what to wear anymore) or "non ci sonopiù le mezze stagioni" (midseason does not exist anymore).

Football. The most popular sport in Italy. All through the year almost all men talk about football: what their favourite team did, bad moves by the coach, how bad the news about fixed games was.

Politics. Talking about politics is fine in Italy but sometimes the conversation can become unpleasant, as some people may be defending their party too eagerly.

Food. If the conversation is between mums or housewives, they will probably talk about the meal they cooked the night before or what they would like to try cooking. Food and eating well are fundamental aspects for most Italians.

I would say there are no taboo topics in normal or formal conversation. Obviously no one talks about sex or private aspects of his or her life in public. As for religion, a topic to avoid in some cultures, it is not a controversial subject in Italy, but it's not very common either.

2 - Events of great significance for the community, deeply stored in everyone's mind

On the 17 March 1861, **the birth of the Italian kingdom** was declared, with the crowning of Vittorio Emanuele II. A desire for freedom from the Austrians and other invaders and the need to be united as a state led Italians to uprisings and revolutions. The Carbonari movement was one of the first signs of something about to change. This was followed by the revolution of 1848 and by the important Spedizione dei Mille (the Expedition of the Thousand) led by Garibaldi, which marked the final stage in the unification process called Risorgimento. Rome became the capital in 1870 replacing Turin. In 2011 the 150th anniversary of national unity was celebrated.

On 25 April 1945, **World War II ended** with the surrender of the German Army occupying northern Italy. During the war Italy was allied with the Nazis, but from 1943 the Partisan (resistance) movement opposed Fascism (Mussolini was first arrested and then escaped till he was caught again and killed). This event is very vivid in everyone's mind especially because there are still survivors of that war willing to keep the memory alive. Grandparents who lived that tragedy first hand, museums or monuments and commemorations are all important reminders of that despicable period of our history.

3 - Nouns and Figures from the past / present that you use in colloquial expressions

Pinocchio. The famous character by Collodi is used for example when trying to explain to children that lying is not right. You can say to a child "don't tell lies or your nose will become longer like Pinocchio's."

Cicerone. When you say "fare da Cicerone" ("I'll be your Cicero") it means that you will be someone's guide, for example when sightseeing in a city or visiting a museum. This image is probably linked to the fact that Cicero used very rich and precise descriptions. He also wrote a book about Greece that could be considered a tourist guide in the modern sense of the term.

Calimero. "Mi sento come Calimero" ("I feel like Calimero") when you think the entire world is against you and you are having bad luck. This is because Calimero was an unlucky black chicken born into a family of yellow chickens. Calimero often blurts out, "It's not fair!"

4 - Words used to designate a type of person, animal, things

Giù. This preposition is used to describe the South of Italy. A Milanese would ask a Neapolitan "sei stato giù per le vacanze?" ("have you spent the holidays in Naples/in the South?").

Perla. The translation is pearl but in Italian this word is also used to indicate a very funny story or expression, or a very interesting piece of information.

5 - Common phrases and fun expressions in your native language and their translation in English

- *Avere il braccino corto.* Literally "to have a short arm," it means that a person is penny-pinching.

- *Raccontare balle.* Literally "to tell balls," it means to lie.

- *Fare un quarantotto.* Literally "to make a 48." It means to make a mess, as it refers to the revolutions in 1848.

- *Ci sono quattro gatti.* Literally "there are four cats," it means that there are just a few people.

- *Non c'è un cane.* Literally "there is not even a dog," it means "there is no one."

- *Alzare il gomito.* Literally "to raise the elbow," it means "to drink too much."

- *Bello come il sole.* Literally "beautiful like the sun," it means "extremely beautiful."

- *Braccia rubate all'agricoltura.* Literally "arms stolen from agriculture," it means that someone with an intellectual job should do a more practical job because he or she is not particularly smart.

- *Due di picche.* Literally "two of spades," it indicates a refusal, especially in love relationships.

- *E compagnia bella.* Literally "and nice company," it means etcetera.

- *Idem con patate.* Literally "the same with potatoes," it's an expression used to confirm what was just said.

6 - Songs and games you remember from your childhood, that are generally passed on to the next generation

- Nascondino (Hide and seek)
- Girotondo (Ring a Ring o' Roses)
- Il gioco del silenzio (The game of silence)
- Mondo o campana (Hopscotch)
- *Ma che bel castello marcondiro ndiro ndello, ma che bel castello marcondiro ndiro ndà...*
- *La bella lavanderina, che la vai fazzoletti per i poveretti della città. Fai un salto, fanne un altro, fai la giravolta, falla un'altra volta. Guarda in su! Guarda in giù! Dai un bacio a chi vuoi tu!* A counting-out rhyme. The literal translation: "The beautiful washer girl washes handkerchiefs for the poor people of the city. Jump once. Jump again. Cut a caper. Do it again. Look up! Look down! Kiss anyone you like"

7 - Legends/ stories or famous characters of the Imaginary / Folk tales

Dante and his journey through hell, purgatory and heaven guided by Virgilio and Beatrice, and described in the Divine Comedy. In Italy you study the entire poem at school and everybody knows this story.

Garibaldi e i Mille are very vivid in the Italian imaginary, as their expedition was fundamental in unifying Italy. There is also a song: "Garibaldi fu ferito, fu ferito ad una gamba, Garibaldi che comanda, che comanda i suoi soldà" (Garibaldi was injured, his leg was injured, Garibaldi who is a commander and commands his soldiers).

8 - Products or goods that represent 'the national treasure'

Caffè espresso. It's the quickest, yet most important rite we have in Italy. You drink it hot, short and standing at the bar. Be careful in Naples: they serve it in an extremely hot cup!

Pizza. It was created in Naples and therefore Italians do it better!

Moda. Fashion is one of the leading sectors of the Italian economy and Italians in general are famous for their good taste in clothing.

The Coliseum. Probably the most representative monument in Italy is in Rome, the eternal city which represents the Roman Empire and Italy's long history.

Aperitivo. Typically from Northern Italy (Milan is the place of birth and capital city of the *Aperitivo*) is the custom of meeting friends or colleagues after work and drinking something together at a bar. The aperitif is served along with many appetisers and even proper dishes (if you are lucky in Milan, you can also find hot pasta or risotto).

Vespa. The famous scooter by Piaggio. Its name means "wasp."

Portugal

FIRST NAME: MANUEL
FAMILY NAME: BENSAÚDE FERREIRA DEUSDADO
HTTP://WWW.PROZ.COM/PROFILE/637512
&
FIRST NAME: MARINA
FAMILY NAME: TAVARES
HTTP://WWW.PROZ.COM/PROFILE/112325

Capital	Lisbon	Population	10,781,400
Government	Republic; parliamentary democracy	Currency	Euro (EUR)
Religion(s)	Roman Catholic and others		
Language(s)	Portuguese		

Manuel: I am a Portuguese translator from Lisbon. From an early age, translation was an obvious career choice for me. I worked freelance for a while, but dealing with stressed out clients, huge translation requests with tight deadlines, working late in the evening was not what I was expecting. So, to ease the pain, I started working at a translation agency, where I stayed for nearly two years. There I had the chance to develop myself as a professional translator. When I felt ready to deal directly with clients again, I restarted working as a freelance translator.

Besides translating, I have also written two books, "No Meu Tempo - Estórias de Amor e Humor" and "No Meu Tempo - Festas, Romarias, Lendas e Cantigas," and translated another one: "O Pintor Ricardo Bensaúde."

Marina: I was born in Viseu, a cozy city in the north of Portugal, in 1976. At the age of fourteen, I realised I wanted to be a translator, so that I could help break language barriers. During university, I applied for the Erasmus Program and finished my Degree at Queen's University of Belfast, in 1998/1999. Afterwards, I started a postgraduate qualification in Translation Studies, completed in 2004.

As for work, I started out as both an administrative assistant and translator, mainly translating manuals on several subjects. In 2009, I had the opportunity to take a subtitling and dubbing course, which enabled me to start working full-time as a translator. I started translating mainly scripts for cartoon series and animations, which made me realise working in translation can be really good fun!

I believe that all my experiences help me in my work as a translator, as the more information we have, the better we can be in our job. Those experiences made me a creative, responsible and organised person.

1 - A typical conversation – what are the common/ universal topics people go for? (weather, politics, etc.) - And some topics that you should avoid discussing with the locals?

In Portugal, we like to talk about food as much as we like to eat! And we have a lot to choose from: tasty soups, excellent meat, fresh fish and traditional sweets. If we don't know where or what to eat, we can always ask for some suggestions.

Football is a favourite topic. While not everybody watches or even follows football, most people do. And depending on your team, sometimes you would prefer not to be a football fan! First thing to do is try to find out which football club of the person we are talking to supports. It's highly probable that it is one of the traditional "big 3": Benfica, Porto or Sporting. In recent years, other football clubs have become more important and have more fans, like Sporting Clube de Braga, Vitória de Guimarães or Vitória de Setúbal. If your team loses its Sunday match, you know how tough Monday is going to be.

Weather is a true universal theme. In most situations, if there's a need to break the silence, it's always a good option.

Topics we usually avoid in more formal contexts

Money – Although, nowadays, the economic crisis is a hot topic, people don't like to discuss personal money issues and avoid revealing their own situation.

Politics – Almost everyone has an opinion regarding politics, but it may be sensitive subject matter. Perhaps due to the recent transition to democracy, we tend to be very politically correct. This is especially true when talking about social and labor rights. Or even when talking about the former dictatorial regime which Portugal was under for the majority of the 20th century. If someone dares to say they think the Estado Novo Regime had one or a few good aspects, they are instantly referred to as a "fascist."

Religion – The vast majority of the population is Catholic and, although there is freedom of choice, this topic may offend religious sensibilities.

Sex – As most families are still conservative, this is not a topic mentioned in a normal/formal conversation.

2 - Events of great significance for the community, deeply stored in everyone's mind

1926 – 1974: Dictatorship - Especially strong from 1933 to 1974, when António de Oliveira Salazar began a new regime called "Estado Novo" (New State). With no political parties, very strong censorship and a secret politic police, PIDE, people were dominated through fear and ignorance.

25 April 1974: A group of military officers organised a coup d'etat to end the dictatorship. In the end, it was a bloodless revolution, which became known as "Revolução dos Cravos" (Carnation Revolution), as bullets were replaced by carnations. Through this revolution, Portugal recovered its freedom.

Carnival – This religious celebration is deeply rooted in Portugal and we've been celebrating it since the Middle Ages. In those days, people would dress in home-made costumes, play tricks on each other and do other funny things. Although the Brazilian Carnival has its origin in Portuguese colonisation, some Portuguese cities are now being influenced by Carnaval do Rio and feature Rio's famous samba parades.

Dia de Portugal, de Camões e das Comunidades Portuguesas is a National holiday celebrating the Nation, Camões, our most famous poet and Portuguese Emigrants. Held on 10 June, this date originally signaled the death of Luís Vaz de Camões, one of the most important Portuguese poets and author of Os Lusíadas, an epic poem from the 16th century, exalting the country's achievements overseas. Afterwards, it also became the Portuguese National Day, paying special attention to the emigrant community.

3 - Nouns and Figures from the past / present that you use in colloquial expressions

- Pinga: Sometimes, we refer to wine as "pinga"; for example, "esta pinga é da boa" ("this is a really good wine").
- Pitéu: Similarly to "pinga," we can refer to food as "pitéu"; for example, "que pitéu magnífico" ("this is delicious").
- Bófia ("Cop"): Another name by which police officers are known.
- Marialva: It can have two meanings. A more literal one, representing a man interested in horse riding and bullfighting who takes life easy and a second pejorative one which refers to womanisers.
- Calmeirão ("Big boy"): A nickname for a person of tall stature.
- Alfacinha – Nickname given to a native of Lisbon. Literally translated: "Little Lettuce."
- Tripeiro – Nickname given to a native of Oporto. Literally translated: "tripeman."

4 - Words used to designate a type of person, animal, things

Velho do Restelo (Old Man from Restelo) – A character from "Lusíadas," probably the most important book in Portuguese Literature, written by Luís Vaz de Camões about the discoveries. When the sailors are getting ready to set sail towards India, this old and savvy man speaks, censuring the option to sail the seas, looking for fame and heroism, not thinking of the negative consequences that could have. Thinking about this character and what he represents, we say that pessimistic people are like the "Velho do Restelo."

Zé Povinho. A symbol of social criticism created by Rafael Bordalo Pinheiro, a 19th century Portuguese artist. This character is often seen as the embodiment of the Portuguese people. It represents a submissive, patient, naïve, humble and indifferent people, who will always be a victim of those who are more powerful. The main feature of the character is a gesture he makes with his arms, called "manguito." This gesture is an expression of his anger and indignation, however, besides that gesture, he hardly does anything else to change the situation.

5 - *Common phrases and fun expressions in your native language and their translation in English*

Como cão e gato ("Like dog and cat") – This phrase is used when two people don't get along very well…

Puxar a brasa à minha sardinha ("to roast one's sardine better than someone else's") – We use this funny phrase (original sense might get lost in translation) when we want to refer to someone whose only interest is their own benefits and who takes the actions necessary to achieve them.

Vender gato por lebre ("To sell a cat as a hare") – Another funny phrase. This one means to deceive someone, particularly by selling an item that doesn't correspond to what one expected.

Cai o Carmo e a Trindade ("To hit Carmo and Trindade") – Carmo and Trindade were two churches destroyed in the Lisbon Earthquake of 1755. When you say that someone struck Carmo and Trindade you're saying they did something amazing, surprising or terrible.

Vai dar banho ao cão! – This expression is used when someone is making fun or trying to cheat us and we are tired of it or don't believe it. Literally translated: "Go bathe the dog"!

Dar com a língua nos dentes – This expression is used when someone knows a secret and reveals it, either intentionally or unintentionally. Literally translated: "To hit with the tongue in the teeth."

6 - Songs and games you remember from your childhood, that are generally passed on to the next generation

- Jogar ao pião – Playing spinning top
- Apanhada – Playing tag
- Jogar às escondidas – Playing hide and seek
- Stop (Países) – On a sheet of paper, players draw a few columns, each for a different theme (like names, countries, animals, colours, brands or objects). Then, one of the players recites the alphabet in his or her head and other player has to say "stop"! When the player says "stop," the one that was saying the alphabet stops and says the letter which he or she was thinking at that moment. After that, all players have to fill the columns with words starting with that letter, corresponding to the theme. Afterwards, all players reveal their answers. There is a score system for each column: 5 points when the answer is the same, 10 points when answers are different, 20 points when only one player answers.

Children's songs

- A saia da Carolina

- Atirei o pau ao gato
- Eu vi um sapo
- Machadinha
- Malhão, malhão

7 - *Legends/ stories or famous characters of the Imaginary / Folk tales*

Legend of Barcelos Rooster – Legend says that a man who was wrongfully accused of being a thief said that he was so innocent, and that if it were true the roasted rooster on the judge's table would sing at his hanging. When the man was about to be hanged, the roasted rooster did sing, thus proving the man's innocence and saving him from death. This is one of the most famous Portuguese legends and inspired one of the most emblematic Portuguese icons, the Barcelos rooster, which can be found in any souvenir shop and is a symbol of faith, tranquility, confidence and honour.

Legend of the Miracle of the Roses – This is a legend about kindness. According to the legend, King D. Dinis didn't like to see the Queen, Saint Elizabeth of Portugal, devoted to the poor and sick, spending all her time with the poor and he also though that charity was costly to the country, so forbid her from helping more people. One day, the King saw her leaving the palace and asked her what she had under her robe. She was going to hand out some bread, but, afraid of the King's reaction, she answered: "Roses, my Lord." But the King doubted that, because it was January. The King made the Queen open her robe and when she did, the bread had turned into roses, the most beautiful roses ever seen. Later, the Queen was canonised and became Saint Elizabeth of Portugal.

8 - *Products or goods that represent 'the national treasure'*

Azulejo (Portuguese Tiles) – "Azulejos" have played an important role in Portuguese architecture since the end of the 15th century. They can be used on both the inside and outside of buildings, for example covering façades of churches or private houses. There is a wide variety of shapes, colours and patterns.

Fado – The national song, UNESCO Intangible Cultural Heritage since November 2011. In a way, this mournful song depicts the Portuguese way of life, with a deep connection to the past. The biggest Fado singer, a reference for all, is Amália. After her death in 1999, a new generation of Fado singers emerged, like Marisa, Camané, Ana Moura or Carminho and Fado is gaining new listeners.

Pastéis de Belém – A pastry believed to have been created before the 18th century by Catholic monks in the Santa Maria de Belém, in Lisbon. Though it has been spread, it is believed that the original recipe is kept by only one pastry shop, located in Belém.

Vinhos do Porto e da Madeira (Port and Madeira Wines) – Port wine is produced exclusively in the Douro Valley in the north of Portugal.

Romania

FIRST NAME: AURELIA
FAMILY NAME: POPESCU
A.POPESCU@TRADONLINE.FR
&
FIRST NAME: FLAVIA
FAMILY NAME: IVAȘCU
FLAVIA.IVASCU@GMAIL.COM

Capital	Bucharest	Population	21,848,500
Government	Republic	Currency	Romanian lei (RON)
Religion(s)	Eastern Orthodox		
Language(s)	Romanian		

Flavia: I have been working as a translator for 8 years now, both in Romania and in Canada (English, French, Romanian, also some Spanish). I work both as a freelance and an internal translator for GS1 Canada. I received my BA in Translation in Romania back in 2004. I do interpretation (English, French, and Romanian) and some terminological work.

As for hobbies, I will list only one, because it encompasses so many others that I enjoy doing with him, namely my Rogue, a 4-year old Chocolate Labrador.

Aurelia: I'm 27 years old, I studied French, Spanish, Portuguese and English and I am a certified translator and interpreter. I'm a dynamic person, with good communication skills. I can easily adapt to different technologies and working environments. My choices tend to favour work in a multicultural environment because I'm passionate about exploring new cultures and it is important to keep practicing my three active languages.

1 - A typical conversation – what are the common/universal topics people go for? (weather, politics, etc.) - And some topics that you should avoid discussing with the locals?

Common subjects

Romanians are shy and quiet when you first meet them, and they admire modesty and humility in themselves and others. Weather is a major icebreaker (especially when you don't find any other). Romanian people also enjoy exchanging ideas about the latest local news and TV shows. We usually complain about corrupt politicians. Conversations may also include the well-being of the participants to the conversation, including their children. Many families have relatives working or living abroad so there is usually something interesting to bring up in a conversation.

To avoid in a formal conversation:

Once you develop a personal relationship Romanians will open up slightly. We do talk about everything: sex, politics, religion, death, etc., but we find it delicate to talk about our sexual education or about events that happen abroad. Reactions to these topics might not always be diverse and interesting, but we usually keep an open mind about everything.

2 - Events of great significance for the community, deeply stored in everyone's mind

The 1977 Vrancea Earthquake - The earthquake was felt in the whole Balcanic area. There were 1528 deaths (1424 of them in Bucharest), 11,300 injuries and 35,000 buildings collapsed or severely damaged. Zimnicea town was destroyed. The brilliant comedian and well known performer Toma Caragiu died during the earthquake.

The Romanian Revolution of 1989 overthrew the communist regime and its dictator Nicolae Ceaușescu. Under Ceaușescu's rule the people of Romania had experienced severe food rationing, power cuts and fuel shortages, the abolishment of contraception and abortion, state controlled censorship of the media, visitors and travel restricted. People still remember the "colectivizare," the expropriation of farms and land, and "Securitatea," Ceaușescu's secret police. Women will never forget the Romania's 1966 Anti-Abortion Decree or the term we use for children born in that period: the "decreței."

Romania became a Member State of the European Union on 1 January 2007.

3 - Nouns and Figures from the past / present that you use in colloquial expressions

- Vlad Țepeș - Prince Vlad, or as he was called even in his own time, Dracula (which means "Son of the Dragon") fought to keep the Muslim-faithed Ottoman Turks out of their country. He ruled his military kingdom of Wallachia — southern Romania — with a heavy and blood-soaked fist. Not only the Turks but also to many of his own countrymen he was Vlad The Impaler.

- Lișița/Azurul - CFR "Săgeata albastră" (The blue arrow): I travel a lot by train and I heard these funny words describing the latest Romanian train "Săgeata albastră" (The blue arrow). Lișița is a bird (lișița means "coot") and the speaker found some kind of resemblance between the modern shape of the train and the curve of the bird's body. The second word, Azurul, is more poetic, it means "blue" or "the blue sky."

- "Terchea Berchea" is used to refer to a person who doesn't have a prominent social status: *Cine-i tipul ăsta? Ai auzit de el? / Nu, e un terchea berchea...* ("Who is this guy? Do you know him?" / "No, never heard of him...he's a terchea berchea.")

4 - *Words used to designate a type of person, animal, things*

Nea Caisă: literally "apricot guy." We use this word to speak about a person that has no importance in our life, but who can give us a hand if needed. It also designates somebody that we don't know.

Robocop: ironically, we call someone a Robocop if he is hilarious as he attempts to show off his bravery or power. We use it in many contexts, for example when a boy is trying to impress a girl, when a lawyer wants to make an impression in his legal activity or when we want to create a stereotypical business man who exaggerates his actions so it remains clear to the audience who he is.

5 - Common phrases and fun expressions in your native language and their translation in English

A se uita ca mâța-n calendar (literally "to stare like a cat at a calendar.") To stare at something/someone and not understand anything)

A tăia frunza la câini (literally "to cut leaves for the dogs.") To loaf around

A-și pune pofta-n cui (literally "to hand one's appetite.") You can whistle for it

A-i pica cuiva cineva cu tronc. To fall for somebody, head-over-heels

Când mi-oi vedea ceafa (literally "when I will be able to see my nape of the neck.") When pigs fly

Socoteala de acasă nu se potrivește cu cea din târg. Don't count your chickens (before they are hatched)

Găina bătrână face ciorba bună – (literally "the old chicken makes the soup taste well.") There's many a good tune played on an old fiddle.

6 - Songs and games you remember from your childhood, that are generally passed on to the next generation

I used to play ȚOMAPAN (we would think of a letter and then each of us had to find names of a country, a river, of animal etc that began with that letter), Hide & seek, or *Flori, fete sau băieți, melodii sau cântăreți* (Flowers, girls, boys, songs or singers), *123 la perete stai* (1, 2, 3 to the wall – Stop when I turn back.) When we wanted to pick someone out of a team or to pick that first person to start the game we would sing:

Una mie sută lei
Ia te rog pe cine vrei
Din grămada cu purcei
A lui Moș Andrei!
Dacă n-ai pe cine
Ia-mă chiar pe mine

Game for several children

Podul de piatră s-a dărîmat.

A venit o apă și l-a luat.

Vom face altul pe ram in jos,

Altul mai trainic si mai frumos.

7 - Legends/ stories or famous characters of the Imaginary / Folk tales

My grandmother once told me that Saint Ilie is the patron of the clouds; he brings the rain, lightning and thunder, which are the weapons he uses to kill demons. Being a somewhat vindictive saint, he also sends the storms when he's angry with people for having forgotten his birthday.

There is this story about how Ilie always waits anxiously for his birthday, constantly asking God when it will be. The Lord always tells him: "It will come, Ilie. Just be patient a while longer and it will come." But this is just a trick that God plays on St. Ilie every year. After some days have gone by, God tells the saint that his birthday has already passed. Of course, Ilie gets very angry at having missed his birthday yet again. In his fury, he hurls violent hailstorms and thunder and lightning at the earth. These are referred to as the "storms after St. Ilie."

During the night between the 5th and the 6th of December Saint Nicholas comes. In the evening children love to place a pair of clean boots at the windows or doors. They used to write Saint Nicholas a letter in which they tell him how they behaved during the year. Saint Nicholas brings them presents: fruits, candies or toys; the next morning, the children will find them. According to tradition, children who don't behave well receive... a small twig! On the 6th of December we also celebrate those named Nicolae, or similarly.

8 - Products or goods that represent 'the national treasure'

Dacia – most Romanians drive a Dacia, it is the "national car." It started somewhere in the '60s, with the communist regime: at one moment Renault made a deal with Dacia (or the other way around) and we started to produce a car that was a copy of Renault 12. Later, we produced the long waited model, Dacia Logan, with air conditioning, "servo-direction," electrical windows both front and back, ABS system. I know that there are also new models too, Dacia Sandero, Duster and Lodgy.

Țuică/Pălincă (plum brandy). A generic name for a strong alcoholic drink; every flavour has a different name, for example we have "afinată" which is cranberry brandy.

Romanian wines are also very popular on the international market: *Tohani, Sauvignon Blanc, Muscat Ottonel, Tămâioasă Românească, Grasă de Cotnari, Riesling, Chardonnay, Fetească Albă.*

Many of our medieval castles have been restored almost to their prime, monasteries and churches too. A common misconception about Dracula's castle is that it is situated in Bran. Vlad's castle was actually the Poenari Castle (849 m high) – there are 1,480 steps leading to this castle.

The Danube Delta is the Europe's largest remaining natural wetland and the unique ecosystems are under legal protection including floodplains and marine areas. The core of the reserve (312,400 ha) was designated as a "World Natural Heritage Site" in 1991.

***

If you are interested in discovering the specific legends, myths of the Romanian community, from very concrete data to folklore, you should visit a small town or a village, where tourism means no ATM machines and no shopping centres. You could start by joining a medieval festival in Transylvania or participating at a wedding. Romania is home to a number of festivals, both religious and cultural, and May and June are the best months to visit, followed by September and early October.

Fun fact: before WWII, Bucharest (Romania's capital) was known as Little Paris, or Paris of the East.

Gheorghe Marinescu, a professor at the Bucharest Faculty of Medicine, was the first to see living nervous cells with a microscope.

Romanian researchers from "Victor Babeș" Institute have discovered a type of cell that could promote the regeneration of the heart muscle affected by heart attacks. They are called "Telocite Cells," and can be used effectively to treat heart attacks.

Spain

First name: Eva
Family name: Estrany
estrany@yahoo.com
&
First name: Nora
Family name: Berasategui
n.berasategui@tradonline.es

Capital	Madrid	Population	47,042,000
Government	Parliamentary monarchy	Currency	Euro (EUR)
Religion(s)	Roman Catholic and others		
Language(s)	Castilian Spanish (official), Catalan and others		

Nora: I was raised in Mallorca, an island I used to like until I became a teenager – then, it became quite boring for a girl wanting to know more about the world. Living in a small island can be a lot of fun, but for a young girl an island can also feel quite isolated. I always had to take a boat or plane to go anywhere. When I was little, whenever we traveled in mainland Spain by car, I would see the signs pointing to different cities, sometimes even 500 kilometres away, and I would get all confused. I used to think: "Is it possible that if I follow that road I can reach Madrid, without taking a plane or a boat?" That was amazing for me! Sometimes I even saw signs pointing to France, and it made me wonder if I could go from country to country on foot!

I have lived in many different cities and countries: Bilbao and Madrid in Spain, Bristol and London in the United Kingdom, Mexico, Nicaragua and Chile. I have now lived in or around Barcelona for 10 years and sometimes I wonder if it that is too many already! I still have 'wanderlust' and I look forward to a new future adventure. Maybe your country will be next!

Eva: I am a Spanish/Catalan translator and interpreter with over fifteen years' experience in the business. After graduating from the University of Barcelona, including one year at Cardiff University, I completed my studies with an MA in Cultural Politics and became a member of the Institute of Linguists.

Since then I have been involved in a range of interesting and exciting projects and events, meeting some fantastic people along the way. Examples of my work include The European Commission Future of Europe Conference, the European Language Boards Network Conference and the '99 Under 19 Rugby World Cup.

1 - A typical conversation – what are the common/universal topics people go for? (weather, politics, etc.) - And some topics that you should avoid discussing with the locals?

Spanish people vary a lot between regions. Some are extremely open and talkative and others are very secretive and closed. People in Mallorca usually make a strange guttural sound by way of greeting when they bump into each other in an elevator, while in other parts of Spain you just cannot leave the elevator for 15 minutes regardless of how much in a hurry you are, because your neighbour has all the latest news that you HAVE to learn about…

The topics covered by Spanish people when having a formal/cordial/casual conversation are like in any other country, weather, football between guys, or the unacceptable rise in the price of groceries. Football is certainly given a place of honour in the collective consciousness and a staggering 40% coverage on most TV news programmes. Lately, most conversations revolve around the economic crisis, politicians, corruption and banks.

Something which is quite differentiating from Northern European countries is the 'loudness' of the people. Many times I've been told by foreign friends that Spanish are loud and 'invasive' with each other's living space. I must say that I was quite shocked when getting on the public transportation of other European countries, people are quiet, almost as quiet as a Spanish hospital waiting room, and not only that, people avoid not only any sort of physical contact- it's even eye contact! I must agree with this generalisation of Spanish character, we are loud, talkative, touchy and a bit more spontaneous that most of our fellow Northern Europeans.

2 - *Events of great significance for the community, deeply stored in everyone's mind*

Spain had a 40 year dictatorship that ended in 1975. My parents' generation grew up under a dictatorship. My grandparents' generation suffered the Spanish civil war. Mine was the first generation of people who were born in a democracy. The huge changes that came with democracy and entering the European Union were of course welcomed by the vast majority of the population.

The 1992 Barcelona Olympics were responsible for transforming the city into the modern iconic landmark we know today. Not only did it trigger a crucial development of infrastructure, what is more important, it brought a whole nation together in celebration of sportsmanship, hard work and the drive to move forward.

Ten years after the end of a dictatorship and the inauguration of a new promising era of democracy in the history of Spain, the Catalan singer songwriter Lluís Llach, armed with lyrics full of passion and craving for freedom, became the first and only singer with a sold out gig at the magnificent Football Club Barcelona stadium. It was a memorable concert that still resonates in the minds of a whole generation who has learnt to look at the future with hope and determination.

3 - *Figures from the past / present that you use in colloquial expressions*

¡Viva la Pepa! It is a very common expression in Spanish which is used to refer to any situation of chaos or carelessness. The origin of the expression is very interesting. It has to do with the first Spanish constitution from 1812. King Fernando VII abolished it and banned any mention of it. Since the constitution was originally approved on May 19th, Saint Joseph's Day, supporters of the constitution began calling it "Pepa" (Pepe is a familiar version of Joseph in Spanish and Pepa is its feminine form). The expression ¡VIVA LA PEPA! (Hail the constitution!) was written on the walls of many cities as a way to express support for the constitution without using its proper name, which was banned.

4 - Words used to designate a type of person, animal, things

Juan Palomo. A famous andalusian 'guerrillero,' whose name nowadays is used in a popular rhyme which is used to refer to people who like to do everything themselves. "Eres como Juan Palomo, yo me lo guiso, yo me lo como" (You are like Juan Palomo, I cook my meal and I eat it myself).

Some common idioms make reference to historical or religious personalities. Some examples:

- *Ser alt com un Sant Pau* (to be as tall as Saint Paul): It is understood the idea of physical height comes from a more spiritual sense of the significance of Saint Paul's position within the Catholic Church.
- *La mare d'en Tano* (literally: for Tano's Mother's sake): an expression of shock, outrage, or indignation.
- *Semblar el cul d'en Jaumet* (literally: to be like Jaumet's behind): to be restless, always on the move.
- *Ser una Senyora Maria* (to be a Mrs Maria): considered the most popular female name, Maria is used to depict the common housewife, with a negative connotation of a gossiping nature.

5 - Common phrases and fun expressions in your native language and their translation in English

Déu-n'hi-do (impossible to translate, literally or not). This is by far one of the most common expressions in the Catalan language that one often wishes could be transferred onto any other language to convey its particular meaning, that of a sense of admiration, or indignation, or simply a statement of something exceeding our expectations, an idea of quantity, significance or achievement.

You can't translate it though; unfortunately you have to settle for a mere 'wow' or a more bland 'awesome.'

Se veía de una hora lejos (I could see it coming, literally "You could see it one hour away"). In Spanish we would simply say "se veía venir."

En boca cerrada no entran moscas (Flies don't enter a shut mouth). By abstaining from unnecessary talk one prevents many evils.

No por mucho madrugar amanece más temprano (Getting up very early won't make the sun rise any sooner). Your effort will only take you so far. Not everything is in our hands. Know when it's time to let go, relax and let things take their course!

En tierra de ciegos, el tuerto es rey (In the land of the blind, the one-eyed is king). Even a mediocre person can stand out if surrounded by lesser people.

6 - Songs and games you remember from your childhood, that are generally passed on to the next generation

There are 3 schoolyard games that seem impervious to the technological revolution:

Escondite (hide and seek) - I think the rules are the same in all countries... are they not?

Canicas (marbles) - This game goes in and out of fashion every few years. These small marbles are quite mesmerising to look at, and I for one remember looking at my personal collection much like Gollum looked at his ring! Children compete, argue and get dirty on the floor, doing what kids should do, in my opinion – have good fun, without screens!

Rayuela (hopscotch) - A classical game more seen in towns than in cities but that have a place in every person's memory. You only need to draw in chalk your playing squares on the ground and… jump!

Songs in Catalonia:

En Joan Petit Quan Balla (Literally, "When Little John dances…", a "heads, shoulders, knees and toes" kind of action song).

"El Gegant del Pi" ("The Pine Tree Giant," evocative of the traditional Giants that fill the streets on every major festivity).

Lots of tongue-twisters: "En Pinxo li va dir a en Panxo / vols que et punxi amb un punxó? / I en Panxo li va dir a en Pinxo / punxa'm però a la panxa no" (for practicing the /ʃ/ phoneme, eg. the 't' in the English word 'motion'; the 'x' in Catalan).

7 - Legends/ stories or famous characters of the Imaginary / Folk tales

My grandmother used to tell me stories about a mountain in the Basque Country called Amboto, located in a region famous for its witch activity. Legend says that witches performed Akelarres (Basque term for Sabatt, or ritual meetings of witches.) In the caves of the mountains, their leader was a supposedly fearful witch called Mari, who performed satanic rituals and orgies and was accused of engendering storms, ruining the peasants' harvest lands and killing the cattle of the surrounding villages. The legend says that one knows that Mari is at home when the peak of the mountain is covered by clouds.

"En Patufet" is one of the most endearing stories passed through generations. It is the story of a little kid the size of a chickpea dressed in the traditional Catalan outfit, including the L shaped red hat "barretina," who demands a bit more responsibility to prove he's worthy of his parents' trust. It contains a much loved popular song that children love to hear and sing, "Patim, patam, patum…"

8 - *Products or goods that represent 'the national treasure'*

Spanish people take pride in the country's gastronomic delights, its weather and its way of life. Spain's main exports are gastronomy-related, e.g. olive oil, Jamón serrano, Turrón de Jijona, wine, cava, fruits and vegetables. Fuet is a Catalan thin saussisson with a very distinct and unique flavour. Pa amb tomàquet - the more mundane and yet not-to-be-missed, quintessentially Catalan spreaded tomato and olive oil on bread: the best way to eat a toast and a good companion to tapas.

Spain has had its fair share of contributions to highbrow culture (flamenco, Picasso, Dalí, Velázquez, Gaudí, Calatrava, etc.). We also export many textiles. For example, Spanish-owned Inditex (Zara) is the largest high-street clothes manufacturing company in the world.

Sweden

FIRST NAME: EMMA
FAMILY NAME: HALLBERG
EMMAHVANDA@YAHOO.FR

Capital	Stockholm	Population	9,103,000
Government	Constitutional monarchy	Currency	Swedish kronor (SEK)
Religion(s)	Lutheran and other		
Language(s)	Swedish (official)		

I was born in a small town called Tillberga, near the city of Västerås, in Sweden, where I spent part of my childhood. Another part, from age 3 to age 8, then from age 15, was spent in France and the French-speaking part of Switzerland, where I learned to read and write in French before starting to write in Swedish. After studying chemistry and physics as well as a little biochemistry and biophysics in Sweden (Uppsala University, Masters level) and in France (Paul Sabatier University in Toulouse, first two years and fifth year (DEA) of university studies), I gradually decided to live permanently in Sweden, where I'm now well settled in the southernmost region.

My professional activity has been full-time translation since 2006-2007, when I realised my passion for languages was a lot healthier for me personally than handling chemicals in a laboratory, and started to test my wings as an interpreter (hospitals, schools, asylum seekers) in Sweden.

I recently upgraded my self-employment status to a 1-person LLC, whose activity mainly consists of translating documentation and software within the fields of medicine, science, software, teaching, legal, etc.

1 - A typical conversation – what are the common/universal topics people go for? (weather, politics, etc.) - And some topics that you should avoid discussing with the locals?

Swedish people are generally very open, and can talk about many different topics, however, it's well known in Swedish society that this happens only after a while. This phenomenon is sometimes called the "ketchup bottle effect": in society, Swedes tend to be rather shy and discuss mainly very neutral subjects, such as the weather, "and how is your family?" "did you watch that football game?" Therefore, a French person in Sweden may feel these people are terribly quiet and distant. However, after a while, the same French person may experience the opposite shock, and find them almost disturbingly familiar. This is when the ketchup comes out of the shaken bottle, all at once. At this point, people relax totally and act almost like brothers and sisters, which can be pleasant as long as it's not interpreted as a lack of respect.

Just like in many other countries, religion, politics, money, etc., are usually avoided.

2 - Events of great significance for the community, deeply stored in everyone's mind

Swedish history, at least lately, has not been as filled with contrast as the rest of Europe. Of course there were battles and disagreements, but no revolutions or wars affecting everybody equally.

Society is characterised by a term used in politics since the 1920s: *folkhemmet* (Swedish Welfare State), which is among the ideals that Swedes generally value the most. Initially, it implied that people with little means should receive newspapers and books at a reduced cost. Even today, there is a strong opinion that all should have equal rights to education, medical care, and good standard housing, and that this should be done partly using revenue from taxes.

The idea is so deeply rooted in society that all Swedish political parties consider this a matter of course, although to variable extents. As a result, the average Swede can be perceived as a little naive. Society is often there to help out when something happens.

In the 1970s, a decision was made that everybody should call each other by first name and/or second-person singular rather than using second-person plural. This is the case also between, for example, a managing director and employees. Only a few positions (king, queen, etc.) are exempted from this rule.

Sweden is a monarchy; however the king has only a representative role, no political power. The royal family is very popular, although there are sometimes discussions regarding the use of such a role in a modern society.

3 - Nouns and Figures from the past / present that you use in colloquial expressions

Among the real persons from the past that had an influence on people and society in Sweden, one should mention Carl von Linné (17th century), who studied plants and created a naming and classification system that is applied even today. The first person to ever cross the Atlantic in an airplane was Charles Lindbergh, who achieved this in 1927. He was American, but Swedes tend to consider him a Swede, as his grandfather was a wealthy farmer who lived in Smedstorp, near Simrishamn in Sweden. Everybody also knows the name of Alfred Nobel, the chemist who established a number of prizes to be awarded for significant achievements in a number of fields. This event is followed closely every year.

In the field of literature and theatre, there are a few names that are very well known throughout Sweden and even abroad: August Strindberg, Selma Lagerlöf and Wilhelm Moberg, among others, and there is a rather strong tradition of reading. More recently, we have Astrid Lindgren, a writer who focused mainly on books for children, and had an enormous impact. Her stories are widely loved by both children and adults. Her work also led to a number of films about Pippi Longstocking, the children in Bullerbyn, Ronja Rövardotter, etc. She recently passed away and holds a place in people's hearts.

Films made by Ingmar Bergman have had a great influence, and most Swedes can tell you where he spent the last years in his life, on the island of Gotland.

Raoul Wallenberg and Dag Hammarskjöld, who are highly respected in society, make most Swedes feel very proud. They give us a sense that this country always wants to protect human rights.

- Sweden -

There is a very well-known story with a linguistic touch that is told at history lessons:

When King Karl XIV Johan welcomed his French wife Désirée in Sweden, in the early 1800s, she travelled through the south of Sweden, called Skåne, where people speak a thick local accent. They had suffered from the long drought and called out "Vi vill ha regn!" (We want rain!) over and over again, which sounded like "Vive la reine!" (Hail the Queen!), and so the queen was happy. (There are a couple of versions of this story, one where the people were instructed to shout "We want rain" to welcome the queen, as they didn't speak any other language.)

4 - Words used to designate a type of person, animal, things

- "Ankdamm" (literally duck-pond): a closed group of people/small community where everybody knows everybody, with such a lot of conflicts and loyalties that rational decisions are no longer made and nothing ever changes.
- "Svensson" (a Swedish family name): a person who is completely average in society, or "normal" in every single aspect of society.
- "Spela Allan" (to play Alan): to consider oneself very tough, smart and superior; thought to derive from the character roles played by Alan Ladd in the past.

5 - Common phrases and fun expressions in your native language and their translation in English

"Få ändan ur vagnen" (to get one's behind out of the wagon): to finally get something done (e.g. finally write that letter that you've been thinking about for ages).

"Ha tummen mitt i handen" (to have the thumb in the middle of one's hand): to be terribly clumsy, specifically when it comes to practical things around home, the opposite of handy.

"Dum som tåget" (stupid like the train): describes someone really dumb.

"Få för gammal ost" (to have it for old cheese, usually "Now I'll let you have it for old cheese"): someone who is angry because of something the other person did to him or her may say this right before getting his or her revenge, by pouring a glass of water on him or her for example.

6 - Songs and games you remember from your childhood, that are generally passed on to the next generation

I'm convinced Swedish children spend more time playing outdoors than in many other countries. Sweden consists mostly of small cities, countryside, fields, a lot of forests and lakes. Nature and outdoor activities are highly valued by Swedes in general. This is reflected in legislation by a right called "allemansrätten" (the right of everybody), which gives everyone the right to spend time outdoors, pick berries, camp, make a fire, fish in the ocean, or swim in lakes when in the wild, under the condition that they respect their duty to protect nature and keep it clean. Children often also join clubs (scouts, sports, etc.) to learn about forests, sailing, how to make a fire in the wilderness, fishing, etc. This may also be due to the importance of leisure time in Swedish society. Leisure time is almost considered sacred.

As in many other countries, football, swimming and other sports are very popular, and because of the climate, most children and adults practice skiing and ice-skating. Classical games such as chess and cards continue to entertain all generations, and are often taught by a grandmother to a grandson.

Today, of course, electronic games have become very widespread, and this is considered a problem by some. An increasing number of nursery schools are teaching small children how to use an electronic reading pad as an educational tool.

7 - Legends/ stories or famous characters of the Imaginary / Folk tales

Stories told by the older generations live on, and often talk about imaginary creatures living in nature, e.g. fairies, elves. I believe a decreasing number of children actually believe in them though.

Many of these stories were told to teach children about dangers. One of them is about a man (called **"Näcken"**) who sat in the river and played the violin to draw people into the river where they would drown.

8 - Products or goods that represent 'the national treasure'

Sweden has a long history of engineering. For example, the production of cars such as Volvo and Saab has been of high value to the economy. The country also produces important volumes of wood and minerals, mainly in the northern regions. Highly skilled services play an increasing role in Swedish exports, which also comprises the film and music businesses, and many talented songwriters.

Ukraine

First name: Nataliya
Family name: Yena
contact@yena.de
www.yena.de

Capital	Kyiv (Kiev)	Population	44,854,000
Government	Republic	Currency	Ukrainian hryvnia (UAH)
Religion(s)	Ukrainian Orthodox		
Language(s)	Ukrainian (official), Russian		

"Nataliya Yena Simultaneous Interpretation" is the eponymous trade name I use as a sole trader. I am a conference interpreter and translator for the Ukrainian and Russian languages, paired with German and English. I've been in the business of translating and interpreting since 1991, and have been operating under my own trade name since 2011. I am based in Frankfurt am Main, Germany and Kyiv (Kiev), Ukraine. I have a pool of approximately 30 translators and 10 conference interpreters with whom I collaborate on a regular basis.

During my career, I've interpreted for presidents of Ukraine (Leonid Kuchma and Viktor Yushchenko), Ukrainian prime-ministers (Yuliya Tymoshenko and the acting PM Mykola

Azarov), as well as German chancellor Gerhard Schröder, other politicians, entrepreneurs, businessmen and public figures.

I graduated from the London School of Economics and Political Science (LSE) in 2001, working regularly since for international organisations such as the European Commission, European Parliament, Council of Europe, UNHCR, OSCE, OECD and multinational companies from Russia, Ukraine, Germany, United Kingdom, Italy, the US and Canada.

1 - A typical conversation – what are the common/universal topics people go for? (weather, politics, etc.) - And some topics that you should avoid discussing with the locals?

In a formal conversation in Ukraine, it is always correct to ask how things are, how life is; about your interlocutor's job and his or her ongoing projects. You should be prepared to hear "And what about you?" in return. Be ready to give an answer in the same way. It is simply a matter of politeness.

Topics to avoid:

- Politicians
- Religion
- The current government
- Government projects
- Elections

2 - Events of great significance for the community, deeply stored in everyone's mind

1917 – 1920 – Formation of the Ukrainian State (Ukrainian National Republic) in Central, Eastern and Southern Ukraine under President Mykhailo Hrushevskiy

1932-1933 - Holodomor in Ukraine, a famine induced deliberately by the central government of the USSR. Millions of Ukrainians died of starvation in a peacetime catastrophe unprecedented in the history of Ukraine.

1936-1938 – Onset of mass repressions and terror in Ukraine. Huge numbers of writers, painters, other artists as well as scientists, political activists and regular citizens vanished during those years.

April 26th, 1986 – The Chernobyl disaster, a catastrophic nuclear accident at the Chernobyl Nuclear Power Plant in Ukraine, which was under the direct jurisdiction of the central authorities of the Soviet Union. An explosion and fire released large quantities of radioactive contamination into the atmosphere, which spread over much of the Western USSR and Europe.

October 2-17th, 1990 – Revolution on Granite, hunger protest campaign of Ukrainian youth. A direct consequence of the protests was the resignation of the head of the Council of Ministers of the USSR, Vitaly Masol. A hunger strike played an important role in the development of Ukraine's independence.

August 24th, 1991 - Verkhovna Rada of Ukraine adopted the Act of Independence of Ukraine.

- Ukraine -

2000-2001 – "Ukraine without Kuchma" campaign of protests in Ukraine organised by political opposition with the ensuing resignation of the President of Ukraine Leonid Kuchma.

November-December 2004 – Orange Revolution, campaign of protests, pickets, strikes and other acts of civil disobedience in Ukraine, organised and conducted by the supporters of Viktor Yushchenko – one of the candidates in the presidential elections and subsequent President of Ukraine.

3 - *Nouns and Figures from the past / present that you use in colloquial expressions*

- **Pavlik Morozov** – means traitor, betrayer.
- **Yanuchary** – paraphrase of a historical term and an onomatopoetic misinterpretation of the name of the acting President of Ukraine Viktor Yanukovych; means low-level government officials, ignorant people. Actual historical term is "Yanychary," native Ukrainians who were abducted by Ottoman Turks as young children, or even born and raised in Turkey and who were particularly fierce warriors in Ottoman Turkish forces during military raids upon what was then Ukraine.
- **Kravchuchka** – a hand-pulled truck, a sort of a trolley; the term is derivative from the surname of the former President of Ukraine Leonid Kravchuk, when the kravchuchka has became popular as well as widespread.
- **Troya** – short name of the district of Kyiv "Troyeshchina," which has a bad reputation.

4 - *Words used to designate a type of person, animal, things*

- Pani – address for women, elder and young ladies
- Pane – address for men, mostly of elder age

- Kohanyy (kohana) / liubuy (liuba) – manner of referring to someone whom you love or like
- Dorohuy (doroha) – a different manner of referring to a person you like; can be used in an ironic way

5 - Common phrases and fun expressions in your native language and their translation in English

Пропав, як у воду впав (Went missing, as though fallen into the water) – Meaning: to get totally lost

Переплив море, а в калюжі втопився (Crossed the sea, but drowned in a puddle) – Meaning: failed due to something insignificant

Везе йому, як тому втопленику (As lucky as a drowned man) – Meaning: to have no luck

Всякий свого щастя коваль (Everybody is the blacksmith of his own happiness) – Meaning: everyone has a chance in life, whether we use it depends on us

Хто в світі не бував, той і дива не видав (If you have not travelled, you will not have witnessed wonders) – Meaning: the proverb stresses the importance of education, travelling and a broad mind

Совість гризе без зубів (Conscience gnaws without teeth) – Meaning: pangs of conscience (moral pain) are sometimes worse than physical pain

6 - Songs and games you remember from your childhood, that are generally passed on to the next generation

Songs:

Lullabies ("Kotyku sirenky" (Gray Kitty), "Oj spy dytja" (Sleep, My Baby), "Oj baju mij baju")

Songs from the cartoon "Petryk Pjatochkin"

Games:

Khovanky (Hide-and-seek)

Kvach (Weakling)

7 - Legends/ stories or famous characters of the Imaginary / Folk tales

"Ivasyk Telesyk" is the story of an old couple without children. Once the old lady told her husband to go to the forest and bring a wooden log to put into the cradle. The next morning, they saw a little boy, not a piece of wood in the cradle. Cerastes later kidnaps the boy Ivasyk, but he outwits and destroys Cerastes.

Other well-known fairytales:

- Koza-dereza
- Kotygoroshko
- Yajtse-rajtse
- Sirko
- Lesychka-sestrychka i vovk-panibrat
- Legends:
- Zmij i ruska tsarivna
- Legenda pro Dovbusha (Legend of Dovbush) – a story of a leader of the national liberation struggle in the Carpathians, a kind of Ukrainian Robin Hood, who fights the rich and spreads their property to the poor

8 - Products or goods that represent 'the national treasure'

Banosh: a dish in Western Ukraine which is made of corn, sour cream, cheese, and eggs

Kvas: traditional drink, the main ingredient of which is bread, and which has some alcohol content

Uzvar: traditional drink made of dry fruits, traditionally prepared at Christmas

Kutja: sweet grain pudding, prepared for the Christmas Eve, Malanka, Baptism of Jesus; a mix of honey, dry fruit, wheat and poppy seeds

Varenyky: square- or crescent-shaped dumplings of unleavened dough, stuffed with sauerkraut, cheese, mashed potato, cabbage, meat, hard-boiled eggs or a combination of these, or with a fruit filling

Deruny: potato pancakes, with onions and eggs

***

Ukraine is a country well worth a visit. In the West, there are the beautiful Carpathian Mountains, a region with a unique culture, traditions and cuisine. There are also the Crimean Mountains in the South, brimming with ancient caves and remnants of old dwellings – a superb location for hiking and biking.

United Kingdom

First name: Christina
Family name: Hewitt
UK.LINKEDIN.COM/IN/CHRISTINAHEWITT
CHRISTINAHEWITT@YMAIL.COM

Capital	London	Population	63,047,000
Government	Constitutional monarchy and Commonwealth realm	Currency	British pounds (GBP)
Religion(s)	Christian		
Language(s)	English		

I am a twenty-five year-old British Mexican, born in the US, raised in London. When asked where I am from, I say London- after all, I grew up there; although as I see a puzzled look forming slowly on the other person's face (I am dark, foreign-looking and generally more outwardly friendly and smiley that most British people), I reveal the whole story. I have lived in Italy and Spain as an English teacher and I am (slowly) making my way into the translating world. After a lifetime of negotiating between two cultures at home and on my travels, it only seemed natural to move into translation. The opportunity to learn about different subjects is not something that is available to most. The complexity of translation also attracted me. However easy it may seem, it is always a challenge and it always will be: there are not enough hours in the day or years in a lifetime to ever learn any language 100%.

1 - A typical conversation – what are the common/ universal topics people go for? (weather, politics, etc.) - And some topics that you should avoid discussing with the locals?

In order of appropriateness:

- Weather is the most important topic of conversation and provides the basis for polite small talk. In a country that is covered by grey cloud most of the year, it is understandable that we complain and/or endlessly hope for the sun to come out.
- Work
- Sport
- TV, films, music
- Politics. It is best to keep the conversation revolved around general complaints about the state of our society, the government or politicians. Most people fall asleep at the first mention of anything too serious.

It is best not to mention: the state of your finances, personal problems, or bodily functions!

Note: The Brits are not as right and proper as foreigners are often made to believe. It depends on the social class, age group and who you are in the company of, but generally among younger generations we are very frank about most things. At a dinner party, most do not have any qualms about discussing drinking habits, their (or their friend's, flat mate's, mortal enemy's, girl on the bus', etc.) sex life, farting, etc.

2 - Events of great significance for the community, deeply stored in everyone's mind

7 July 2005 terrorist bombings in London

1969 Monty Python was first aired on the BBC and had a huge influence on British comedy.

1964 the swinging 60s and the Beatles

1948 the creation of the National Health Service

1940-1941 the Blitz: a period of sustained bombing on the UK by the Germans during World War II

1916 the Battle of the Somme: one of the largest and bloodiest battles of World War I

1913 the suffragettes gained the right to vote for women

1859 The Origin of Species published by Charles Darwin

1807 abolition of the slave trade

1688 the Glorious Revolution. King James II was overthrown by Parliament and never since has a monarch held absolute power

1666 the Great Fire of London

1605 Guy Fawkes' gunpowder plot to blow up the Houses of Parliament

1066 the Battle of Hastings

3 - Nouns and Figures from the past / present that you use in colloquial expressions

Cockney is a type of East London slang based on rhyme and popular culture and often references famous places and people. It is constantly evolving and updating itself. Some examples:

Brahms and Lyst: pissed (drunk)

Hank Marvin (a famous guitarist): starving

Conan Doyle (an author): boil

Andy McNab (a novelist): cab

Duke of York: cork

Shakespeare has to be one of the most quoted people in the English language (except for the King James Bible perhaps). He is our most famous playwright and wrote plays such as Romeo and Juliet, a Midsummer's Night Dream and Macbeth. Some commonly used phrases from his works include: "it's all Greek to me" (I don't understand); "we have seen better days"; "in my mind's eye"; "Romeo, Romeo, wherefore art thou Romeo?" and "what's done is done."

4 - *Words used to designate a type of person, animal, things*

The English language is blessed with a wonderful adaptability. British people have a propensity for combining and adapting words to describe cultural phenomena. Here are just a few:

- Chav/Chavette: Stereotypically, the male 'chav' wears a Burberry-effect baseball cap placed at an angle and cheap rip-off sportswear; is covered in 'bling' (cheap and tacky jewellery); socialises outside McDonalds or other fast food outlets with a can of lager in one hand and a cigarette in the other; has a propensity to punch anyone who appears to be minding their own business; has a pregnant 14-year-old 'chavette' girlfriend with large, fake-gold hoop earrings and two-tone hair. Both are typically unemployed and uneducated, with little ability to read or write and mostly live on council estates.

- Pikey: Derived from the word 'turnpike' and originally a

- United Kingdom -

harmless slang term for a gypsy or traveller. It can also be used as a term of abuse to mean any person displaying behaviour or engaged in activities associated with gypsies.

- Toff: Posh or upper class people usually educated in a private school and from wealthy families.
- Wigga: A mixture of 'white' and 'nigga.' This word signifies a white person who pretends to be black.
- Bobby: policeman
- John: the toilet
- Quid: British pounds

5 - *Common phrases and fun expressions in your native language and their translation in English*

- All right? Informal, used instead of "Hi, how are you?"
- I can't be bothered: used when you are too tired, or don't feel like, doing something
- Big girl's blouse: a person who is pathetic or a wuss (scared of many things)
- Cheesed off: upset
- The dog's bollocks: amazing. A more polite version is 'the bees knees'
- To spend a penny: to go to the toilet
- Bob's your uncle: added to the end of phrases to mean, 'and that's it!' or 'voila!'
- A piece of cake: easy
- To take the piss: to make fun of
- To waffle: to talk on and on about nothing
- To know your onions: knowledgeable
- Dressed up to the nines: well-dressed

6 - Songs and games you remember from your childhood, that are generally passed on to the next generation

Ring a-round the roses, a pocket full of posies, atishoo, atishoo, we all fall down (supposedly about people dying in the plague).

Oranges and lemons, say the bells of St. Clements...

There once was a woman who swallowed a fly, oh my, she swallowed a fly...

Baa baa black sheep have you any wool, yes sir yes sir three bags full...

Jack and Jill went up the hill to fetch a pail of water, Jack fell down and broke his crown and Jill went tumbling after.

Intsy wintsy spider climbed up the water spout, down came the rain and washed the spider out...

Games

Conkers: horse chestnuts are tied to a string and knocked against each other until one breaks.

Marbles: marbles are rolled along the floor to hit each other.

Hop, skip and jump: throw a stone into the box and hop, skip and jump past the other boxes to collect it.

Hide and seek

7 - Legends/ stories or famous characters of the Imaginary / Folk tales

Stories:

- Peter Rabbit: a fictional character in Beatrix Potter's children's stories. He has many adventures with his other animal friends.

- Winnie the Pooh: Winnie is a bear who just loves honey and this gets him into all sorts of trouble

- The Wind in the Willows: Ratty and Mole enjoy the quiet life by the river boating and having picnics until they have to save their friend Toad from trouble.

- The Chronicles of Narnia: The series narrates the adventures of three children who enter the fictional realm of Narnia through a cupboard where there are magic, mythical beasts, and talking animals.

- Alice in Wonderland: A young girl falls down a rabbit hole and enters a whole new world of weird and wonderful characters.

- Harry Potter: we all know these stories!

- All stories by Roald Dahl such as Charlie and the Chocolate Factory, the BFG, the Twits and Matilda.

Legendary characters:

Jack the Ripper. An East London mass murderer that never got caught.

Guy Fawkes. He tried to blow up the Houses of Parliament with gunpowder, but his plot was foiled and now we burn an effigy of his body and let off fireworks on the 5th of November every year.

Loch Ness Monster (Nessie). A monstrous, snake-like creature that lives in Loch Ness Lake in Scotland

King Arthur, Merlin the Wizard and the Knights of the Round Table. Legend has it that from their base at Camelot they performed acts of chivalry and set out on the Quest for the Holy Grail. Arthur also obtained a magic sword by pulling it out of a stone.

Robin Hood. A heroic outlaw in English folklore. He lived around Sherwood Forest in Nottingham with his Merry

Men and is famed for taking money from the rich to give to the poor.

8 - Products or goods that represent 'the national treasure'

It is slightly paradoxical that most quintessentially 'British' things come from abroad. However, I'd say it is appropriately representative of the melting pot that is our culture:

Tea. Our forefathers travelled to the East and brought tea back to England. It now lays the foundation for any social occasion: when someone comes to your house to visit; when you sit down for a chat; when you have a problem; when you are happy, or at the end of a meal. English Breakfast taken with milk is the standard variety but most people stock other types of tea at home.

Curry. Originally from India, it arrived in the UK and underwent a metamorphosis. We now have many types of curry that would not be found in India, namely the Balti that was invented in Birmingham and the Tikka Masala that claims origin in Scotland.

Fish and chips. An English tradition. The fish is battered and deep fried and served with chunky potato chips and reconstituted peas that go mushy when cooked.

The London Underground. Here we call it the 'tube' and it is the oldest underground railway system in the world.

Scottish tartan. A woollen, checkered fabric worn as part of Scottish traditional clothing.

***

Many particularities of British culture are well-documented, such as the weather, overuse of the words "please," "thank you," "sorry," and our love of queuing. Others are not so well-known but equally as important:

A) Sarcasm is an important part of British culture often misunderstood by foreigners. Generally, the rule is that it is humorous to say something derisive about something, someone or a situation with ambivalence (the other person does not know if you are being serious or not); or to say something ironically e.g. you just crashed your car and your friend says, "well done, mate."

B) Taking the piss out of oneself. This is a defining characteristic of Britishness. One must also be self-deprecating. Unlike in America, the English do not take kindly to a person who outwardly praises themselves.

C) Happy tolerance of physical discomfort. Camping. Music festivals. Beach holidays. Wearing very little clothing on a night out. We don't have the climate for any of these things, but we insist on doing them anyway.

D) Anything you do while drunk (or if it is to raise money for charity) is acceptable.

ASIA/PACIFIC

- China
- Indonesia
- Japan
- Lebanon
- Malaysia
- Pakistan
- South Korea
- Thailand
- Vietnam
- Yemen
- Russia
- Turkey

and **New Zealand**

China

FIRST NAME: ALBERT
FAMILY NAME: DENG
ALBERTDENG@HOTMAIL.COM
&
FIRST NAME: CÉLIA
FAMILY NAME: SHEN
SHEN.CELIA@YAHOO.FR

Capital	Beijing	Population	1,343,239,000
Government	Communist State	Currency	Renminbi yuan (RMB)
Religion(s)	Daoist (Taoist), Buddhist, Christian		
Language(s)	Standard Chinese, Mandarin		

Albert: I was born in Shenyang, in the Northeast of China. I obtained my Bachelor of Arts in English and Master of Arts in British and American Literature from Jilin University in Changchun, in the Northeast of China. After working for three years in the southern city of Guangzhou, I migrated to New Zealand. I have been working professionally as a translator-interpreter in Auckland, New Zealand since 2003.

I now work regularly with New Zealand government agencies such as the courts, police, Immigration and Protection Tribunal, Customs, Employment Relations Authority and Auckland City Council. I also work for private businesses and individuals. Occasionally I do some cultural consultancy work mainly for business people in New Zealand who want to overcome cultural barriers while working in a Chinese environment.

Célia: After graduating from China University of Political Sciences and Law (Beijing) in 2004, I came to France in 2005 to study administrative law at the University of Metz. In 2008, I graduated with a Master's degree in financial and legal translation at the Sorbonne Nouvelle University (Paris). Currently, I work for translation agencies, law firms and newspapers.

1 - *A typical conversation – what are the common/ universal topics people go for? (weather, politics, etc.) - And some topics that you should avoid discussing with the locals?*

In China, the topics that people like to talk about vary according to age and origin. Generally speaking, hometown, tourism, cuisine, movies, TV series and entertainment programmes are topics that Chinese people like to talk about. Competitive sports, widely covered in state media, are closely followed and discussed by large numbers of people. Sports that China is good at in international competitions draw the most attention.

Relatively speaking, the older generation likes to talk about their grandchildren, because in China it is very common for grandparents to take care of their grandchildren. Middle-aged people like to talk about their children, or how to become richer.

Young people like more fashionable topics, such as tourism, entrepreneurship, luxury or the hardship of life.

As for the topics to avoid, like in many countries, these include a woman's age, a person's wage or a family's property which are sensitive topics. In addition, asking a 30 year-old single woman why she is not married is very annoying and embarrassing. In Chinese cities, women generally work. So, unless the husband is particularly rich, being a housewife is not a thing to show off. So never ask a housewife why she does not get a job or if she is bored at home.

Religious topics are officially confined to within government-approved religious institutions. The subject of death is not appreciated, especially when people or their relatives happen to be sick or when people do types of work prone to accidents and fatalities.

2 - Events of great significance for the community, deeply stored in everyone's mind

In the 6th and 5th centuries BC, a great scholar, thinker and philosopher, Confucius, preached his principles of how an ideal society should operate. In his lifetime, he taught students and traveled the various feudal kingdoms of China to spread his messages, which emphasised universal love, loyalty, hard work, frugality, education, devotion and sacrifice and priority of group over individual, responsibility over rights, and long-term over short-term gains. The fruits of his decades of teachings, compiled into a set of classic literature still revered in many Asian countries today, would shape the whole culture of Eastern and Southeastern Asia.

In 2008, a shocking earthquake occurred in China and affected most of the provinces of southwest China such as Sichuang, Guizhou, Chongqing and Yunnan. In the earthquake, more than 80,000 people lost their lives and countless others were injured. Chinese people were deeply touched by the courage of residents in the earthquake zone in face of the disaster. There is a very sad and moving story: A mother, when rescuers found her in the ruins, had unfortunately died. But rescuers were surprised to find that under the mother's body, there was a sleeping baby. In the last minute of her life, this mother created a safe space for her child with her arms, upper body and knees. Rescuers found a cell phone in the deceased's possessions. There was a written message: "Dear baby, if you can survive, do remember that I love you."

3 - Nouns and Figures from the past / present that you use in colloquial expressions

Not many people born outside China know who Lei Feng was and what "learn from Lei Feng" means, but for the Mainland Chinese, Lei Feng is as familiar as "gutter oil" (poisonous cooking oil extracted from leftovers of the restaurant kitchens). According to the official propaganda, Lei Feng was a model young soldier in the late 1950s and early 1960s. He is said to be loyal to the Communist Party and Chairman Mao, work hard, lead a plain lifestyle and go all out to do good deeds for the people. Though Chinese society has undergone tremendous changes since Lei Feng's days, the personality has entered Mainland Chinese vocabulary. If someone is said to be a "living Lei Feng," he or she is selfless, compassionate, helpful and philanthropic. To "learn from Lei Feng" simply means to be a good Samaritan.

4 - *Words used to designate a type of person, animal, things*

"Sheng Nan" and "Sheng Nu" are words that have appeared in recent years. They are words for single women and men who are supposed to be getting married. Sheng Na - Chinese: 剩男, literal: man who is left; Sheng Nu – Chinese: 剩女, literal: woman who is left. Generally speaking, if a person is 30 years old and not married, he or she will be considered as Sheng Nan or Sheng Nu. In Chinese cities, life is very stressful; people work hard to afford the high cost of life so they have no time for love. However, many young people refuse to be called Sheng Na or Sheng Nu, because they feel that although they are single, although they are "left," they are still happy. It is their choice.

5 - *Common phrases and fun expressions in your native language and their translation in English*

There is a unique way of informal greeting in Mainland China today which means: "Have you had your meal?" This is used especially during meal time, when the speaker supposedly does not know whether the other person has had his or her meal. While the other party will provide a direct answer as to whether he or she has had a meal, the speaker is not particularly interested in the answer as much as just extending a greeting. This phrase came into more frequent use in the 1980s but was to some extent discouraged by the political establishment early this century. However, there is evidence that it is still in use today.

6 - *Songs and games you remember from your childhood, that are generally passed on to the next generation*

Over the years, childhood games and songs have undergone a lot of changes. Due to the boom of the residential building industry children have less outdoor group activities and are more confined indoors. Group games have given way to modern electronic games that can be played by a single person. Group games among children that have not died out include card games and Hide and Seek. Sports matches such as football and badminton are also quite popular. As the Chinese government limits the number of children born to each couple to only one (with some variations) and people are living in housing complexes with more privacy for individual households, it is harder for the children (in the cities in particular) to find playmates nowadays.

Little mouse on the lampstand (小老鼠上灯台) is a popular Chinese children's song. The lyrics are very simple and interesting, suitable for a baby just beginning to learn to sing. This song is familiar to children especially in the north of China, and almost every child can sing it:

> 小老鼠上灯台,
>
> 偷吃油下不来,
>
> 喵呜喵呜猫来了,
>
> 叽里咕噜滚下来。

Little mouse, on the lampstand,

He steals oil and cannot get down.

A cat purrs and comes,

Oops, little mouse rolls down.

7 - Legends/ stories or famous characters of the Imaginary / Folk tales

The remote years up until the 5th century BC[1] were a period of numerous legends. While some of those legends are too mythical to be true, some seem to have more credibility. Those years were said to be a period of innocent and unsophisticated people and selfless and judicious leaders. Yu the Great might be the last such leader. In his days, there were big floods causing tremendous miseries to the people. His predecessor did not succeed in controlling the floods, because he tried to achieve it by simply building higher dykes. When Yu assumed his position, he worked tirelessly outside home with the people, day and night to conquer the natural disasters. He was famous for being so preoccupied with his work that he passed by his own home three times without entering it, including once when his baby was born and he actually heard the cry of the baby. He was also famous for employing a strategy of dredging and diversion, rather than embankment as his successor had done. By digging many irrigation canals, the strength of the flood was reduced, until no major destruction was caused by the floods.

Zhou Bapi is a famous character from writer Gao Yubao's fiction **Ban Ye Ji Jiao** (半夜鸡叫: the cock crows at midnight). Zhou Bapi is a bad boss, a symbolic bad landlord. In ancient days, there were no clocks. People got up when the cock crowed and slept at sunset. So according to their contract, farmhands had to get up and go to

---

[1] China has a recorded history of nearly 4,000 years, but archeologists have traced the beginnings of human civilization in China to a much earlier time.

work when the first cock crowed. To make his farmhands work more, he got up at midnight and made the cock crow to wake them up.

Now, Zhou Bapi is a word for a tight-fisted and demanding employer. When we say that someone is a Zhou Bapi now (现代周扒皮), it means he is very mean.

8 - Products or goods that represent 'the national treasure'

Mao Tai is produced in the town of Maotai, a city of Ruairen in Guizhou Province. It is considered to be China's best liquor: the "National Spirit." It is made from sorghum and wheat. The particular climate and vegetation conditions in its place of origin give Maotai a unique taste and a mild, mellow soy sauce-like fragrance. Its alcohol content is about 54% to 55%. Maotai become a luxury brand and the most expensive Chinese alcohol.

The Chinese government sees a protected animal, **the panda**, as a national treasure. The panda has in some way obtained a national animal status. Many important sports events held in China like the Asian Games and Olympic Games have it as the mascot. The Chinese government also gifts pandas to other countries and areas as goodwill. With decades of efforts in protecting the animal, it has been saved from the brink of extinction. In the 1980s, a farmer was executed for killing a panda and selling its skin.

Here are some things to keep in mind when dealing with Chinese people.

- It is offensive to give someone a clock as a gift, because "to give a clock" sounds the same as a phrase that means sending someone to death.

- Eight is considered the luckiest number, while 4 is considered an unlucky number. 666, instead of being associated with Satanism as in the West, is also a lucky number series in China.
- "Going Dutch" (sharing dining and shopping bills) is usually not a welcome practice. Some see it as selfish and alienating. Instead, people take turns in paying whole bills on different occasions.

Indonesia

FIRST NAME: IKHSAN FERI
FAMILY NAME: SAPUTRO
LINKEDIN.COM/PUB/IKHSAN-FERI-SAPUTRO
&
FIRST NAME: RATNA
FAMILY NAME: WIDJAJANTI WUSONO
HTTP://WWW.PROZ.COM/TRANSLATOR/1234417

Capital	Jakarta	Population	248,645,000
Government	Republic	Currency	Indonesian rupiah (IDR)
Religion(s)	Muslim		
Language(s)	Bahasa Indonesia (official, modified form of Malay), English, Dutch, local dialects		

Ikhsan: I was born in 1984 in the capital city of Indonesia, Jakarta. I studied English Literature at Gadjah Mada University and graduated in 2008. During the time I was a student, I held several part-time occupations, one of them as a freelance interpreter & translator for a local NGO. After I graduated, I was hired as an interpreter for a consultant management company, CCI. I thus got the chance to visit several of their 33 production plants as interpreter. This experience was wonderful: I met people from various levels in company, while also improving my translation skills, and travelling around Indonesia. In August 2011, I was offered the position of Indonesian translator at booking.com in Singapore, and now I've moved on to working for SDL.

Ratna: I am a professional translator and interpreter (Indonesian – Spanish – English) with a Degree in Translation/Interpretation and 20 years of experience in this area. I was born in Indonesia but grew up, studied and worked in several countries for many years. Client satisfaction is the most important thing for me.

1 - A typical conversation – what are the common/universal topics people go for? (weather, politics, etc.) - And some topics that you should avoid discussing with the locals?

Common conversation topics

Latest news: Indonesia is a huge country consisting of a diversity of cultures and ethnic groups. Thus, lots of news fills the media every day.

Football: Although the achievement of Indonesian Football Team has never been popular outside South East Asia, the fanaticism surrounding football is undoubtedly frantic.

Food: Indonesians are proud of their food. You will find that the western part of Indonesia produces hot and spicy food, generously flavoured. In the central part like Java, the food is sweeter. In the eastern part like Sulawesi or Papua, you can find extremely exotic food ranging from barbecued bats to sago palm worms.

Music: Since MTV and the gadget market boomed, Indonesian popular music is heavily influenced by Western music such as Rock, Indie, Alternative.

Topics to avoid

Religion: Since Indonesia has a history of religious conflicts, it's highly advised to avoid this sensitive issue.

Financial condition: Some people will be extremely open about their financial condition in Indonesia. They will be considered as not polite and arrogant. Also, don't brag about your wealth because it may lead you to be prey for criminals.

Sex: Indonesia is not liberal yet. There are also many fundamentalists and conservative people. Try to avoid this issue.

2 - *Events of great significance for the community, deeply stored in everyone's mind*

1928: Sumpah Pemuda (Youth Pledge). After hundreds of years being oppressed by colonialists, this second youth congress declared a unity pledge and put this congress as a milestone in the people of Indonesia's struggle to gain independence.

1945: Proklamasi Kemerdekaan Indonesia (Proclamation of Indonesian Independence). Soekarno, the first president of Indonesia, declared the independence of Indonesia in Jakarta.

1945: Battle of Surabaya. The battle is the greatest single battle after the declaration of independence. It was marked as an act of resistance towards the return of colonialists.

1965 – 1966: Mass Murder of Indonesian Communist Party Members. Around one million people were murdered in an attempt of political cleansing. It happened mainly in Central Java, East Java, Bali, and North Sumatra.

1966 – 1998: The New Order. Also known as the Era of Soeharto, second president of Indonesia, it was the era when the economy grew fast while corruption developed sharply.

1998: Reformation Era. The economic crisis hit Indonesia hard. Student demonstrations occurred mostly in big cities, demanding changes in politics. In May, demonstrations broke into riots in several locations.

Triggered by the deaths of several student demonstrators, the riots culminated with mass violence in major cities. Thousands of people were killed and a massive exodus of Chinese Indonesians was reported after hundreds of rape cases.

3 - Figures from the past / present

Munir Said Thalib is famously known by his first name, Munir. He was known as a determined human rights activist in Indonesia. He was assassinated during his flight to the Netherlands, poisoned. After a series of human rights violations in Indonesia, Munir became a prominent activist. He received threats from people who felt uneasy about him and was finally assassinated at the time when democracy and optimism started to rise in Indonesia. Since 2005, the day of Munir's death has been the Human Rights Defender Day.

4 - Words used to designate a type of person, animal, things

- Tuan – this word is used to refer to a respectable man, master, employer, or an owner (e.g. tuan tanah means landlord). From this word emerges the word Tuhan, which means god, that is used in the Bible translation. Before it became Tuhan, the bible used tuan, which created controversy because the word tuan only describes human characteristics instead of divine elements.

- Anda – The word Anda is a second person pronoun, or "you." Although it is the common translation for the English word "you," Anda (using a capital "A") has a respectable tone. The word was coined in the early period of post-independence. It was "invented" after a demand for a second person pronoun that was sufficient to address the second person in a respected way. At that time, several words were used as a second person pronoun but none of these was considered adequate to cover the intention of respect:

- Bung, it was used only for the matter of egalitarian status among soldiers.

- Tuan, respectable and already used in the military sphere but rejected since it reminded people of colonialism.

- Bapak, literally means father. Today, this word can be used not only for the biological father but also for a respected older man or leader, something that was considered weird in the early period after independence.

5 - Common phrases and fun expressions in your native language and their translation in English

Anak bawang (Onion child) – An underestimated person in a group or a competition.

Cinta monyet (Monkey love) – love or crush among teenagers, first love, love that changes easily.

Menghitamkan negeri (To blacken the country) – leave the country forever due to conflict with family.

Kalah jadi abu, menang jadi arang (Loose and be ash, win and be charcoal) – Describing a situation which has no benefit at all.

Bagai telur di ujung tanduk (Egg at the edge of a horn) – Someone in a very dire situation, dangerous.

6 - Songs and games you remember from your childhood, that are generally passed on to the next generation

- *Congklak/Congkak* – A game of the mancala family. This mental calculation game is considered as a game for girls.
- *Panjat pinang* – A race climbing a palm tree covered with oil to get the presents hanging on the top of the tree log. During the colonial era, this game was an entertainment for the Dutch. They put valuable gifts on the top of a tree log covered in oil and let the natives race to get the gifts. Due to its history, there are some pros and cons regarding this game.
- *Mobil-mobilan dari kulit jeruk bali* – A very rural toy for boys. It is a car toy made of pomelo skin and sticks from coconut leaves.
- *Galasin/ galah asin* – Group game of team working, played in a field as big as a badminton court. In this game, each group must employ strategies to defend their area and yet conquer the other group's area by running across the borders.
- *Lodong* – A game that is heavily influenced by a cannon used in a battle, lodong is made of bamboo with no bullets. It is usually played to celebrate school break, religious festivals, or during a communal party.

7 - Legends/ stories or famous characters of the Imaginary / Folk tales

Sangkuriang is the main character in the legend of Bandung Lake and Mount Tangkuban Parahu creation. The story involves the marriage between human and god/goddess, a common myth among Indonesian stories.

Genderuwa is a ghost story told by parents from generation to generation, describing a ghost with a huge and hairy body. Genderuwa will kidnap children who are still playing outdoors at dusk. In Indonesia, which is heavily influenced by Islam teaching, dusk is a time when Muslims should pray.

8 - *Products or goods that represent 'the national treasure'*

Angklung. A traditional musical instrument made of bamboo. The name itself is onomatopoeic. Angklung is played by shaking it, creating a unique hollow sound. It is usually played in a group as one player can only produce one note.

Jamu. Undoubtedly one of many national treasures that Indonesia has. Basically, jamu is an herbal drink which consists of different kinds of roots, seeds, fruits, barks and leaves such as ginger, key lime, turmeric, tamarind, galangal, cinnamon, cardamom. It's proved to be healthy- an ancient remedy for several types of discomforts and pains. Jamu is a traditional heritage from the Javanese Kingdom back in the 8th century. At the beginning it was kept as a secret among the aristocrats and the recipe was passed from one generation to another, whereas now it has spread to all levels of society.

Japan

FIRST NAME: YUZO
FAMILY NAME: KAMEI
SPEAKINGLANGUAGESJP-9199@YAHOO.CO.JP
HTTPS://WWW.LINKEDIN.COM/PUB/YUZO-KAMEI/3A/177/908

Capital	Tokyo	Population	127,369,000
Government	Parliamentary government with a constitutional monarchy	Currency	Japanese yen (JPY)
Religion(s)	Shintoism, Buddhism, Christianity		
Language(s)	Japanese		

I was born in Yokohama, a port town with a population of three million and situated 30 km south of Tokyo, in 1969.

After graduating from a public high school, I began my studies at the University of Tokyo in 1987. My special field was Germanic studies (Germanistics). My hobbies were listening to classical music, studying foreign languages, and reading about astronomy including such topics as the Big Bang, galaxies and stars, dark matter, quarks and particles.

The 1980s was a period when Japan reached the peak of its flourish as one of G7 economic powers. As a citizen of one of world's leading countries, I was dreaming about the future of the country during my teens, imagining what magnificent future will await me. That sense stimulated me to apply myself by learning foreign languages at college: English, German, French, Italian, Latin, Greek, Chinese, Korean, and others.

After acquiring a B.A. in 1991, with a thesis on Mozart (in German) and an M.A. in 1993, with a thesis on the social music history of Vienna (in Japanese), I completed my doctorate study in 2001 (but not yet a D.A. holder). The topic of the doctoral thesis (to be completed soon) is the historical conditions of the formation of the world music capital Vienna. I studied at the University of Vienna from 1996-2001, receiving a scholarship from Austria, Spain and the Czech Republic (with German, Spanish and Czech research plans). One-month language courses I attended in Europe included Italian, German, Spanish, Czech, Hungarian, Bulgarian and French. Besides taking private lessons in Greek and Slovak, I have studied almost all the European languages.

After returning home from Vienna in 2001, I took a long break, as I felt exhausted at having done so much. Recently, I've been feeling an itch to go back to Europe and travel the whole world.

Please see my Linkedin profile and my Geocities page too[1], you can find my detailed CV, and more on Japan.

1 - A typical conversation – what are the common/universal topics people go for? (weather, politics, etc.) - And some topics that you should avoid discussing with the locals?

---

[1] http://www.geocities.jp/catspeaklanguages/000japanese.html#profile

Common Topics

Weather: in combination with daily greetings, one prefers saying, "Every day, it is really cold/hot/warm/cool, isn't it?" in high winter/summer/spring/autumn, "It has become colder/hotter/warmer/cooler, hasn't it?" at the beginning of winter/summer/spring/autumn and "It's been raining a lot, hasn't it?" in the rain season in June/July. Talking about today's and yesterday's weather and about next days' forecast is common, too.

Sports: Baseball is the most popular sport. However, recently, football (soccer) has become more popular particularly among younger people. Sumo, a traditional fighting sport, is popular among middle-aged and older people. The professional football league has a history of less than two decades (J-League since 1993), so older generations are not so enthusiastic. If you can talk about baseball as a foreigner in Japan, you will be warmly welcomed by people.

"Football" means American football in Japan, so please use "soccer" to talk about European football.

Economics and financial issues: these are popular themes between people. Greetings are sometimes followed by a conversation like "How have your economic conditions been recently? - not good, but not too bad" "Are you earning well lately? - Well, so-so." Such a conversation can function as a lubricant in personal relations.

Topics to avoid

Politics/Religion: People tend to avoid discussing politics, as it is too complicated and can easily lead to misunderstandings.

Sex: As people are generally conservative, this theme should be avoided.

2 - Events of great significance for the community, deeply stored in everyone's mind

794 Opening of the ancient capital Heiankyou (meaning "capital of peace and order") in today's Kyoto, 480 km west of Tokyo. The family of Tenno, Japan's emperor, lived here since 794 until 1868, when it moved to Tokyo.

1192 Start of the samurai government. MINAMOTONO Yoritomo (1147-99), the leader of the most powerful samurai family of that period, was named Shogun and opened his government in Kamakura.

1853/54 Visit of US Navy ships in 1853 to conclude a trade treaty between samurai-reigned Japan and USA. The treaty was concluded in the following year. Japan "opened" its door to occidental countries. The advent of the powerful US Navy ships fatally accelerated the tempo of the country, culminating with the end of samurais' feudal reign (1867).

1867/68 End of samurai government (feudal period) and start of Meiji period (1868-1911). This is the beginning of the modern era in Japan. Rapid westernisation and industrialisation of its state and society were promoted under a powerful leadership of the Meiji government.

1941.12.8 (12.7 in Hawaii time) Japan's attack on Pearl Harbor in Hawaii, USA.

- Japan -

1945.8.6/8.9 Explosion of the atomic bombs, the first and, at the same time, the last ones used ever in human history, in Hiroshima/Nagasaki, killing hundreds of thousands of citizens.

1945.8.15/9.2 End of World War II. Japan accepted its unconditional surrender to the Allied.

3 - *Nouns and Figures from the past / present that you use in colloquial expressions*

Sekigahara: In 1600, a crucial battle was fought in Sekigahara. Today, we speak of "Tenka wakemeno Sekigahara" (the decisive and fateful battle of Sekigahara) when one must go into a crucial battle (or make a life-changing decision) in various social, economic and political fields in our daily life.

Kurofune: The US battleships, made from iron and running with vaporised machinery, that visited Japan in 1853/54, brought an enormous surprise to the people. Today, we speak of "kurofune" when foreign companies "invade" the inland economic market by achieving a surprising success. iPhone was, for example, a "kurofune for the Japanese, as it destroyed the former customs of the inland mobile phone market.

Iza kamakura ("Let's depart to Kamakura now"): The obligation of lower class servant samurais was to rush to Kamakura to support the government and to fight for it when it met territorial threats or other kinds of political difficulties. Today, it is used when important difficult issues arise in various fields of our life that require the concentrated cooperation of many persons.

4 - Words used to designate a type of person, animal, things

- Gohan/meshi: It is used to talk about breakfast, lunch and dinner. It literally means "rice," a Japanese staple food, but we use it not only for rice, but for every kind of food served as a meal.

- Oyaji: A vulgar way of talking of "father." It is widely also used for elder men. "Oyaji gyaru" is a word combination that expresses a young woman or a teen girl who behaves and thinks like an elder man.

- Ojisan: It literally means "uncle," but it is widely used for elderly men and for those younger men who behave in an old-fashioned way.

- Jijii: This is a variety of "ojisan," but it sounds pejorative and offensive. It is used as a curse word directed to unmoral or annoying men (no matter the age).

- Kusojijii: A word that sounds more pejorative than "jijii." Kuso means "shit."

- Obasan: It literally means "aunt," but it is widely used for "elder women" or those who behave like older women. It is the female equivalent of ojisan.

- Kusobabaa: A word that sounds more pejorative than "babaa." It is the female equivalent of kusojijii.

5 - Common phrases and fun expressions in your native language and their translation in English

- Itadakimasu: A word used when starting eating breakfast, lunch and dinner. It literally means "[I am about] to receive [your food] reverentially."

- Gochisousama: A word used when finishing breakfast, lunch and dinner. It literally means "[It was] a great dish [for me]."

- Tadaima: A word used when coming back from outside

and entering home, saying it at the entrance. It literally means "[I've come back] just now."

- **Okaeri:** A word said from inside home by a family member when someone comes back from outside, saying "tadaima" at the entrance. The one inside responds then "okaeri." It literally means "You've (safely) come back."

- **Otsukaresama:** A word directed to someone who has put a lot of work into something. It literally means "You've done tiring work," or "You've got tired!" as "tsukare" means "being tired."

- **Sumimasen/suimasen:** it is a word of apology meaning "sorry" or "pardon me." But it is not only used for apology, but widely also in the meaning of "Thank you." The spirit underlying it is that a thanking one feels "sorry for having spared no efforts and been willing to do such a gratifying thing for such a less worthy person like me."

6 - Songs and games you remember from your childhood, that are generally passed on to the next generation

Jinsei game ("game of life"): a board game played by 4 to 5 persons. One goes through the steps according to the numbers given by the roulette. The purpose is to reach the goal of life first.

Pacman: an originally Japanese, nowadays worldwide popular display game of an eating yellow globe that continually eats cookies, fruits and monsters. I liked it, and played it well at shops during my childhood.

Momotarou: the cute theme song of the story and the hero boy "Momotarou," explained in Topic 7. It is, together with the songs named below, famous nationwide, and loved particularly by small children.

Urashimatarou: the theme song of the story and its protagonist "Urashimatarou," explained in Topic 7.

Usagi to kame ("rabbit and tortoise"): the theme song of the story "Usagi to kame (rabbit and tortoise)," explained in Topic 7.

Inu no omawarisan ("a policeman dog, a police-dog"): a song of a police-dog and a wandering kitten that can only meow and weep, cannot explain herself, give neither name nor address, which makes him endearingly embarrassed.

Yuki ("snow"): a song of appreciating and enjoying the falling snow, a dog running joyfully in the garden and a cat preferring the warmth of the inside home and sleeping underneath a heating table (called kotatsu).

Mori no kumasan ("a bear in a forest"): a song of a heartwarming encounter of a girl with a gentle-hearted bear in a forest.

Kaeru no uta ("a song of frogs"): a song of the croaking voices of a party of frogs.

Nanatsu no ko ("seven crow children"): a song of crows. It is a romantic and melancholic excellent song, singing: "Why do crows cry? Because they have seven cute children in the mountain," but a comical version was broadcast several decades ago, saying: "Why do you cry, Crows? - It's none of your business. We cry of our own free will! (Karasu naze nakuno? - Karasu no katte desho!)" As a child, I loved this version and often sang it.

7 - Legends/ stories or famous characters of the Imaginary / Folk tales

The followings are nationwide famous fairy tales.

Momotarou: a story about a boy, Momotarou, born from a giant peach. Momo means "peach," tarou is a common boy's name. One day, an old woman found a giant peach floating in the river near her house in a countryside. Her husband cut it, and a baby boy came out. As they had no child, they were very glad to finally have one. The boy grew up and decided to go to attack an island where a devil lived and required the people to dedicate him treasures, foods and girls. The boy was followed by a dog, a monkey and a bird as his servants. They fought well and won the fight. The devil finally surrendered and was sent out from the island. He became a hero of the countryside. His cute theme song, named in Topic 6, is famous, too.

Urashimatarou: a story about a young fisherman, Urashimatarou, who saved a tortoise at a beach and was carried by it to a dreamland castle in the deep sea. The tortoise was in fact the beautiful princess of that land, who provided him with a thanksgiving invitation, welcoming him to a gorgeous party. Having enjoyed several days there, he went back home, but he found no friends anymore. Society had totally changed. The fact is: the several days corresponded to several centuries in the human world. Transformed into a crane, he desperately flew away into the sky. His theme song is named in Topic 6.

Kachikachiyama (a ticktock mountain): a story of revenge taken by a good-hearted, wise rabbit in place of a sorrowful old countryman, upon a mean raccoon dog that brutally killed the man's gentle wife. It teaches us about justice, and the idea that a criminal is punished inevitably.

8 - Products or goods that represent 'the national

treasure'

- Kimono: Traditional apparel. It was common daily wear until the first half of the 20th century. Today, it is fondly worn on special festivals and social outings.

- Sumo: A traditional fighting sport. It comes from a holy religious ceremony, consisting of dedicating strong men's physical battle to natural gods (similar to the Olympic games in Ancient Greece). Rikishis are professional and highly respected. Six tournaments are yearly held, bimonthly from January to November, each consisting of 15 days. Several hundreds participate in them. The most successful earns more than [the equivalent of] a million US dollars. I love to watch it on TV.

- Mt. Fuji (fujisan): A 3776 m high volcano. The highest mountain of the country. Its surprisingly beautiful conic form has always been loved by the Japanese. It became a theme of many literary and artistic works. It can be seen from many places- from a hill near my house, too. When seeing it, I feel more brave when thinking about my future.

- Manga/anime: Manga meaning "cartoon," anime "animated cartoon," both are known worldwide today. Anime derives from "animation," which is pronounced "animeeshon" in Japanese. Its abbreviation is "anime."

- Cats: A cat is an animal traditionally loved by the Japanese people. *Maneki-neko* ("an inviting cat") is a doll that sits like a human and raises one of her arms, meaning "invitation" in Japanese custom. Widely popular is today a tricoloured cat that acts as a "station master" in railway stations in the countryside, wearing a uniform hat, welcoming travelers with her cute meows and bringing wealth to the less prospering community.

***

Japan is a country that integrates a millennia-long history and centuries-long modern civilisation with its futuristic spirit of advancing the wealth and happiness of everyone in the world, while promoting a peaceful coexistence of the whole globe in the 21st century of high industrialisation, rapid transportation and internet.

Airports look modern. High-rise buildings occur more and more in main towns. But if you go into a narrow back road just behind a modern building, you'll find people's houses, standing simple, modest and reserved. High buildings were traditionally avoided owing to the severe natural conditions of the Japanese Archipelago: typhoons and earthquakes. In 2011 you could see the catastrophe in Tohoku caused by strong quakes (I felt them, too, even in the Tokyo area very far from the epicentre), and the following tsunamis, earthquakes can so easily destroy our daily life, often in a second, often in a minute…

Wooden-made, low houses are the expression of the nation's wisdom of living on this Pacific island, moderately and less pompously, with less persistence as regards the material aspects, and with deep thanks for our fleeting life. Such a life philosophy was formed throughout our history. The profound long-stroke sound of Buddhist temple's bell, often referred to as "bell of 'Nothing Is Perpetual,'" will give you a hint as to what that philosophy is.

If you have a Japanese friend, ask him or her to take you, when travelling to Japan, to a temple or a shrine that he or she knows well since childhood. You will find a peaceful quiet spot that is totally isolated from the clamour of main roads. Wherever people live, a temple or a Shintoist shrine stands. You will be the first visitor there from your country.

In general, the Japanese get shy when meeting a foreigner. This is mainly due to their sense of inferiority that they cannot speak English or other foreign languages well. Japanese is a linguistically isolated language at the East margin of Far East. It is generally believed that English is a language of unbelievable difficulty. If you want to know the country and the people more, the best way is to just speak to them, even in English, also armed with basic greetings in Japanese like Kon-nichiwa (Hello) and Arigato (Thank you). They will then gradually open their mental "door" to you. They will pull out a dictionary, seek someone who speaks English, or try to speak their less refined English to communicate with you.

They are a "closed box," and you are trying to open it. The key lies in the "box" itself. An encounter with the people and the country will be quite challenging and adventurous for you.

Lebanon

First name: Pamela
Family name: Ammoury Maalouf
www.pamela-maalouf.globtra.com
&
First name: Bernadette
Family name: Bou Rjeily Choueiry
berna.bourjeily@gmail.com

Capital	Beirut	Population	4,140,000
Government	Republic	Currency	Lebanese pounds (LBP)
Religion(s)	Muslim, Christian		
Language(s)	Arabic (official), French, English		

Pamela: Fond of literature and poetry, I started writing at the age of 11, expressing my thoughts in Arabic, English and French. My poems were published locally as well internationally: I was the first poet in "The Best Poems and Poets" of 2003, and "Who's Who in Poetry," two books grouping the best poets and poems from all over the world. I now hold a Masters in Translation and a Diploma in Interpretation, while also pursuing a PhD in... translation!

I work as a freelancer with various individuals, companies and organisations, such as the United Nations (in Lebanon, Qatar, Abu

Dhabi, USA and Europe); this enables me to broaden my horizons in different fields.

Bernadette: I was born in Al-Chiyah, a small area in the Southwest suburbs of the capital Beirut. A few years later, and due to the civil war, we had to move to Fanar, a safer place. I studied at the College des Soeurs Antonines, where I learnt Arabic, French and English. As I loved to learn languages, I decided to study for a B.A. in translation at the Lebanese University. I also studied Spanish at the Cervantes Institute in Beirut.

When I first graduated, I couldn't find a decent job in my field, but I managed to work for a magazine, where I was responsible for international Public Relations. I had to visit many international exhibitions, conduct interviews with existing clients, and meet up with prospective clients. A few years later I started to translate press articles from Arabic into English. Three years later, I found a job as a translator with the United Nations Relief and Works Agency for Palestine Refugees in the Near East (UNRWA) in Beirut, where I stayed for 3 years, until I got married and moved to Dubai. Once in Dubai, I worked as an Arabic copywriter with an advertising agency, then I was contacted by UN OCHA – IRIN (Integrated Regional Information Networks) to work with them as an Arabic Editor to post humanitarian news on their website.

1 - A typical conversation – what are the common/universal topics people go for? (weather, politics, etc.) - And some topics that you should avoid discussing with the locals?

During a common conversation, it is normal to talk about work, family and life in general, besides any current exceptional event that is occurring on the national or the international levels. Lebanese people are very sociable and like to get to know people and create a friendly relationship with everyone. Therefore, asking too many questions and talking about oneself is not considered rude but it is better rather to have interest in others.

Unlike many other nationalities, Lebanese people are known for their love of politics. Every time they sit together, they will discuss their national issues as well as the Arab Spring and any other international topics. They also have a passion for sports. You can find for example people supporting the German soccer team more than the Germans themselves. As for the Lebanese women, they are very concerned about their beauty and fashion.

On the other hand, discussions related to sexual topics are usually avoided especially if people around are a bit old.

2 - Events of great significance for the community, deeply stored in everyone's mind

1956 is the year of the foundation of the "Baalbeck International Festival" by President Camille Chamoun. It is the oldest and best-known cultural event in the Middle East and the eastern Mediterranean.

A series of clashes erupted in 1975 between Lebanese Christians and a few Palestinians in the streets of central Beirut, which is presented as the spark that set off the Lebanese Civil War, in the mid-1970s, marking the painful memory of every Lebanese citizen.

A few other events also affected Lebanon but were unfortunately also very sad. One of them took place in 1982 when the Lebanese president, Bachir Gemayel was assassinated in Achrafieh. The other, more recent, in 2005, when former Prime Minister Rafic Hariri was assassinated in Beirut.

In 2009 Beirut is nominated by UNESCO as World Book Capital and in 1997 Pope John Paul II did the historic visit to Lebanon followed by another one, in 2012 - this time by Pope Benedict XVI.

However, there is one extremely important event that took place around 2,000 years ago in Lebanon. It is actually the first miracle of Jesus Christ, when He turned water into wine during a marriage in Cana of Galilee in South Lebanon.

3 - *Figures from the past / present that you use in colloquial expressions*

Ayub is the name of a prophet (Job) who was famous for his righteousness and for his patience. In fact, he is a man who suffered a lot due to the death of all his children, bankruptcy and disease while only his wife was struggling to make a decent living. Later on, God granted him blessings and peace after all that he went through. Therefore, whenever one shouts "صبرك يا أيّوب" (your patience Ayub), this means that he or she is asking for Ayub's patience.

Hatem Tay (in Arabic: حاتم الطائي أو حاتم طيّ) is the symbol of generosity in the Arab world for he was known for his big-heartedness and generosity. Thus, when calling someone Hatem Tay, this reflects how generous he or she is.

Bou Zahra (in Arabic: بو زهره) designates a wolf and when someone is called "bou zahra" this indicates how wily he or she is.

Abou Melhem is an old TV personality, very well-known in Lebanon. He used to live in one of the Lebanese villages, where he would solve the problems of the villages' citizens. And from then on, whenever anyone solves someone's problem they call him Abou Melhem.

Not to forget the famous Beiruti personality, **Abul Abed** (أبو العبد) also known as Abul Abed El Beiruty. Abul Abed is a fictional character who is the theme of many jokes. In illustrations, his most notable features are a large moustache and the red fez he wears on his head.

4 - Words used to designate a type of person, animal, things

Asfouriyé: (in Arabic: عصفوريّي) There was in the past a park called "asfour" meaning "a bird," where a psychiatric hospital was built later on. Ever since, and whenever a person acts foolishly or insanely, he would be described as if he got out of the "asfouriyé."

Chitan: (in Arabic: شيطان) meaning "Satan" or "the demon" usually addressed to children who are hyperactive or very smart. In this context, the word "mzar'at" (in Arabic: مزرقط) originating from "zor'ta" (in Arabic: زرقطة) and meaning a "bee" can also be used to indicate how active someone is.

In Arabic, most names have meanings. I will cite a few:

- Habib: a male name meaning lover
- Reem: a female name meaning white gazelle
- Adel: a male name meaning just and correct
- Assaad: a male name meaning happier
- Labib: a male name meaning intelligent

- Siham: a female name meaning arrows
- Ibtissam: a female name meaning smile
- Farah: a female name meaning joy
- Nour: a unisex name meaning light
- Nagham: a female name meaning rhythm

5 - *Common phrases and fun expressions in your native language and their translation in English*

Masha'Allah or Smallah: (in Arabic: ما شـاء الله أو اسـمالله) this expression is widely used in Lebanon and reflects appreciation, joy, praise or thankfulness.

Enkasar el charr: (in Arabic: انكسـر الشـرّ) when a glass or a plate is broken, people say this expression as a good sign since a crisis was about to happen and was avoided thanks to that 'thing' that was broken (evilness was broken).

Tolii men l ard aktar ma nezil men l sama: (in Arabic: طلع مـن الأرض أكتر مـا نـزل مـن السما) a unique and beautiful expression that is used when it rains too much, literally meaning "what is coming out of the ground is way more than what is falling from the sky."

Tarboosh bayak maalla' aal tour Eiffel: (in Arabic: طربوش بيّك معلّق عَ بـرج إيـفل) literally meaning "your father's fez hangs upon the Eiffel Tower." The fez (or Tarboosh) is a traditional red felt cap with a silk tassel that represents a part of the oriental cultural identity and which is associated in this expression with the Tour Eiffel that symbolises a very high summit. In fact, this is a very funny expression meaning that the person in question is very arrogant.

Chou jeib Tarazan aa Vegas? (in Arabic: شـو جـاب طـرزان عَ فـيغاس؟) literally meaning "what brings Tarzan to Vegas?" an expression criticising the fact of relating two very different issues or things to each others.

El kalb lli beddo jar aal seid, baleh w bala saydo (الكلب اللي بدو جر عالصيد بلاه وبلا صيدو) means literally no need for the dog that needs to be dragged to the hunting. This expression is used in Lebanon to say that it is better not to force anyone to do anything they do not want to do, and it is especially used to tell girls that if a man has to be pushed for marriage, it is better not to marry him.

6 - Songs and games you remember from your childhood, that are generally passed on to the next generation

Yalla tnam (in Arabic: يلّا تنام): meaning "May she sleep"; sung to little babies to fall asleep.

Ya zghiri leich aam tebki (in Arabic: يا زغيري ليش عم تبكي؟): meaning "Little girl, why are you crying?"

Scout songs are also best known by everyone. They're mostly in French, such as Chevalier de la table ronde, Santiago, Ce n'est qu'un au revoir, Le coq est mort.

Games

La'ita (in Arabic: لقّيطة): one must catch the others

One of the games that never dies in Lebanon is "hide and seek" - Ghammida (in Arabic: غمّيضة). It keeps passing on from one generation to another.

There is also the prison ball game that is better known in Lebanon as "ballon chasseur" in French. But nowadays, all kids prefer electronic indoor games and rarely play in the streets like we used to do.

7 - Legends/ stories or famous characters of the Imaginary / Folk tales

Abou kis (in Arabic: أبـو كــيس): meaning "a man holding a bag" used when a child is being naughty, and to scare him, grandma would tell him: "If you don't stop what you are doing right away Abou kis will come and take you away!"

El wéwé (in Arabic: الواوي): also used to scare children (The wolf).

Folk tales:

When a tooth falls from a child's mouth, mothers usually take the tooth and tell the child that a gift will replace it and that it will show under his or her pillow. When children fall asleep, parents replace the tooth with a gift or simply with a small sum of money. This method is adopted to prevent children from crying after losing their tooth.

And as we are a country where several religions and civilisations coexist, almost every kid in Lebanon (including non-Christians) believes in Santa Clause and waits for gifts from him on Christmas Eve.

Not to forget mentioning Grindizer, the super robot that amazes all kids at all times. In addition, there is the famous character called Jongar, also representing a super robot.

8 - Products or goods that represent 'the national treasure'

As Egyptians are proud to be the descendants of pharaohs, we Lebanese are proud to be descendants of Phoenicians. At that time, Cadmus, a Phoenician prince was the first to introduce the original Alphabet to the whole world.

- Lebanon -

In addition, Lebanon is a touristic country, known for its hospitality and good food. It is very well known for its two starters (*mezzeh*), hummus and Tabbouleh. Tabouli (in Arabic: تبولة) is a famous Lebanese salad with chopped flat parsley, mint, diced tomato, green onion, lemon juice olive oil and a hint of cracked wheat.

Moreover, we have very high quality wine and *arak* (an Arab alcohol based on grape and aniseed) that are exported to many European countries.

It is also worth mentioning our handmade stoneware (فخار) in which our ancestors used to cook as well as the rigid cedar woods that were even used in the decoration of many well-known old churches in Europe.

***

Lebanese people attach great importance to family, religion, education and marriage. They are very caring and show sympathy towards others and at the same time, they know exactly how to enjoy their time with their families, friends and loved ones.

Lastly, and despite all wars and conflicts which have occurred in Lebanon, this beloved nation has always been protected by the Lord through the many Lebanese Saints and Beatified Brothers protecting this country: Saint Charbel, Saint Rafqa, Saint Nimatullah Al-Hardini, Beatified Brother Estephan Nehme, Beatified Father Yaacoub as well as Venerable Patriarch Estephan Douaihy.

Before I conclude, allow me to reiterate what Pope John Paul II said during his visit to Lebanon: "Lebanon is more than a country, it is a message"

Malaysia

First name: Maisarah
Family name: Ariffin
MAI.ARIFFIN@GMAIL.COM

Capital	Kuala Lumpur	Population	29,180,000
Government	Constitutional monarchy	Currency	Malaysian ringgits (MYR)
Religion(s)	Muslim (official), Buddhist, Christian, Hindu, Confucianism, Taoism		
Language(s)	Bahasa Malaysia (official), English, Chinese, Tamil, Telugu, Malayalam, Panjabi, Thai and others		

I'm a chemist, currently working at a private laboratory in Malaysia and previously studied in France for almost 7 years. Funded through a government scholarship, the first two years were spent studying the fundamentals of French (an uncommon language to be used in Malaysia), and the next five years I devoted to getting the Diplôme d'Ingénieur in Chemistry, which I obtained in 2010.

1 - A typical conversation – what are the common/ universal topics people go for? (weather, politics, etc.) -

And some topics that you should avoid discussing with the locals?

If you are meeting a person for the first time, the first couple of things that are always asked are "Where do you work?" and "Where did you complete your studies?" People asking about universities you might have attended is an expected occurrence, but asking about secondary schools might be baffling to foreigners. We do it though, since so many schools are well-known here (especially the "elite" and full-boarding schools), so we get an idea of the other person's background and personality by finding out where they spent their youth (13 to 17 years old). Besides, we are attached to our alma mater and can relate easily with people who have the same background as us (like some people from different full-boarding schools knowing each other through events, sports competitions, etc). This can be quite an interesting topic to talk about.

2 - Events of great significance for the community, deeply stored in everyone's mind

The 16th Commonwealth Games which were held in Kuala Lumpur, the capital city of Malaysia in 1998 hold a very special place in the hearts of Malaysians. Being the first Asian country to act as host for the last Commonwealth Games of the 20th century, we were so proud and determined to do our best. At that time, the whole country became one. We cried and laughed together. Everyone was supporting the athletes and especially during finals where we were competing, everyone was tense and so focused on the games. We ended up coming in at fourth place among all 70 participating countries- the best result we have got so far. Have you ever heard our theme song for this event? It was "Standing In

The Eyes Of The World," sung by Ella, our rock queen. Every time we hear this song, it brings back memories of the atmosphere surrounding the Commonwealth Games.

3 - *Figures from the past / present*

When talking about **Tunku Abdul Rahman**, the first thing that comes to our mind is independence. He was the first Prime Minister of Malaysia and played a very significant role in obtaining the independence of Malaysia (known as the Federation of Malaya at that time) from British colonial rule in 1957. Because of that, he is now known as Bapa Kemerdekaan (Father of Independence).

A brief history of the colonisation of Malaya: In 1511, a Portuguese fleet led by Alfonso de Albuquerque sailed into Malacca (one of the states in Malaysia) harbour and captured the city with canon fire. A century later in 1641, the Dutch captured the city from the Portuguese and controlled the spice trade. In 1819 British administration replaced the Dutch and established a trading post in Singapore. The British administration in Malaya lasted 138 years until our independence in 1957.

4 - *Words used to designate a type of person, animal, things*

Bandung is actually a name of a city in Indonesia, but when we talk about mi bandung (bandung noodles) and air bandung (bandung water), these refer to a food and a type of sweet drink, that have no relation whatsoever with the Bandung city.

Belanda is the Malay name of The Netherlands. But *ayam belanda* (turkey) is a type of bird which is not even related to the country

Belanda. (Interestingly enough, the English name "turkey" is not related to the Republic of Turkey either!)

5 - Common phrases and fun expressions in your native language and their translation in English

Instead of fun expressions, these are some funny riddles that are quite known, like:

Question 1: How do you put an elephant in a refrigerator?

Answer 1: Open the refrigerator, put in the elephant, and close the door.

Question 2: Then how do you put a giraffe in?

Answer 2: Open the refrigerator, take out the elephant, put in the giraffe, and then close the door.

6 - Songs and games you remember from your childhood, that are generally passed on to the next generation

Do you know a game where people spread out five small stones or small cloth bags containing sand or beans, and then pick them up one by one? The game is called Batu Seremban and was originally played by girls. The objective of the game is to throw one of the stones, one at a time, and sweeping another on the floor while simultaneously catching the one you threw earlier. This game can get complicated. It is enjoyed by both girls and boys nowadays, no matter whether you're old or young; you can still play this game and have fun.

Another interesting traditional game that has now gained worldwide recognition is Sepak Raga. It was first played amongst the royalty, which the "commoners" later adopted. This game requires a special ball, which is made of rattan. The traditional way of playing this is to have about ten people standing in a circle, passing the ball around. The player can either balance the ball with either of their legs or can head-butt the ball. Whenever the player who is balancing the ball drops the ball he is called out before the game continues, and this will go on until only one player is left.

7 - Legends/ stories or famous characters of the Imaginary / Folk tales

Hikayat Si Tanggang (the Story of Si Tanggang) is one of Malaysians' favourite stories. The story is about an ungrateful son being cursed by his mother into stone. Si Tanggang was a poor boy who lived with his parents by the sea. Despite living in poverty, Si Tanggang dreamed of being rich and living a good life. When he grew older, he left the village to work as a slave in a big ship. He worked really hard and became the captain's favourite and eventually became his adopted son and married his daughter. He became rich. One day the ship docked at a river mouth of a village; Si Tanggang's village. People recognised him and told his parents about their son. Her mother cooked his favourite dish and they rowed a little boat to meet him. They called out Si Tanggang's name and when Si Tanggang realised that they were his parents, he was ashamed and pretended not knowing them. He didn't want his wife to meet his poor parents. He shouted at them and pushed them away. Very sad and heartbroken, the parents rowed back to their village. His mother then said that if it was true that the man was his son, may God punish him. Then the sky turned dark, the wind became stronger, and the waters rough. Si Tanggang realised his mistakes and called out his parents, but to no avail. Si

Tanggang, his wives, the ship and the sailors had then turned into a huge stone, taking the shape of the ship.

Moral of the story: honour your parents.

8 - Products or goods that represent 'the national treasure'

Proton Saga is Malaysia's first ever car, manufactured by Perusahaan Otomobil Nasional Berhad (PROTON). The car was commercially launched on 9th July 1985 by the fourth Prime Minister of Malaysia, Dato' Seri Dr. Mahathir Mohamad, who was the originator of the Malaysian car idea. Saga now comes in variations, but the first-generation Saga is the longest surviving Proton model to date- that's nearly 22 years. The original Saga model was based on the 1983 Mitsubishi Lancer Fiore- Mitsubishi had agreed to produce Malaysia's own national car. The name Saga was actually chosen from the winner of a contest, held before production, to choose the best name for the first national car. The winner, Ismail Jaafar, a retired military soldier, said that "saga" (Abrus precatorius) which is a type of soft, fragile but productive seed commonly found in Malaysia, could represent the car, as in the Proton Saga 1.3 litre engine would be "as strong as the saga seed."

Pakistan

First name: Muhammad Salman
Family name: Riaz
http//:translationstudiesinfo.blogspot.com
salman_riaz@ymail.com

Capital	Islamabad	Population	190,291,000
Government	Federal republic	Currency	Pakistani rupees (PKR)
Religion(s)	Muslim (official), Christian and Hindu		
Language(s)	Urdu (official), Punjabi, Sindhi, Pashtu, Balochi, Hindko, English (official; lingua franca of Pakistani elite and most government ministries) and others		

I am a university lecturer and have taught linguistics and English literature for about six years. I am also an English-to-Urdu-and-Punjabi translator. Though my professional journey as a freelance translator started less than two years ago, hard work and perseverance have won me the confidence of my clients.

The interesting field of translation can easily be divided into two major categories: technical (or non-literary) translation and literary translation. The translation market is largely in need of technical translation, hence I, as a professional translator, mostly get projects from this category; however, it is literary translation that I take much more of a fancy to and that I love to do. It is also my area of research, and my PhD in Translation Studies research focuses on it. To put it more specifically, I am conducting a 'function-based' comparison between selected translations of Saadat Hassan Manto (a leading figure in the history of Urdu short story writing) and their translation into English by Manto's nephew, Khalid Hassan, attempting to identify how effectively the selected translations do justice to the 'purpose/s' which they are assigned by the client or the translator. In short, doing and researching literary translation is my passion, my love. To me, it is more an art than a skill, whose creation is as much contingent upon creativity as on skilfulness.

1 - A typical conversation – what are the common/universal topics people go for? (weather, politics, etc.) - And some topics that you should avoid discussing with the locals?

In Pakistan, a conversation normally opens with people greeting each other. The one opening up a conversation says اسلامُ علیکم – an Arabic expression which means "peace be upon you." This beautiful greeting is returned by the listener/s with وعلیکمُ السلام, meaning "peace be upon you, too." Pakistani society is a close-knit structure, where people live in a joint-family system and hold strong relationship with their kith and kin. Owing to this social allegiance, conversational greetings are normally followed by some typical questions such as "How are your parents?" "How about your wife and kids?" "How is your life going?" This mode of conversation demonstrates solidarity with the interlocutor/s.

The topics that men love to talk about are the same as anywhere else: politics, sports, and business. Another typical subject is religion. Women also share universal topics of conversation, the most important being fashion. People love to meet with each other and engage in chitchat, and spend hours on this favourite pastime of theirs. However, one should avoid certain sensitive topics in ordinary social interactions. For instance, owing to the strong religious influence, sex-related topics are considered taboo and are usually avoided in conversations.

2 - Events of great significance for the community, deeply stored in everyone's mind

The independence of the country in 1947 is the event that is deeply rooted in the minds of the people. The independence movement accelerated in 1940, and for the next seven years, the Muslims of the subcontinent, which was under the British rule, struggled hard towards independence under the commandership of the great leader Mr. Muhammad Ali Jinnah, known by his title Quid-e-Azam (the Great Leader). The movement was based on a "Two Nations Theory," an ideology championed by the then Muslim leaders of the subcontinent. Muslim leaders, especially Quid-e-Azam, made it clear to the nation that Muslims and Hindus of the subcontinent were two nations diametrically opposed to each other in every aspect of life, be it religion, politics, or something else. They made it clear to the people that, owing to this unbridgeable gap between the two nations, it was improbable for them to live together; hence the Muslims not only demanded freedom from the British rule, but also struggled for a separate country for themselves. The dream of the Muslim community came true when, on August 14, 1947, a new country with the name of Pakistan emerged on the map of the world. The declaration of independence was followed by brutal bloodshed and the massacre of millions.

- Pakistan -

We are now in the 56th year since the inception of this new state, but the memory of this special event is still fresh in the minds of the generation that fought for Pakistan, and they have transferred the ideology which was the basis for their freedom movement to their children and grandchildren.

3 - Nouns and Figures from the past / present that you use in colloquial expressions

After independence, **Quid-i-Azam**'s picture was given a permanent place on currency notes. It was a symbol of homage to the great leader. Unfortunately, however, his name came to have a negative connotation in the context of money. Now, if someone, especially an employee in a public or private sector organisation, wants to indirectly ask for bribery, he or she may say do so by saying something like "Quad-i-Azam chale ga" [You will need Quid-i-Azam to get this done], where "Quid-i-Azam" would mean "currency note," or in other words, "money." This is a circumlocution to demand bribery. It is ironic that the name of Quid-i-Azam, whose personality was, and is, a symbol of honesty and uprightness, has now come to be connoted with some corrupt officers in such a wrong way.

4 - Words used to designate a type of person, animal, things

Muhammad Iqbal (1876-1938), the national poet of Pakistan, was a great thinker and philosopher. Without doubt, he is one of the greatest Muslim thinkers of the 20th century. As a tribute to his philosophical matchlessness, he came to be known as Allama (i.e. a great scholar and thinker) Iqbal. Over time, his name has come to be used in educated spheres as a symbol to denote individuals who show great philosophical promise. Mostly, it is used in a light-hearted way in frank conversations, such as:

وہ اکیسویں صدی کا اقبال ہے ارے یار،

Oh buddy, he is Iqbal (i.e. a great philosopher) of the 20th century.

I would also like to point out another example, which is much more interesting and widespread. It is actually not a proper noun that I am going to refer to, it is a phrase: *Eid ka chand* (i.e. the moon of Eid). Eid is the most important religious festival for Muslims (as Christmas is for Christians). There are actually two Eids that the Muslims celebrate: One is called *Eid-ul-Fitr* (celebrated on the 1st of the Islamic month of Shawaal) and the other *Eid-ul-Azha* (celebrated on the 10th of the Islamic month of Zulhaj). As you might know, the Islamic calendar is lunar (known as Hijri Calendar), that is to say, it is based on the movements of the moon, not the sun, as is the case with the Gregorian calendar. According to the Islamic calendar, a crescent moon marks the start of a month. Put in this context, each year, the days of the two Eids are set according to when the crescent moon shows up for the months of Shawaal and Zulhaj. The days in a lunar calendar are not fixed, which means that the new month can start after either 29th or 30th of the previous month; it all depends upon which day the moon is crescent. The beauty of this uncertainty lies in the curiosity that it induces in the Muslims. Men, women, and children, all rush to the roof on the 29th of the months preceding the two months of Eid, and look up to the sky for the crescent moon. Now, my dear readers, our phrase is rooted in this religious practice, and it is used when communicating with a familiar person whom you are seeing after a long, long time (such as your colleague returning to work after a prolonged absence). The meaning it denotes would become clear from the following Urdu idiom.

آپ تو عید کا چاند ہی ہوگئے ہیں۔

Word-for-word translation: You have become the moon of Eid.

Meaning: Like the moon of Eid (which appears only twice in a year), you have been seen after a long time. It is a lighthearted way of expressing how much the speaker has missed the listener during his or her days of absence.

5 - Common phrases and fun expressions in your native language and their translation in English

As in any other society, there are certain commonly-used, funny idioms used in Pakistani society, of which I have cited a couple below. Both examples contain the idiom in Urdu, its literal translation in English, and then a brief explanation of what the idiom means or in which context it is used.

He or she can neither read nor write, but his or her name is Fazil.

Explanation: The name Fazil in Urdu means 'very learned.' The idiom is mockingly used for a person, who does not hold much knowledge of a field, but who behaves as if he or she were profoundly full of knowledge.

The face is of *chureils*, disposition that of fairies.

Explanation: *Chureil* is a fairy-tale character who has big, protruding teeth, a dreadful face, and inwardly-bent feet. The idiom is used to indicate a person, especially a woman, who has a very ordinary personality but who behaves and talks in such a manner as if she were a beautiful and delicate fairy.

6 - *Songs and games you remember from your childhood, that are generally passed on to the next generation*

Though the Internet has brought about a drastic change in the game-habits of children, who no longer take that much interest in mixing with their peers and playing games in groups, one of the results of which is that age-old child songs and games are dying out – some culture-specific songs and games have survived, especially in villages. A few interesting, popular games are:

Gilli Danda: It is a cricket and baseball type of game, but the ball used in it is made of wood, with pointed edges; you can imagine how *brave* a 'fielder' would have to be to 'catch' this wooden ball after it was hit by the batter.

Bantey: A popular game played in villages, whereby a child uses a tiny marble to hit other marbles.

Stapu: A game, popular with girls, which is played by drawing eight equal-sized boxes on ground.

7 - *Legends/ stories or famous characters of the Imaginary / Folk tales*

Before the nationwide interest in the Internet, plenty of tales about imaginary creatures were told by grandmothers to their grandchildren. Unfortunately, most of them have not survived against the tide of the electronic revolution, whereby children now take more interest in playing video games, chatting with friends, watching movies of imaginary characters, etc., than in listening to such stories. A few, nonetheless, have survived, and are still told to children. Those worthy of mention are such moral stories as:

Thirsty Crow, whose moral is "Necessity is the mother of invention"

Greedy Dog, whose moral is "Greed is a curse"

Clever Fox, whose moral is "Grapes you can't reach are sour"

These, and some others, are the moral stories that are mostly told to children in educated families. These are sort of universal moral stories similar to those told in many societies of the world.

8 - Products or goods that represent 'the national treasure'

Pakistan is famous for many products. It exports top-quality footballs (which are used in international football matches, including such mega events as Olympics and World Cup) and leather goods. Gujarat, the city that I come from, is famous for its fan and furniture industries, which are internationally liked for their quality. A special type of rice, which is called Basmati Chaawal in Pakistan, is a very fine quality product, and is in high demand in international markets.

The country is also rich in huge resources of minerals such as copper, marble, gypsum, sulfur, and silica. Especially mentionable are the resources of coal, copper, gas, and gold. The reserves of these minerals are so huge that each of them has been identified as being among the top ten reserves in the world in their respective categories.

Thailand

FIRST NAME: WORAPOT
FAMILY NAME: SATTAPUNKEEREE
HTTP://JUFFY.TRANSLATORSCAFE.COM/
WSAT001@GMAIL.COM

Capital	Bangkok	Population	67,091,000
Government	Constitutional monarchy	Currency	Baht (THB)
Religion(s)	Buddhist (official)		
Language(s)	Thai, English (secondary language of the elite), dialects		

Worapot Sattapunkeeree was born in 1970 in Rachaburi Province and raised in Bangkok in Thailand. In 1992, he graduated from Thammasat University with a bachelor degree in French and English. During his academic life at Thammasat University, he won a one-year partial scholarship from the French Government to be an exchange student at The Center of Applied Linguistics of the University of Franche-Comte in Besancon, and graduated with a diploma in French Studies in 1991. After that, he ventured into the international business banking field at Krung Thai Bank Pcl. in Chiang Mai, Thailand. At the age of 32, he decided to quit his banking job to continue his studies at The University of Auckland in New Zealand. During his academic life there, he did academic yet controversial and rare research. He chose a different route compared to mainstream research on second language acquisition, that has over-researched the "minority, powerless students learning the majority, imperialist language." Instead, he probed a New Zealander of European heritage learning the rare, endangered language Maori. The results are worth reading. He graduated in 2004 with a masters degree in Applied Language Studies and Linguistics. Mr. Worapot has previously been employed in a number of professions ranging from banker and lecturer to interpreter, translator, editor, proofreader and transcriber. Most recently, Mr. Worapot has been working as a contract lecturer in English at Maejo University in Chiang Mai, Thailand, his second home, and working for various companies in the translation industry around the globe. His publication includes Thai translation version of New Media Art from TASCHEN. Mr. Worapot is fluent in English and quite good in French in addition to his Thai mother tongue excellence.

1 - A typical conversation – what are the common/ universal topics people go for? (weather, politics, etc.) - And some topics that you should avoid discussing with the locals?

Thai people are extraordinarily kind to foreigners who don't speak Thai very well. The more you attempt to speak, the lovelier you become! Another thing is that Thai society gives importance to three main words: Sawatdee (Hi), Kho-thot (Apologize / Excuse me) and Khop-khun (Thank you). You may be wondering why La-kon (Goodbye) is excluded!

Actually, most Thais dislike saying the word "La-kon" because it gives the feeling of being away from each other for too long. Of course, the word "La-kon" is often seen used in Thai romances when a leading actor has to pass away or be away from a leading actress, which is a real tragedy. Saying this word is almost like being such a melodramatic actor in real life. That's why Thai people use "Sawatdee" when meeting each other, and when leaving each other as well. One of the specific gestures that you could do when saying "Sawatdee" (promoted worldwide by Miss Thailand Universe) is *wai*, the Thai greeting gesture: a slight bow with the palms pressed together in a prayer-like fashion. You do not necessarily need to do a *wai* and say "Thailand" in an overacting manner like Miss Thailand Universe! Just do a nice *wai* and say a plain "Sawatdee" distinctly, and you will win Thai hearts. Smile is also vital when you greet Thais. Thailand is noted as the land of smile. Therefore, when you visit the kingdom, do not scowl like an angry bird! Keep smiling because that will be the beginning of a good friendship...

"Kho-thot" is used when you need help from someone (Excuse me) or apologise for your mistake (I am sorry/I apologise). For instance, when you want to ask for directions, you should say Kho-thot "Krap" (for male speakers) or Kho-tot "Kha" (for female speakers). Both gendered ending-words are added at the end of sentence to make the conversation polite/formal. But, if you are unsure of the gender, pick one, use it and do not forget to smile! You're asking for help by using "Kho-tot," to start with, and then using English may not work out because Thai people will be too excited every time they have to communicate with foreigners. The secret is to understand body language. We can guarantee that although they do grasp what you say, body language rather than speech will be your answer since they cannot speak English very well. Good luck and hope you get help! The last word is "khop-khun." You already know when to use this word. Do remember that such a word is worthier than money. If you say this and leave a tip, then the recipient will be really grateful indeed!

2 - Events of great significance for the community, deeply stored in everyone's mind

Recently, you must have seen the news about Thailand's political assemblies leading to riots in Bangkok. Several countries strongly advised their inhabitants not to travel to the kingdom. The situation was not actually as violent as it looked in the media worldwide. After the riots, Thai people were in more harmony than before. We did help restore places and rehabilitate some Thai people's terrified minds. We wholeheartedly collaborated in doing so, as though no conflict had ever happened. And, do you know what made this conciliation happen? Our beloved "Nai-luang," King Bhumibol Adulyadej or King Rama IX did! We love The King. Long Live The King!

3 - Figures from the past / present that you use in colloquial expressions

Thais give importance to past Thai heroes and heroines and often use their names to call people who do good things. However, Thais also use some leading actor/actress's names to call bad people too. For example, Khun-pan is one of the leading actors in Thai literature "Khun-chang Khun-pan" and had several wives. His name is used for calling people who have several wives, girlfriends or "giks." If you have several husbands, boyfriends or "giks," you will be called "Nang-kha-khi" because this name refers to a leading actress in Thai literature "Kha-khi" who had several husbands!

4 - *Words used to designate a type of person, animal, things*

If you visit Thailand and do shopping, for example, at minimarts, sales assistants might get puzzled if you call product names in Thai properly! Why? Most Thai people like using a popular brand of a product to refer to the whole class of that product. Such substitution of a part for whole is rhetorically called "synecdoche." We've been doing this for generations. And, believe me there are plenty of them in Thailand's shopping places! Let's practice a few of them:

"Fab" (a powdered detergent brand) is used instead of "Pong-suk-fok" (the complete noun for a powdered detergent product)

"Sunlight" (a dishwashing liquid brand) is used instead of "Nam-ya-laang-chan" (the complete noun for a dishwashing liquid product)

If all these become your catchwords, you certainly will get a Thai wife real soon!

5 - *Common phrases and fun expressions in your native language and their translation in English*

Learning funny Thai words and expressions will let you know who is gossiping about you! Here are a few that people use when talking behind your back!

"Gik" (กิ๊ก) is a pronoun that means "a person who is more than a friend but not your boy/girlfriend."

- *Thailand* -

"Ab-baew" (แอ๊บแบ๊ว) is an adjective that means "in an over-lovely manner."

Another thing you might wonder about is why Thai people end their English speaking with "na." For example, Have a good trip na (นะ). "na" is a Thai particle, and the ending with "na" results from the fact that they are not familiar with ending a sentence too abruptly like in English. Therefore, they add "na" at the end to make the sentence more polite (not too polite like "Krap" or "Kha"). Do not be afraid to use "na" if you have a chance to speak to Thais na.

6 - Songs and games you remember from your childhood, that are generally passed on to the next generation

Most urban Thai children now are technology-savvy. They have iPhones, iPads, and the like. They enjoy them and forget traditional Thai games. However, in the countryside, you can still find those kids who play traditional games that have been passed on to them. One of the games is "Thai-style rubber band rope jumping game." Rubber bands are interwoven to make it like a rope. Then two players hold the rubber band rope at both ends at different vertical levels based on body parts from low to high level. For example, the first or the start level can be hip level and then waist one and so on. The others players have to jump over the rubber band rope. If the rubber rope is touched, that player is dead and out of the game. The game goes on like this and the height level increases until there is only one player left and s/he becomes the winner. This game requires a lot of jumping skills and can make you sweat and lose weight! The reason this game is still so popular in rural parts of Thailand is it is a cheap game. You need only the rubber bands. I used to play this game when I was young. I love it.

7 - *Legends/ stories or famous characters of the Imaginary / Folk tales*

Most Thai legends are stories stemmed from Thai literature. If you want to know what they are like, you have to wait until the weekend at 9 am, turn on your TV in your hotel and choose Thai TV Channel 7. There you will see some Thai characters in very ancient dress, other characters acting as giants, and half-human and half-animals, mystical cities, magic, magical objects and the like. I think they are like Harry Potter in a way. Or was J.K.Rowling inspired by our legends?

8 - *Products or goods that represent 'the national treasure'*

Visiting other countries always means eating their national food. Thailand has a lot of food ranked as the yummiest of the world such as "Som-tum" (papaya salad) and "Kaeng-kheaw-whan" (green curry). The fact is "authentic Thai food" is not available at restaurants where foreigners usually go to. You have to choose the eateries in which there are only Thai customers. Another thing is you have to know this Thai phrase "Mai-phed" (not spicy) if you want to dine out at a real Thai restaurant because Thais love spicy food. Tell them "Mai-phed" so that you can survive another day in Thailand! But, you have to pronounce it correctly. If you pronounce "Mai-ped" instead of "Mai-phed," it means you do not eat duck!

South Korea

First name: Eunjung
Family name: Picard
EUNJUNG@NEUF.FR

Capital	Seoul	Population	50,004,441
Government	Republic	Currency	South Korean won KRW
Religion(s)	Atheist		
Language(s)	Korean		

I was born in Seoul, in South Korea. I have a masters in French language and literature.

My first job in interpreting was in an iron-and-steel plant concerning the disassembling of a train in Charleroi in Belgium (large scale project, lasting 6 months). I discovered that I was full of resources and it all went well. I was given the job of reassembly in Korea having been highly recommended by the managers in Belgium. This was in 1995. Since then I have been both translator and interpreter (among other things: the translation of French books; various documents, and interpreting on behalf of private companies, law courts and the French police).

-THE WORLD IN WORDS-

My first translation was "Le Petit Prince" by St-Exupéry; I translated it for my boyfriend in 1986. It was his birthday present. I spent all summer translating it and making the book myself (writing and drawing it). I can therefore say that it is "the best translated version ever!" Like the original, I drew everything except the Baobab trees in pastel. I made two photocopies: one for me and one for my best friend (one girl). Naturally, I have lost the original.

I adore my job, and I'm proud to be a translator-interpreter.

1 - A typical conversation – what are the common/universal topics people go for? (weather, politics, etc.) - And some topics that you should avoid discussing with the locals?

- Politics. Koreans are well informed of everything that occurs in the political parties of the country. Especially as every mention of the president of the Republic or head of party is recorded. It is enough to mention the name of the President, or that of the head of the opposition party to get a conversation going.

- Chaebols (재벌), economy related. Family-controlled South Korean business conglomerates. When we speak about *chaebols*, it is as if we are speaking about the economy via theses groups. The *chaebols* deal more with the economy than with the country. For example: Samsung, Hyundai, LG.

- The people known in the world of entertainment: Koreans are very interested in singers, actors who incarnate the image of the good father, good mother, or ideal son-in-law. They speak much about them, and always look upon them with tenderness.

- Sports. Baseball is very popular. All corporations

(chaebols) have their own team and they look after it. Football is almost a national sport. Besides, all international competitions have become state business for the Koreans.

- Weather. "Oh, the weather is cold! What is it with this wind?" These are topics to discuss…

Topics to avoid:

Avoid any personal issues. Koreans are friendly, but at heart, adhere to Confucianism. They believe therefore that it is better not to speak about oneself too much. Self-publicity must be avoided and boastfulness, in particular, is very badly considered.

2 - Events of great significance for the community, deeply stored in everyone's mind

1945: An end to Japanese occupation: For 36 years, Korea was under the Japanese occupation.

1950: The Korean War: This lasted 3 and half years and devastated the whole country.

1988: The Seoul Olympic games: This event remains in the memory of the Koreans and is the most important event of the 20th century for them.

1992: Reopening of the discussion between the two Korean countries (South-North dialogue):

Since the armistice of 1953, there have been difficult relationships between North and South Korea. This was one of the great events in the history of Korea. Thanks to Mr Chung (the CEO of the Hyundai group) who started giving rice to North Koreans, the dialogue got kickstarted[1]; though don't quote me on that!

3 - Nouns and Figures from the past / present that you use in colloquial expressions

- **Jaringobi** (자린고비): very well-known in Korea, like Charles Dickens's Scrooge. A term which designates a scrooge-like nature. Synonym with Sujeonno (수전노), Norangi (노랑이), Gudusey (구두쇠) etc.

- **LEE ByungChul** (이병철): The founder of SamSung group, one of the Korean Chaebols. Mostly known as leading electronics manufacturer, Apple's greatest contender. To say that you are not rich, you say that, "You take me for the son of LEE Byung Chul!"

- **KIM Sat Gat** (김삿갓): a gleeman of the Joseon Dynasty (19 c). We say when restricted by daily life, "I wish I were free as KIM Sat Gat…"

4 - Words used to designate a type of person, animal, things

- *Seonsaengnim* (선생님): Polite term used at school when talking to teachers and more generally to elderly people.

- *Ajumma* (아줌마) for women and *Ajeossi* (아저씨) for men: used to address a middle aged person.

- *HarabeoJi* (할아버지): literally grandfather. Also used to address a man advanced in age.

- *Halmeoni* (할머니): strictly grandmother. Also used to address a woman advanced in age.

If we can hardly tell whether the person in front of is Ajeossi or

---

[1] Rice being one of the more expensive cereals with most North Koreans eating mainly corn powder

HarabeoJi, it is better not to use these terms. Polite terms are widely used, and attitude and courtesy are important, but not pronouns necessarily.

5 - *Common phrases and fun expressions in your native language and their translation in English*

Daebak (대박): It is a very common expression used to express that something really awesome has happened.

Aja (아자)! It is an expression that indicates encouragement with gesture. "You can do it, be brave!"

Jeong Mal (정말)? "Really?" Young people often use this expression at the end of each sentence.

Mi Cheoss Oh (미쳤어?): to use between friends: "Are you nuts or what?"

6 - *Songs and games you remember from your childhood, that are generally passed on to the next generation*

Majinga Z (마징가 Z): Song and animated cartoon for children at the end of the 70s and the beginning of the 80s. It is indexed on the large list of all Karaoke places in the country (Koreans love to go sing karaoke with friends).

Candy (캔디): Song and cartoon for teenagers at the beginning of the 80s. All girls know it. Initially a cartoon. The animated version and the theme song were especially popular among teenagers during the 80s.

Taekyon V (태권V) : Animated cartoon for children at the end of the 70s and the beginning of the 80s. Young people would parrot the idiosyncrasies of the main character (an invincible robot) to entertain friends and make them laugh.

7 - *Legends/ stories or famous characters of the Imaginary / Folk tales*

ChunHyang Jeon (춘향전) (The story of ChunHyag) is one of the best known love stories and folk tales of Korea. This is a love story about a courtesan's daughter and a Governer official's son. ChunHyang keeps her integrity till the end at great risk to her life. Happy ending included!

Jangwha and Hongryeon Jeon (장화 홍련전) (The story of Jangwha and Hongryeon): one of the best known folk tales. It is a ghost story about two young women, Jangwha and Hongryeon, who are falsely accused and killed as a result of a trick played by their wicked stepmother. They appear as ghosts to complain to the mayor at night. But he dies of fright. In the end, the mayor finds out the truth and the baddies are punished.

Heungbu and Nolbu Jeon (흥부 놀부전): is a story written in the late Chosen Dynasty (14 c-19 c) by an unknown person. This story about two brothers has been passed down through generations. The older brother, Nolbu is rich but miserly. The younger brother, Heungbu is poor but good-natured. And one day, Heungbu saves a swallow with a broken leg. The swallow returned and dropped a gourd seed to him. This gourd was packed with jewelry and gold. The good man is rewarded for his kindly nature.

All stories with Tigers and Foxes with 9 tales.

8 - *Products or goods that represent 'the national treasure'*

Insam (인삼): Roots of Jinseng called Insam as is well known (in Korea). Known as being able to help cure all kinds of illness. And, Korean Jinseng is the best.

Kimchi (김치): The must of Korean cuisine. Fermented Chinese cabbages. No Korean meal without Kimchi!

Bulgogi (불고기): Second best of Korean cuisine, it is prepared with roasted marinated beef.

K-Pop: Korean pop music influenced by western genres. Adulated in Asia, and, even at this moment in the world with the success of KangNam Style by Psy.

Vietnam

First name: Hoa
Family name: Bui
http://www.vanhoa.info
vanhoabui@gmail.com

Capital	Hanoi	Population	91,519,000
Government	Communist	Currency	Vietnamese dong (VND)
Religion(s)	Buddhist, Hoa Hao, Cao Dai, Catholic, Protestant		
Language(s)	Vietnamese (official), English (increasingly favoured as a second language), some French, Chinese, and Khmer		

Hi everyone, I am Bui Van Hoa from Vietnam. In my country everyone calls me by my last…oops, nope, by my first name, Hoa. Many of you may feel a bit puzzled and think that the order is wrong but in the Vietnamese tradition, the family name is always written before the given name, completely contrary to Western names. So if you are talking with Vietnamese friends, please pay a little attention to their names, otherwise you may easily get confused over which name you should use to address them. Currently I live in Hanoi and am working as an English editor for a newspaper in Vietnam. Sometimes I also work as a freelance translator to earn some extra money.

1 - A typical conversation – what are the common/universal topics people go for? (weather, politics, etc.) - And some topics that you should avoid discussing with the locals?

In everyday conversations, the Vietnamese can talk about almost any topic in the world.

When two people meet for the first time, they usually ask about the other's age first so that they can choose an appropriate way to address each other. As the conversation goes on, Vietnamese people can talk about their hometown, educational level, social and family status. Someone may ask you if you are still studying or already in the workforce, where you are working, and how much you earn. Westerners may feel embarrassed when being asked about their earnings but it is OK in Vietnam and if you do not want to talk about it, you can respond with general statements such as, my salary is enough for my basic needs, and the conversation will automatically move on to a different topic. Vietnamese people also talk a lot about their family. People are rather curious about whether you are married or not and how many children you have. In Western countries, these questions seem to be an intrusion of privacy but in my country people do not mind if someone asks them such personal questions. This does not mean that the Vietnamese want to invade the privacy of others, it just shows that our people are very communicative and want to forge closer relations between everyone in a community.

2 - Events of great significance for the community, deeply stored in everyone's mind

Vietnam is at the heart of Southeast Asia and throughout its long history, the country has witnessed a series of momentous events.

In modern history, one of the most prominent events took place on September 2, 1945, when President Ho Chi Minh proclaimed Vietnam an independent country, an event stored deeply in everyone's memory. On that day, President Ho Chi Minh read the Declaration of Independence in front of tens of thousands of cheering people in the Ba Dinh Square in Hanoi, announcing the birth of a new Vietnam to the entire nation and the world. This day marked the glorious victory of the August Revolution during which the Vietnamese people rose up and defeated the French and Japanese colonialists, opening a new era for Vietnam after over 80 years of hardship under foreign rule. Vietnam's independence is significant to not only Vietnam but also other oppressed peoples in the world since it has encouraged many countries in Asia and Africa to continue their fight against foreign aggressors until they are victorious. On September 2, 1945, Hanoi, the capital of the new Vietnam, was beautifully decorated with red flags, banners and colourful flowers. People from across the nation took to the streets to celebrate the country's triumph after a long and heroic struggle. In his speech, President Ho Chi Minh recalled the spirit of the US Declaration of Independence which states that all men are created equal, they are endowed by their creator with certain inalienable rights, among them are life, liberty and the pursuit of happiness. The proclamation of independence on September 2 ushered in a new age for Vietnam in which all people are in control of their own lives.

3 - *Figures from the past that you use in colloquial expressions*

In my country, when a person is called "**Chua Chom**" (Lord Chom), it means he or she is heavily indebted. Legend has that

- Vietnam -

Chom's mother met King Le Chieu Tong while he was trying to escape from Mac Dang Dung, a rebellious official under the Le dynasty, and gave birth to him. Being born into a poor family, Chom had to borrow money from his villagers to eke out a living. He promised to pay back all the debt when he grew up. Many years later Mac Dang Dung was defeated and the Le dynasty was restored with Chom crowned king. His moneylenders then came to him and asked for their loans to be paid. The crowd of moneylenders grew bigger and bigger. Even those who did not lend money to Chom also joined the crowd to look for favours. Chom, now a king nicknamed Chua Chom, was sitting on his sedan chair and decided to throw bags of coins to the cheering crowd until he disappeared into the royal citadel.

This legend is usually associated with King Le Trang Tong but historical facts prove that it is not true. However, this story is still told from generation to generation and the phrase "Chua Chom" has been widely used since then to refer to a heavily indebted person.

4 - Words used to designate a type of person, animal, things

Like many countries in the world, the Vietnamese also use proper nouns, mostly from literary works, to denote a specific type of person. One of the most famous examples is **Chi Pheo**, the main character in a short story of the same name by writer Nam Cao (1915 - 1951). Chi Pheo is commonly used to describe a man who drinks a lot of alcohol and then forces others to accept his unreasonable requests in a stubborn and threatening way. Chi Pheo also refers to a type of man who always denies his wrongdoings using annoying and unconvincing arguments. In

Nam Cao's story, Chi Pheo is a good farmer forced into being a criminal. When he was released from prison, he was always drunk. Whenever he needed something, he went to the village lord's house and threatened him by staging a sit-down protest against him.

More popular examples include **Hoan Thu** and **So Khanh**, names of two characters in the famous epic poem "The Tale of Kieu" by the celebrated 19th century poet Nguyen Du. Hoan Thu refers to an obsessively jealous wife while So Khanh denotes a promiscuous man who is unfaithful in a romantic relationship.

Another interesting story I want to tell you is the story of the Japanese electronics maker Sony. When a TV is said to be "nét như Sony" (literally, as sharp as Sony), that TV has a sharp, clear and vivid display. In general, Sony is used as an adjective to describe an electronic device of superior quality. You may not know that the Vietnamese strongly prefer Japanese-made goods and the Sony TV is one of them. Due to its high quality images, Sony TVs have become a standard by which Vietnamese people judge an electronic device. Today, although there are a multitude of other TV brands which may have the same or even better level of quality than Sony in Vietnam, the name Sony has already taken root in Vietnam and "nét như Sony" has become an integral part of the modern Vietnamese language.

5 - *Common phrases and fun expressions in your native language and their translation in English*

In recent years, **"chém gió"** has become a buzzword among the youth in Vietnam; it literally means slashing the wind. This phrase means boasting proudly about abilities, achievements or belongings that one does not have or has not achieved. Another meaning of slashing the wind is telling a story with imaginary details, which are invented to make the story more fascinating and entertaining.

Now I will tell you another interesting phrase in Vietnamese: **"buồn như con chuồn."** When someone uses this phrase, they are somewhat sad over their unfulfilled expectations. "Buồn như con chuồn" literally translates as "as sad as a dragonfly." You may ask what is the relation between sadness and a dragonfly, since it seems they do not have anything in common at all. Well, the link between sadness and a dragon fly is the sound. "Buồn" (sad) rhymes with "chuồn" (dragonfly). It is a new way to create unique similes, which has been very popular among youths in recent years. A feeling will be compared to an animal or object whose pronunciation rhymes with that of the feeling. Recently a picture book collecting similar phrases was published in Vietnam. Although this new word formation remains controversial, such phrases reflect a language evolving rapidly to meet the needs of young people to express themselves in a unique and different way.

6 - Songs and games you remember from your childhood, that are generally passed on to the next generation

Despite the appearance of new industrial toys, folk games are still popular and remain an important part in the lives of Vietnamese children. I will list two games, one for girls and one for boys.

In the game of "đánh chuyền," girls need a small ball that can be held in a closed hand and about ten 20-centimetre long sticks. A girl stretches her leg and distributes the sticks along her leg, throws the ball into the air, picks up one or more sticks and then catches the ball. During the game, the players will sing a song that counts numbers from one two ten. The number of sticks to be picked up must be the same as the number recited in the song. As the song counts from one to ten, the number of sticks to be picked up each time also increases from one to ten. The girls will take turns throwing the ball, picking up the sticks and catching the ball. The winner is the one who completes the ten-stick pick-up the first. This game is truly unique because it requires girls to have considerable skills when they have to pick up the correct number of sticks and catch the ball at the same time.

While girls prefer games requiring skills, boys usually play games that depend on muscular strength, one of them being "đánh khăng." Boys will need two small cylindrical logs of wood: one log is around 30 – 40 centimetres long and 2 centimetres wide while the second log should have the same diameter as the long log and a length which is about half or one third that of the first log. The game can consist of several boys playing together in which one will use the long log to propel the short log as far as possible. If the short log is caught by other boys, then it will be another boy's turn to play.

7 - Legends/ stories or famous characters of the Imaginary / Folk tales

One of the most famous fairy tales that has been told from generation to generation in Vietnam is the story of **Tam and Cam**. A little girl named Tam had to live with her wicked stepmother and stepsister Cam, both of whom made many attempts to harm Tam. Cam stole Tam's basket of fish, killing her beloved fish while the stepmother forced Tam to sort a basket of mixed black and green beans to prevent Tam from attending the festival. Later, with the help of the Buddha, Tam became the king's wife, but she had not escaped the nasty plots of Cam and her mother. They killed Tam when she visited her home but Tam transformed into an oriole, a xoan tree, a loom, a golden apple and finally she became a human again. She returned to the royal palace and lived happily with the king while Cam and her mother were punished for their vicious actions. The whole story symbolises the constant struggle between good and bad but in the end, good will prevail over bad. The story also conveys a folk philosophy that blessings will come to those who do good things, and punishment will come to those who do bad things.

8 - Products or goods that represent 'the national treasure'

You may have heard about "nước mắm" or fish sauce, a kind of condiment widely used in Vietnamese dishes. But there is another type of condiment which may be less well-known to foreigners but is extremely popular in Vietnamese meals in rural areas. It is "tương," which is made from fermented soy beans. "Tương" is so familiar with rural people that it has been recorded in a folk song that goes like this: *Anh đi anh nhớ quê nhà, nhớ canh rau muống nhớ cà dầm tương...* The verse translates into "When I travel far from home, I remember my hometown. I also remember water spinach soup and eggplants steeped in soy sauce..." Thus we can see that in Vietnam, water spinach (rau muống) served with tương is a great delicacy, deeply stored in our collective memory. Rau muống and tương are the two things that remind us of our childhood and where we come from. If you have a chance to visit Vietnam, you can visit Ban village in Hung Yen province, just around 30 kilometers from Hanoi, a village famous for its "tương Bần" variety of "tương," to bring home a taste of an excellent Vietnamese product.

Yemen

First name: Wahib
Family name: Farhan
http://www.linkedin.com/in/wahibfarhan
zwahib@gmail.com

Capital	Sanaa	Population	24,772,000
Government	Republic	Currency	Yemeni rials (YER)
Religion(s)	Muslim (Islam - official)		
Language(s)	Arabic (official)		

I was born in Yemen in the very beautiful and calm city of Taiz. I received my bachelor degree of arts in English and translation in 1999 from the University of Sana'a. I made my decision to specialise in English language and translation due to my keen interest in learning about other cultures and participate in making foreign cultures known to my country. I found that acquiring a second language would open doors to endless knowledge. After graduation, I joined several international organisations, working as a translator for their daily work and reports, a job that I enjoyed a lot. Two years later, I had a chance to work in a different but still multicultural field, i.e. human resources. During this job which I also enjoyed and excelled in, I gained much experience that later sharpened my translation expertise. Undoubtedly, during my work in human resources, I did not abandon my translation work and I spent almost equal hours doing both jobs. During that time, I worked with many of the widely known translation agencies from all over the world. Also, I participated in the translation and localisation of many projects, both locally and globally.

To briefly describe my experience in the field of translation, I would say that I am a fully fledged English<>Arabic translator with entrepreneurial sense and a cultural flair. Arabic is my mother tongue. I have spent more than 12 years translating and proofreading for a broad range of well-known agencies, as well as for a long list of direct prestigious clients from all over the world. I believe in long-term relationships so that my work is always directed to achieve this point through quality, commitment, punctuality, confidentiality, and trust. My expertise ranges from business, banking, financial, legal, marketing, educational, and general to medical, computer, and engineering.

1 - A typical conversation – what are the common/universal topics people go for? (weather, politics, etc.) - And some topics that you should avoid discussing with the locals?

Common Topics:

Weather: The weather of my home city of Taiz is unbelievable. It is mild throughout the year. This topic is commonly discussed among people. You may discuss the slight variations and changes of weather with your family members, your friends, your workmates, or even the grocery man when you want to buy your favourite drink. It is no surprise that the topic of weather is the introduction to any conversation.

Politics: This is really a hot topic to talk about during the events of Arab Spring. My country, Yemen, was one of the leading countries in the Arab Spring which ended up with a new president thus ushering in a new era. Not only that, as a cultural expert, I noticed that the rebirth of a new culture was evolving and the new generation was getting mature at an early age. You can see an old man discussing purely political issues of certain complexity with a young boy who is almost 10 years old. Yes, that is the situation. Everybody became aware of his rights as well as his commitments as a good citizen.

History: When you talk about Yemen, it brings to mind a long history which is traced back to hundreds of the thousands of years. Tourists who come to Yemen from all over the world do that mainly in search of historical places and in admiration of ancient cultures. When anyone comes to Yemen, he or she would love to visit the places of ancient kings and queens of Yemen who lived thousands of years ago. You may ask about Queen Bilqis, Hemirite Kings, Queen Arwa, just to name a few.

Food: Everything in Yemen is traditional in the whole sense of the word. Types of food served in Yemen cannot be found elsewhere, and are liked by all visitors of Yemen. You may ask a tourist coming from far west for the first time about his favourite meal in Yemen; he or she would certainly say it is "Salta" or "Fahsa." These are traditional dishes served in a very traditional way. They are made of a mixture of vegetables, soup, and meat and are cooked in a pottery. I cannot describe the enjoyment you would experience about Yemeni dishes. It is a topic that you should discuss in your everyday life. Do not miss these dazzling moments!

2 - *Events of great significance for the community, deeply stored in everyone's mind*

The following events are of high significance to everybody in Yemen:

1962 – The September revolution against the Imam rule.

1963 – The October revolution against the British colonialism in the southern part of the country.

1967 – The departure of the last British soldier for the southern part of the country.

1990 – The reunification of the northern and southern parts of Yemen on the 22nd of May.

2011 – The burst of the Youth revolution to change the regime the ended with a new president for the country.

2011 – On the 18th of March, when the previous regime committed the so-called "Joma'at Alkarama" or "Dignity Friday" and around sixty activists were killed in a nefarious way.

3 - *Figures from the past / present*

Bilqis "Queen of Sheba": She was a monarch of the ancient kingdom of Sheba in Yemen who is assumed to have lived in the 10th century B.C. She is a symbol of the strength of Yemeni women.

Queen Arwa: She is the first queen in Islam, and ruled Yemen during 439 – 533 A.H. She is a symbol of wise and smart Yemeni women.

Ibrahim Al-Hamdi (1943 – 1977): He is the most loved president of Yemen in the modern age after the end of Imam Rule. He ruled Yemen since June 1974 till he was assassinated in October 1977. During his rule, Yemen witnessed major changes in political, economic and social aspects.

Ayoub Taresh (1942): He is a very famous Yemeni singer. His national songs constitute the national heritage of Yemen. He is also the singer of the Yemen national anthem.

Tawakkol Karman (1979): She is a Nobel Peace Prize Laureate in 2011. She is a journalist, politician and human rights activist. She was one of the leaders of uprisings in Yemen during the Arab Spring in 2011. She heads the group "Women Journalists without Chains."

4 - *Words used to designate a type of person, animal, things*

- "Insan": a word to refer to a well-principled man with good morals.
- "Ibn Nass": a word used to describe a man or a woman for being modest and belonging to a family with good reputation.
- "Tayeb": a word to describe the kindness of a man or a woman.
- "Rajol": a word to describe a manhood, strength, and good principles of a man.
- "Raheeb": a word used to describe the magnificence of a scene or situation.
- "Okht": a polite way to address an unknown woman.
- "Izzi": a regular way to address an unknown man.

5 - Common phrases and fun expressions in your native language and their translation in English

- "Qal loh thawr, qal loh Ihloboh": One said it was an ox, the other said "milk it." This saying is commonly used when expressing difficult situations.

- "Ahl Makkah adraa bi shiaabiha": The people of Makkah know their alleys better. This is used to express the fact that outsiders cannot know about things more than insiders.

- "Aáti alkhobz li khabazoh": Give the bread to its baker. This saying is also used to stress on averting from trying to do everything and anything, and to refer everything to its specialist.

- "Ála qadr firashak, mod rijlak": Stretch your leg to the size of your mattress. This is used to advise someone with limited resources not to buy things he can live without.

- "Law habibak ásal ma til hasawsh kolloh": If a friend is very kind, do not fully exploit him or her. This is used as an advice to someone who is being opportunistic.

- "Min tighada bi alkathib ma ti áshabah": He who lied to get his lunch cannot lie again to get his dinner. This saying is used to advocate the principle of truthfulness in everything we do.

6 - Songs and games you remember from your childhood, that are generally passed on to the next generation

Ya qamar qomaira, ya siraj allailah, sirbana sirb alhamam, wa alhamam ramz assalam.

This is an ancient song that passes from generation to generation. It uses the moon and pigeons to denote peace.

Wa baqara sobbi laban, Abdullah safar Aden safar Aden, bint okhto jabat walad jabat walad, samaitu Abdu Assamad Abdu Assamd,

Abdu Assamad yeshti haleeb yeshti haleeb, wal haleeb min albaqar min albaqar.

This is a highly rhythmic song that has been sung for ages to make babies sleep.

Ya dajajat amati, bakbiki lik bakbiki

This is another song used for kids, and uses the symbol of hens to create a mood of joy and amusement.

7 - Legends/ stories or famous characters of the Imaginary / Folk tales

The legend of "**Um Al Sibyan**" is very famous, we use it to frighten kids to sleep. It refers to an imaginary character of a Jinn mother that will come if kids do not sleep or keep quiet.

8 - Products or goods that represent 'the national treasure'

Yemen is traditionally famous for: mocha coffee, raisin, fruits, garnet, incense, Hanna, fish, and honey.

***

Yemen is a country of culture and history. Its people are famous for their hospitality, natural behaviour, and generosity. Nature and vast spaces of greenery characterises many places in Yemen. The cost of living in Yemen is cheap. Accommodation is also cheap but you should not expect a variety of five star hotels; you are coming to smell tradition and culture… Welcome to Yemen!

Russia

First name: Maya
Family name: Sandomirova
MAYA.SANDOMIROVA@GMAIL.COM

Capital	Moscow	Population	142,515,000
Government	Federation	Currency	Russian rubles (RUB)
Religion(s)	Russian Orthodox		
Language(s)	Russian		

Hello, I am Maya, a Russian-native French and English translator. I started to work as a translator as a hobby and to earn some money with my knowledge of foreign languages. One day I thought: why not build my career on it? Now I can't imagine my life without my job and my passion: translation. I have lived in France since 2008 and the more I live here, the more I appreciate my own country, Russia. That is why I want to tell you more about it and maybe destroy some stereotypes!

1 - A typical conversation – what are the common/universal topics people go for? (weather, politics, etc.) - And some topics that you should avoid discussing with the locals?

Like in all other countries, people who do not really know each other or do not have much to say start their conversations with weather questions and tend to be rather reserved. That is true in Russia: at first glance, we can appear a little rude, impolite and unapproachable... but things change when you get to know Russian people and visit their home. Most of us know how to listen and share people's problems and feelings, and we do not leave friends in a difficult situation. In Russia, you are guaranteed to find people who appreciate your opinions and criticisms: Russians like to laugh at themselves and criticise their country even if they tend to be patriots deep down.

But be aware that one of the world's common topics – politics – remains a delicate one, like in many other countries: you never know whether the person you are talking to is a government supporter or adversary.

2 - *Events of great significance for the community, deeply stored in everyone's mind*

The major event of the 20th century was, most definitely, the October Revolution which profoundly transformed our country, changing it from a monarchy to a communist society. The USSR brought Russians many victories, over fascism, space exploration, sporting and scientific developments (physics, biology, genetics, etc.) and more. And all this even though, at the same time, the country was backwards in its development in comparison with other European countries. Nowadays, Russia is trying to overcome the differences and delay in its development with small steps, slowly but surely. Unfortunately, we still have many problems to cope with, such as a lack of financing in major social sectors and corruption; but I am persuaded that our resources and human potential will help us regain our past glory!

3 - Figures from the past / present that you use in colloquial expressions

"Как Мамай прошёл" ("passed as Mamai," "as if an army has marched through the place") refers to a 14th century Mongol military commandant who ruled over the western part of the Golden Horde and caused much devastation to Russian lands.

"(Делать несколько дел одновременно), как Юлий Цезарь" ("make several things at the same time as Julius Caesar") is a common Russian expression referring to this Roman general who, according to legend, was able to accomplish several tasks at once.

"Вот тебе, бабушка, и Юрьев день" ("here's a nice how-d'ye-do!") is said to show one's surprise or disappointment when one's hopes and expectations have not come true. Laws passed in 1497 allowed Russian peasants to move from one landlord to another once a year during a week before and a week after St. Yuri's (St. George's) day on the 26th of November. This limited freedom was banned between 1580 and 1590, and St. Yuri's day entered folklore as a symbol of disappointment.

4 - Words used to designate a type of person, animal, things

Like many other languages, the Russian language is rich in proper nouns used to designate inanimate things: French cook Olivier created the most famous Russian salad "оливье" ("Olivier") which is sometimes called Russian salad in post-soviet countries as well as throughout the world. Continuing along culinary lines, "beef stroganoff," a meat dish from 19th century Russia, took its name from Russian count Pavel Stroganoff. Another example: rolled oats, a very popular breakfast dish (similar to English porridge) is called "геркулес" (Hercules), referring to the famous Roman hero, the son of Zeus. Apparently, children who eat this become strong like him! Speaking of tasty food, let me remind you of the story of "шарлотка," Russian apple pie: the wife of English King George III, Charlotte, loved plants and kept a large garden. She was persuaded of the marvellous benefit of apples for human health. According to legend, she invented the recipe for this tasty apple cake by cutting some fruit and smothering it with butter cream. You have to try this culinary delight!

5 - Common phrases and fun expressions in your native language and their translation in English

It may seem incredible because of the "reserved" Russian character, but we have many jokes and like to laugh very much. We make jokes about everything: politics, sex, mothers-in-law, blondes, Russian realities, national minorities and more. British people like to laugh at the Dutch. We also have a similar favourite target, Chukchas (inhabitants of the most remote Northeast corner of Russia). Here are some jokes about them:

"Chukcha, why did you buy a fridge if it's so cold in tundra?" / "Why, it's minus fifty Celsius outside, minus ten inside, and minus five in the fridge — so it's a warm place!"

A Chukcha comes into a shop and asks: "Do you have colour TVs?" "Yes, we do." "Give me a green one."

To maintain our reputation as vodka consumers, we also make fun of drunkards:

Drunk n°1 is slowly walking along, bracing himself against a fence and stumbling. He comes across Drunk n°2, who is lying next to the fence. "What a disgrace! Lying around like a pig! I'm ashamed of you." "You just keep on walking, demagogue! We'll see what you do when you run out of fence!"

6 - Songs and games you remember from your childhood, that are generally passed on to the next generation

Children in Russia play games very similar to other games played throughout the world. Russian children enjoy games that involve chasing and role-playing, as well as card games. An example of a chasing game inspired by Russian historical characters is "Cossacks and Robbers" (Cossacks are an East Slavic people who created semi-military communities and recently formed part of the Russian army). Basically, the purpose of this game is to seek out hidden robbers and take them to prison.

When I was a little child, I used to listen to records, because tape recorders were not common in the late 1980s. One of my favourite songs was "Golyboj vagon" ("Blue car") from a famous Russian cartoon. The song is really touching, optimistic and makes think of a happy future… in particular, for my country! Well, you can judge it for yourselves[1].

---

[1] http://www.youtube.com/watch?v=_4m-jXuQHLg (with English subtitles)

7 - Legends/ stories or famous characters of the Imaginary / Folk tales

The force and power of Russia's glorious past is represented by the "bogatyrs," warriors from Russian legends who defended Russia from its enemies. The bogatyrs embody all the best qualities of Russians: courage, force and inventiveness. They inspired many Russian fairy tales, movies and even artists.

8 - Products or goods that represent 'the national treasure'

In three words, Russia's national symbols are petrol, ballet and vodka.

Speaking more seriously, not many people know that our "traditional" drink arrived in our country only in the late 14th century with Genoese ambassadors bringing the first aqua vitae ("the water of life") to Moscow and presenting it to Grand Duke Dmitry Donskoy. The traditional Russian alcoholic drink before that was mead ("medovukha"), a honey wine much appreciated by our ancestors.

However, Russia's real national treasure is not very well known on the global scene. We have 22% of the world's wood resources, we are number 1 in the world with our diamond reserves and we are also one of the top fur producers.

I hope our little trip to my motherland has been both pleasant and instructive!

Turkey

First name: Nuray
Family name: Yürek
nurayyurek90@gmail.com
&
First name: Buket
Family name: Yilmaz
BuketYilmaz@gmail.com

Capital	Ankara	Population	79,745,000
Government	Republican parliamentary democracy	Currency	Turkish liras (TRY)
Religion(s)	Muslim		
Language(s)	Turkish (official), Kurdish		

Buket: I am a Turkish translator, proofreader and QA tester.

My education means I can work on a variety of subjects using both my linguistic and technical knowledge. I have published 19 books translated from French classics, including Molière, Hugo, Gide and Daudet.

Currently, I mostly work on IT related subjects.

Nuray: I was born in a town called Lüleburgaz, near the city of İstanbul, in Turkey. I spent my childhood and my primary, secondary, and high school years in that town with my family. When the time came for me to choose a program for my undergraduate education, I followed my passion for languages. I decided to apply for French Language and Literature program at Selçuk University, I was accepted and moved to Konya for my education. Besides English and French, I also take Russian language courses in the university. Now, I am in my final year.

I like learning languages and exploring different cultures. When I have time, I also like visiting historical sites of Konya, such as the Museum of Rumi. I am working as a freelance translator as well as an English teacher in a private teaching institution. I hope I will focus on practicing translation and interpretation after graduation.

1 - A typical conversation – what are the common/universal topics people go for? (weather, politics, etc.) - And some topics that you should avoid discussing with the locals?

Turkish people are generally very friendly and they are proud of being described as hospitable by their visitors. They can talk about many different topics, but favourite ones are the weather, traffic, soccer, and the economy. They become friends so quickly and easily that it is possible to see them talking about their families, friends and jobs just a few minutes after the first introduction. They may also ask you questions about your own family and job (even about your salary). So, it is useful to keep in mind that they are just trying to develop intimacy by this kind of conversation, thinking that you will feel better and safer with them. However, if you do not like talking about personal issues, you can just ask them to change the subject. You can be sure that they will show respect. Turkish people enjoy learning about lifestyles and customs of different countries as well as informing foreigners about their own culture. It may be a good idea to ask them about

Turkish culture, cuisine, or talking about your own country and traditions.

Just like many other countries, political and religious topics are generally avoided. "Sex" might be considered the most taboo subject in Turkey.

2 - Events of great significance for the community, deeply stored in everyone's mind

The Turkish Republic stems from the Ottoman Empire, whose founders were descendants of the Great Seljuk Empire, and who came to Anatolia from Central Asia. As a result, Turkish history is full of battles and migrations. However, among those battles, the most important one is the Turkish War of Independence (1919-1922), which resulted in the founding of the modern Turkish Republic in 1923. The founding of the republic is celebrated on the 29th of October every year since then.

After the foundation of the republic, a range of reforms were enacted to transform social, political and legal institutions. They are considered as milestones for the Turkish community. Some of them include abolition of the sultanate, the right to elect and be elected for women (1934), abolition of the caliphate (1924), the alphabet reform (1928), and language reform (1932).

Undoubtedly, among the real persons from the past that have had an influence on people and society in Turkey, the most significant person is Mustafa Kemal Atatürk, the founder of the Turkish Republic. He died in 1938, but he is still seen as a political leader by many people in Turkey. His aphorisms are placed on the walls of many public institutions.

- Turkey -

After a couple of attempts, a multiparty system was also accomplished in 1946. This is considered as the starting point for the Turkish democracy.

3 - Nouns and Figures from the past / present that you use in colloquial expressions

"Fasulye" (green bean): a young child who is included in a group game by the elder children, but for whom the rules of the game are not applied due to his or her age. Elder children include him or her in the game only to let him or her have fun. He or she is not seen as the winner or the loser of the game.

The names of some objects, animals or foods are used to refer to people with both positive and negative connotations.

- Aslan, aslanım: (lion, my lion) – refers to strong or successful men or boys (positive).
- Sazan: (carp) – refers to a person who's fooled by someone (negative)
- Inek: (cow) – refers to a hardworking student with no social life (negative)
- Fıstık: (nut) – refers to a beautiful woman or a sweet girl (positive)
- Taş: (stone) – refers to a sexy woman (positive)
- Kaşar: (a kind of cheese) – refers to a woman with a lot of sexual experience (negative)

4 - Words used to designate a type of person, animal, things

Generally, in Turkey we name our children after nature and emotions, thus almost every name has a meaning, such as my name, Buket, which means 'a flower bouquet'- Nehir (River), Su

(Water), Deniz (Sea), Doğa (Nature), Çiçek (Flower) Tayfun (Typhoon), Saadet (Happiness), Kader (Destiny), Arzu (Desire), Gaye (Intent), etc.

Alex de Souza (a famous football player): used in the phrase "not an alex" to refer to something or someone average. This phrase has been popular among young people recently.

5 - Common phrases and fun expressions in your native language and their translation in English

"Öküzün trene baktığı gibi bakmak" (to stare just like an ox does): to gawk

"İpe un sermek" (hanging flour on the clothes line): to swing the lead

"Damdan düşer gibi" (as if falling from the roof): out of the blue

"Laf söyledi balkabağı" (the pumpkin spoke): to talk nonsense

"Etekleri zil çalmak" (skirts ringing bell): being extremely happy

6 - Songs and games you remember from your childhood, that are generally passed on to the next generation

There are many outdoor games passed on to the next generation. One of them is "yakan top" (literally, burning ball). This game is played between two groups. Group members try to hit the members of the opponent group by using a ball. When all the members of the opponent group are hit, the ball passes to the opponent group.

Hide and seek (Saklambaç) is also a common game among the children. Turkish children like gathering with the other children from their neighbourhood and playing this game. They find it more exciting to play hide and seek at night. This may happen in small villages which are safer, but in the cities that is not common anymore.

7 - Legends/ stories or famous characters of the Imaginary / Folk tales

Just like many other cultures, there are stories that are told children to teach them about dangers. In Turkish, these stories are generally about "öcü" (bogeyman) that comes and punishes the misbehaving children. However, nowadays, there are only a few children who take these stories seriously.

Nasreddin Hoca (Nasreddin Hodja) is a witty, wise Sufi figure. Turkish people have a large repertoire of jokes about him.

Keloğlan (Bold guy) - adventures of a simple boy with some sense of humour but no hair on his head, fighting with giants and witches.

8 - Products or goods that represent 'the national treasure'

Turkey's Mediterranean shore, called the Turquoise Coast, Aegean coast and historical sites in Anatolia have a high touristic value. There are many holiday destinations which offer various activities, such as sightseeing tours in Ancient Ephesus, Ürgüp (fairy chimneys), Topkapı Palace, Museum of Rumi, etc. There are also cruise tours.

Turkish cuisine is also regarded as a "national treasure" and it is seen as a part of tourism. Many people who visit Turkey try Turkish food, such as kebap, döner, çiğ köfte, and rakı (Turkish alcoholic drink). Therefore, restaurants around historical sites and hotels are important sources of income for Turkish people. Yoghurt is probably the only Turkish word known by the world. It's a food developed by Turkish nomads to carry milk with them wherever they went. It is used as a side dish in almost every meal and mixed with garlic. Contrary to its usage in the rest of the world, in Turkey we rarely eat it mixed with sugar.

There are also goods that are exported abroad or bought by foreign visitors. These include rugs and carpets that can be found especially in the Grand Bazaar in Istanbul. Some of them are hand-crafted, and therefore very valuable.

New Zealand

First name: Kathryn
Family name: Malan
k.malan@tradonline.fr

Capital	Wellington	Population	4,327,900
Government	Parliamentary democracy and a Commonwealth realm	Currency	New Zealand dollars (NZD)
Religion(s)	Protestant, Roman Catholic and others		
Language(s)	English (official), Maori, and New Zealand sign language		

I am a French to English translator from New Zealand. I started working as a freelance translator in 2011 and moved to France in 2012 to take up a position as an in-house translator for Trad Online. I love translation and the challenges it poses, as well as the fact that I am helping the world to communicate!

1 - A typical conversation – what are the common/universal topics people go for? (weather, politics, etc.) - And some topics that you should avoid discussing with the locals?

New Zealand conversations often revolve around the weather, who won the rugby or netball (or other current sporting event), where you are planning to go for your summer or Christmas holidays, and of course what you do for a living. In fact, it is generally in that order too!

2 - Events of great significance for the community, deeply stored in everyone's mind

Our country is still quite young (the Treaty of Waitangi – our founding document – was only signed on 6 February 1840), but we have already experienced quite a few significant events and have achieved great things. All Kiwis, as we call ourselves, know about New Zealand being the first country to give all women the vote in 1893, Sir Edmund Hillary being the first to climb Everest in 1953 with Sherpa Tenzing Norgay, the bombing of the Rainbow Warrior (Greenpeace vessel) by French secret service agents in the Auckland harbour in 1985, the Springbok rugby tour of 1987 with its anti-apartheid protests, Team NZ winning the America's Cup in 1995 with their boat Black Magic, and more recently the earthquakes which have rocked Christchurch for over a year now and which continue even today.

3 - Nouns and Figures from the past / present that you use in colloquial expressions

We have few instances where a name for something is derived from a famous person. However, we do have many words that are used to name places or people from places:

Poms: English people. The origin of this name is uncertain, and is commonly used in New Zealand, Australia and South Africa. It can be an offensive word.

JAFA: People living in Auckland (Just Another F*cking

Aucklander, or alternately, Just Another Fantastic Aucklander). This term has a double meaning though, as it also refers to a round, candy-coated chocolate sold in New Zealand (Jaffa).

The Ditch: The Tasman Sea separating New Zealand and Australia.

A Remuera Tractor: This is a pejorative term for an SUV. Remuera is an affluent suburb of Auckland, the largest city, and many families living there drive around in huge SUVs even though they never go off-road (which is what SUVs were designed for!).

Rogernomics: This is a political term applied to the so-called "economic reforms" of the 1980s and continuing worldwide today. It was named in honour of the politician who spearheaded it, Sir Roger Douglas, and involves selling off public assets and property to private interests in order to generate short-term, one-off profit.

4 - *Words used to designate a type of person, animal, things*

- Boy racer – a teenage boy who drives a fast, noisy car with a loud stereo.
- Budgie-smugglers – tight-fitting speedo-style male swimwear
- the Dreaded Lurgy – this is a familiar way of saying "a head cold/influenza"
- Kiwi – this is what we New Zealanders refer to ourselves as. The kiwi is a flightless nocturnal bird which is native to New Zealand and has become one of our national icons.
- A wally – an idiot, a clown
- A wharfie – a stevedore, a person who works on the

shipping wharfs.
- Pakeha – a person of European descent
- Anklebiter – a small child or toddler
- The wop-wops – in the middle of nowhere, in a very rural location with few inhabitants

5 - *Common phrases and fun expressions in your native language and their translation in English*

Nek minit – this is a phrase which was made popular thanks to YouTube. It is a contraction of "and the next minute…" and is used as part of a tale where something unexpected and funny or ironic occurs as a consequence.

Raining cats and dogs – this means it is raining a lot.

#8 wire approach – this saying goes back to our country's farming roots as farmers used to use #8 wire for fencing and to fix anything else on the farm, and the saying has come to mean a person who can turn their hand to anything.

She'll be right – this phrase basically means that something will go well, whether you are talking about the weather threatening an event or the piece of timber balanced on your trailer which looks like it might fall off.

Rattle yer dags – this means "hurry up!" and comes from the fact that when sheep run, the dirty wool around their bottoms swings around and "rattles." Another farming-related saying!

In two shakes of a lamb's tail – meaning quickly (in a second or minute is a less poetic way of saying it). This needs no further explanation, just picture a lamb shaking its tail twice.

Bob's your uncle – this phrase means you are guaranteed to succeed, for example, simply hammer this nail in there, and bob's your uncle! You've got a table.

Can you handle the jandal? – Firstly, a jandal is what Kiwis call "flip-flops" (or if you are Australian, "thongs"). This phrase is a fun way of saying "can you handle it?" and works in many situations.

6 - Songs and games you remember from your childhood, that are generally passed on to the next generation

Childhood games, songs and books form an important part of your cultural heritage, and my memories include playing bull rush at school (a game played on a field where one "tagger" tries to tag as many people as possible while they are all rushing across the field to the safe area) as well as stuck in the mud (if you get tagged you are stuck and cannot move until someone frees you), elastics (a game played by girls with a long piece of elastic around two girls and a third jumping it in the middle) and knucklebones (originally played with real knucklebones, but we played with metal ones – throwing them with one hand in a fixed pattern and catching them). For songs, every Christmas, schoolchildren sing the Twelve Days of Christmas, New Zealand-style! For example, on the first day of Christmas my true love gave to me – a Pukeko in a Ponga Tree! A favourite Kiwi children's book series follows a fictional dog, Hairy Maclary, written by Lynley Dodd who makes good use of rhyme and accompanies the story with great drawings.

7 - Legends/ stories or famous characters of the Imaginary / Folk tales

New Zealand is lucky to have the Maori Culture which is rich in mythology. As such, I grew up reading tales of Maui catching the sun or fishing up New Zealand's islands. Of course, the Easter Bunny provided Easter eggs every year, the Tooth Fairy took your tooth from under your pillow and left a coin, and Santa Claus brought presents on his sleigh at Christmas. In addition to that, my favourite phrase from adults was "Eat your crusts, it'll put hairs on your chest!" Or the variation "Eat your crusts, it'll make your hair go curly!"

8 - Products or goods that represent 'the national treasure'

New Zealand is still a very agricultural country, so the main goods we produce include: wool, lamb and milk. Our wines are becoming known around the world too, as is our kiwifruit. Recent events (the Christchurch earthquake) have made us realise that Marmite (a savory yeast spread) is also a national treasure as the current shortage has sent everyone into panic-mode and we are all eagerly awaiting the Mamite factory reopening in Christchurch so we can enjoy our Marmite fix!

Another national treasure we have is the Maori culture. Around the world, we are known for the 'haka' (performed by the All Blacks before a rugby game) and when performed well it has a spine-tingling effect. The haka is most often a challenge, and can be responded to by a haka of your own. It can be a prelude to a battle or to discussions between parties. Nowadays, it is also performed as a celebration (for example, after winning a game).

***

New Zealand has two official languages, English and Maori. It is part of the Commonwealth and has Queen Elizabeth II as its head of state. It also has two names for itself: New Zealand and Aotearoa. The latter is the Maori name, and is translated as "the land of the long white cloud." This is descriptive of the view that greeted the first Polynesians to travel to New Zealand, as clouds tend to form over landmasses and New Zealand is an elongated country comprised of three main islands surrounded by sea, meaning that clouds form along its length and look like one long white cloud. New Zealanders pride themselves on their hospitality, friendliness, sense of humour and can-do attitude. This country is well worth a visit!

THE RESPONSE

The originality of the idea and the simplicity, which makes it reader-friendly, were the main reasons for the 50 translators from 50 different countries to accept the writing effort. For some translators, real effort was necessary as the massive storm Sandy was going to hit their homes, while for others good quality of the content meant documentation and some time spared from their work projects. They were determined to immerse themselves into random moments of their life and society, consulted their family and local community, to provide an authentic perspective of their country.

"I liked the opportunity of showing our country to the world, in a new way."
- Chile

"I love the fact that it gives me the opportunity, as a translator, to write about my points of view and about the different experiences I have had growing up in my country."
- South Africa

"It brings together the community of translators and uses our knowledge to let people around the world know about our cultures and lives."
- United Kingdom

"I really enjoyed working on this project, trying to pick subjects that would be interesting, representative of my country and not too cliche, and now I am really curious to read what the other translators had to say about their homes."
-France

THE AUTHORS

Katherine Parks – *United States*

Johanne Tremblay - *Canada*

Osvaldo Rocha - *Mexico*

Gabriela Castro – *Costa Rica*

Maria A. Benzo – *Dominican Republic*

Gabriela Leverón - *Honduras*

Angeles Bermudez - *Nicaragua*

Rolando Ernesto Tellez - *Nicaragua*

Mariela Cacurri - *Argentina*

Gonzalo Palacios Tarqui - *Bolivia*

Tatiana Perry - *Brazil*

Marcos Monteiro – *Brazil*

Andrée Goreux Boyens - *Chile*

Luis Javier Otoya - *Colombia*

Evelyn Tinajero - *Ecuador*

Erika Pacheco - *Peru*

Emiliano Bentancur - *Uruguay*

Mónica Algazi - *Uruguay*

Mary Olsen - *Venezuela*

Gert Geysels - *Belgium*

Karla Bronselaer – *Belgium*

Evelina Sharapanova - *Bulgaria*

Lisa Hersild - *Denmark*

Steen Johnsen - *Denmark*

Eva Estrany - *Spain*

Nora Berasategui - *Spain*

Kersti Skovgaard - *Estonia*

Eva Seris - *France*

Stephanie Taif - *France*

Claudia Salamone - *Italy*

Marina Tavares - *Portugal*

Aurelia Popescu - *Romania*

Flavia Ivaşcu - *Romania*

Emma Halberg - *Sweden*

Nataliya Yena - *Ukraine*

Christina Hewitt – *United Kingdom*

Shirley Finkel-Hall – *South Africa*

Thabani Ngwane – *South Africa*

Carlos T. Djomo - *Cameroon*

Clementine Agbor - *Cameroon*

Eyob Fitwi - *Ethiopia*

Bonface Andenga - *Kenya*

Brahima Ouologuem - *Mali*

Eric Lamine - *Senegal*

Shushan Adamyan - *Armenia*

Albert Deng - *China*

Celia Shen - *China*

Pamela Fouad Ammoury Maalouf - *Lebanon*

Bernadette Choueiry – *Lebanon*

Maisarah Ariffin - *Malaysia*

Salman Riaz - *Pakistan*

Maya Sandomirova - *Russia*

Worapot Sattapunkeeree - *Thailand*

Eunjung Picard - *South Korea*

Buket Yilmaz - *Turkey*

Nuray Yürek - *Turkey*

Hoa Bui Van - *Vietnam*

Ratna Wusono - *Indonesia*

Ikhsan Feri Saputro - *Indonesia*

Kathryn Malan - *New Zealand*

www.tradonline-books.com

www.ingramcontent.com/pod-product-compliance
Lightning Source LLC
Chambersburg PA
CBHW071258110426
42743CB00042B/1089